Global Visions of Violence

Global Visions of Violence

Agency and Persecution in World Christianity

EDITED BY JASON BRUNER AND
DAVID C. KIRKPATRICK

RUTGERS UNIVERSITY PRESS

NEW BRUNSWICK, CAMDEN, AND NEWARK, NEW JERSEY, AND LONDON

LIBRARY OF CONGRESS CATALOGING-IN-PUBLICATION DATA

Names: Bruner, Jason, editor. | Kirkpatrick, David C., editor.
Title: Global visions of violence : agency and persecution in world Christianity /
   edited by Jason Bruner, David C. Kirkpatrick.
Description: New Brunswick : Rutgers University Press, [2023] |
   Includes bibliographical references and index.
Identifiers: LCCN 2022009400 | ISBN 9781978830837 (paperback) |
   ISBN 9781978830844 (hardback) | ISBN 9781978830851 (epub) |
   ISBN 9781978830868 (pdf)
Subjects: LCSH: Violence—Religious aspects—Christianity. | Persecution. |
   Suffering—Religious aspects—Christianity.
Classification: LCC BT736.15 .G59 2023 | DDC 241/.697—dc23/eng/20220815
LC record available at https://lccn.loc.gov/2022009400

A British Cataloging-in-Publication record for this book is
available from the British Library.

References to internet websites (URLs) were accurate at the time of writing. Neither
the author nor Rutgers University Press is responsible for URLs that may have expired
or changed since the manuscript was prepared.

∞ The paper used in this publication meets the requirements of the American
National Standard for Information Sciences—Permanence of Paper for
Printed Library Materials, ANSI Z39.48-1992.

www.rutgersuniversitypress.org

Manufactured in the United States of America

CONTENTS

Global Visions of Violence

Introduction

Locating Christian Agency in a World of Suffering

JASON BRUNER AND DAVID C. KIRKPATRICK

On the night of April 13–14, 2014, armed men affiliated with Boko Haram raided the government secondary school in the town of Chibok, located in the state of Borno in northeastern Nigeria. Most nearby schools were shuttered that month due to security concerns, but teenaged girls from across the region had gathered at this school to take their final exams. Several hundred girls were kidnapped that night, but Nigerian authorities struggled for weeks to arrive at an official count of 276. The event garnered immediate international headlines. For some, it presented clear evidence of the effete Nigerian state and its inability to protect its citizens. For others, the fact that Chibok was a predominantly Christian area of Borno further illuminated the real dangers that Christians faced at the hands of Islamic insurgents, both in Nigeria and across the globe. For others still, the event embodied gendered violence—the girls were coerced into marriage or servitude (including sexual servitude), and in some cases were forcibly converted to Islam. With these narratives reinforcing one another, the story went viral.[1]

The hashtag #BringBackOurGirls quickly spread across social media, becoming one of the most prominent of the year. Facing pressure from mobilized constituents, governments worldwide pledged forms of aid—troops, surveillance, expertise—to locate the girls and battle Boko Haram. For many American Christians, the severity of violence in Nigeria constituted a genocide, another piece of evidence of a "global war on Christians."[2] This persecution narrative, which is understandably compelling to many American Christians, cannot capture the entirety of the story of Christianity in Nigeria, however. Nigeria now boasts more Anglicans than the United Kingdom, and Southern Nigeria likewise holds some of the largest church buildings on the planet, with local Pentecostal denominations even establishing their own cities.[3] In this way, Nigeria is caught in the politics of how evidence is framed. Is it a poster child for global Christianity, with Christianity blossoming rapidly in novel tessellations of the faith?

1

Or is it an overlooked front of the global war on terror, with Islamist groups in the Magreb seeking to obliterate Christians? Is Christianity the most persecuted religion on the planet, or is it growing and thriving in the Global South?

Within a particular global imaginary, Christianity has become the primary victim of violence worldwide. This narrative stands in contrast to other perceptions that Christianity is rather a source of violence, as found in long-established narratives regarding the faith's justification of the Crusades or the colonial conquest of the Americas. While Christians face discrimination and persecution in many parts of the world from state and parastate actors, religious groups, and neighbors, Christian antipersecution activists and religious freedom advocates in the West have often framed these conflicts as collective evidence of concerted anti-Christian animus, priming victims' religious identity in relation to perpetrators' motives for violence. This narrative uses violence to draw lines of spiritual affiliation and political obligation based on claims of shared Christian identity. As a result, this imaginary blends descriptive accounts of anti-Christian persecution with normative claims of Christians' global interconnectedness.

The subject of this book intersects with three claims about contemporary Christianity that tend to originate from distinct scholarly literatures: the perception that Christianity is increasingly and pervasively persecuted; academic presentations of the global demographic expansion of the religion; and Western foreign policy objectives that are often framed in terms of assisting religious minorities. These dynamics present a complex interweaving of power, affect, expertise, and identity. They are not combined uniformly, but rather interact with local and global networks, beliefs, cultures, histories, and power structures. The contributions in this book illuminate the myriad of ways that violence, persecution, and suffering have impacted Christians and the imagination of Christian identity globally in recent decades. We contend that this subject is necessarily interdisciplinary, requiring the integration of multiple subfields of academic inquiry pertaining to the study of World Christianity.

In the example that opens this chapter, the story of Boko Haram and Nigerian Christianity challenges the uniformity of the causes, effects, and imaginations of this violence. Like other regions and instances examined in the following chapters, the Chibok abductions do not offer an easy parsing of presumed dichotomies: between the local and global; between being victims and possessing agency; between a narrative of Christian persecution and Christian growth. Rather, these factors suggest the plurality of world imaginings concerning the themes of violence and persecution and how Christians, both locally and internationally, have replied to them. In these responses, local contexts have shaped, and continue to shape, the expression of global narratives. They also reveal a host of normative and analytical discourses regarding Christians and Christianity that employ similar thematic elements in contrasting ways.

Global War on Christians

Since the mid-1990s, scholars and activists concerned with international religious freedom have spoken of the unique severity of the global persecution of Christians. Dramatic statistical claims animate this line of analysis and the normative claims it makes with respect to Christianity and Christian theology. Figures from the World Christian Database suggest that there have been, on average, in excess of 100,000 Christian martyrs each year for approximately the past three decades, and the International Society for Human Rights recently claimed that Christians experience 80 percent of all incidents of religious discrimination worldwide.[4] This field of inquiry casts Christianity as having entered a period of severe global duress, amounting to a "global war on Christians."[5] While there is a global dimension to this analysis, certain geographical regions feature more prominently than others, such as Christians living in the Middle East and North Africa. The experiences of Christians in China, North Korea, and parts of South and Southeast Asia also garner outsized attention. With one important exception, this literature generally demands a political or spiritual response to the expansiveness and severity of the problem but pays less attention to the ways in which local Christians respond to the various forms of persecution or violence they face.[6] Furthermore, it often leaves little room to imagine that Christian faith in many regions of the world is constituted by more than persecution, as suffering appears to define the whole of their religious experience. In this literature, Christians worldwide tend to be cast as mere victims, whose plight must be addressed by Christians in the West. In other words, this literature can produce a vision of non-Western Christians as helpless hordes that require American saviors. In most literature on anti-Christian persecution, it is typically the actions of persecutors that matter (or, in some cases, the humanitarian or spiritual or devotional responses from Western audiences), as the persecutors are the ones with the power to inflict damage, pain, suffering, imprisonment, and death.

Nigeria, our example here, has featured prominently in this literature over the past decade. Conflicts in the region are often presented to Western audiences as arising from religious difference. In *The Martyr's Oath,* a recent book on global anti-Christian persecution, Johnny Moore claims that Boko Haram is "far more lethal to Christianity than ISIS, to whom Boko Haram has pledged allegiance. Human rights advocates note that Boko Haram killed 6,644 people in 2014—more than even ISIS did."[7] The Christian advocacy organization Open Doors International states that "more Christians are murdered for their faith in Nigeria than in any other country," and rate the level of persecution in Nigeria as "extreme."[8] The United States Commission on International Religious Freedom's 2020 report recommended designating Nigeria a "country of particular concern," with commissioner Gary L. Bauer's personal statement included in the report claiming that "Nigeria is quickly becoming a 'killing field' for that nation's Christians."[9]

Seen in this light, #BringBackOurGirls fits within a prepackaged narrative of religious warfare.

By intervening in this literature, the analyses contained within this volume share a critical attention to agency in different forms. For example, as in the Nigerian case, these chapters illuminate the "cultural work of the discourse of anti-Christian violence," in Melani McAlister's words in the afterword to this volume. Here, we do not suggest that violence is not destructive, or that the experience of religious persecution or other forms of suffering is thereby excused or justified. The purpose of violence is indeed often destructive, and experiencing violence inflicts harm on Christians and church structures. Such violence, however, can also—and often does—generate new theological reflection, develop distinct Christian identities, foster new forms of political engagement, and result in the creation of new institutions.

Furthermore, Christians experiencing violence can foment novel forms of activism, provide motivation for donations and missionary mobilization, and create new local and international coalitions and networks. Such an approach does not mean neglecting the facts of religious discrimination, persecution, or suffering. In a cover story titled, "The Girls Who Would Not Bow," the flagship evangelical magazine *Christianity Today* highlighted the religious faith of the kidnapped Chibok girls. With the subheading, "How Secret Prayers and Hidden Bibles Sustained Boko Haram's Hostages While the Whole World Waited," the article highlighted the fact that many of the Chibok girls who were eventually released clung to their beliefs, shared Bible verses, and sang secretly in order to sustain their faith and morale.[10] As the authors noted, "[The abducted girls'] faith provided twin anchors of identity and hope during a period when their captors were trying to erase both."[11] Such experiences of enduring faith are compelling and reverberate, even when they occur in less well-known contexts. For example, in this volume, Christie Chui-Shan Chow explores how one controversial Chinese Christian church used the occasion of their persecution in China to develop an expansive global network facilitated by the internet and other media technology. Such complex causes and effects of violence with respect to Christians and Christianity cannot be captured under the purview of a single literature or a single methodological approach. Agency in Santa Muerte, in Kate Kingsbury's chapter in this volume, highlights a transforming Christian practice in light of violence that existing Christian structures cannot seem to remedy or ameliorate. And Candace Lukasik's examination of the Coptic Christian diaspora illuminates the complex ways in which persecution, race, and political power intersect to provide new political opportunities for Coptic mobilization even as these same forces constrain them within categories largely determined by Americans. At its core, agency with respect to persecution often draws on deeper assumptions about the righteous innocence of Christians generally. Christians in these contexts of persecution are almost unanimously presented as victims, while those with power are the aggressors. A fundamental question we pose in this volume considers the ways in which Christians living amid persecution and severe violence, broadly defined, wield agency—that is, in what ways are they shaping their responses to their contexts and communities? The reality is layered, dynamic, and complex.

World Christianity

If the literature on global Christian persecution sounds elegiac, scholars writing within the field of World Christianity can take on a celebratory—even triumphalist—tone. As a field of inquiry, World Christianity emerged in the second half of the twentieth century amid the era of decolonization. Scholarship on World Christianity tends to describe Christianity globally as a "spreading fire," with predicted global growth for the foreseeable future.[12] Research by scholars such as Andrew Walls and Dana Robert compellingly argued that the demographic center of gravity has shifted dramatically from the Global North to the Global South over the course of the twentieth century.[13] The World Christian Database, for example, claimed that while Africa contained merely 10 million Christians in the year 1900, 360 million lived there by the year 2000.[14] For scholars of World Christianity, the expansion of the faith signifies more than simple demographic dominance. Rather, they argue Christianity empowered as it embodied dynamic localized expressions of the faith, which then voiced powerful critiques of a secularizing West or Global North.

Nigeria has likewise featured prominently in this trajectory of scholarship, serving even as a synecdoche of the demographic transformations, religious entrepreneurialism, and political power of Christians in the Global South. Nigeria was home to the first African Anglican bishop (Samuel Ajayi Crowther) in the late nineteenth century, as well as a host of African independent churches that were autonomous from Western Christian missionaries. In the late twentieth century, its Anglican hierarchy was among the bishops from the Global South who criticized the Church of England and the Episcopal Church for their policies of blessing same-sex unions and ordaining openly gay and lesbian clergy. More recently, the massive Pentecostal and charismatic churches of southern Nigeria have received large amounts of attention due to their astronomical size, ebullient style, media savviness, international missionary efforts, and attempts to found their own cities.[15] In this literature, one finds Nigeria fully identified with the dynamic growth of Christianity worldwide, a representative case study of the global transformations of the faith and of processes that are reshaping Christianity as younger, charismatic, and (globally) southern. Scarcely mentioned in much of this literature are themes such as religious persecution, militias, or violence (other than spiritual warfare).

While this paradigm illuminates remarkable developments in sub-Saharan Africa and parts of South Asia, it has nevertheless suffered from some lacunae. As a field, World Christianity struggles in regions where Christianity has declined (the Middle East and North Africa) or has already been indigenized for a millennium or more (Eastern Europe). As a result, these regions remain peripheral to or completely absent from this literature. Among these cavities are not simply the Orthodox and other Christians of Eastern Europe and the Christians of the Middle East, but also those from Latin America. The field has also tended to avoid topics such as international religious freedom, persecution, and violence. Even where such issues are present, the methodological inclination of World Christianity scholars is to insist (not without good reason) on agency rather than suffering, indigenization rather than oppression, and creativity rather than structural constraints.

Harvey Kwiyani speaks into these gaps by engaging the complex intersection of race, missions, and empire in his native Malawi. Kwiyani argues that white supremacy and colonial violence run alongside the demographic expansion of the faith, placing into question the future of global Christian unity and cooperation. While Kwiyani emphasizes the enduring legacies of colonial Christianity, Joel Cabrita speaks to the ways colonialism's gross imbalances of power were inscribed in the dynamics of the scholarly encounters that took place within it, exploring how violence shaped theories of so-called Indigenous religion in twentieth-century Africa. She suggests that the violence of the colonial encounter caused many African intellectuals to craft newly indigenized theories of Christianity. As a result, the field of World Christianity cannot be narrated independently of a chronology of violence, including the ways in which women's many contributions to both movements and scholarships tend to remain occluded.

As they pertain to the study of World Christianity, questions of agency have often followed an attention to the roles of those non-Western people who converted to the faith rather than assuming that the whole story could be understood through the actions and intentions of Western missionaries.[16] In this literature, the actions, beliefs, and institutions of those who converted are often the ones that tend to matter, including especially their creation of new theologies, religious practices, and institutions in the process, often in the context of the real constraints and violence of colonialism. This literature has often referred to these agentive acts as the *indigenization, enculturation*, or *contextualization* of the Christian gospel, processes that were made possibly through translation, dissention, and the development of new church structures.[17] The final three chapters of this book (by Kwiyani, Sunder John Boopalan, and Chow) are intended to respond to these assessments of the field of World Christianity, in terms of geography as well as methodology, offering close examinations of different Christian communities responding to contexts of persecution and violence.

Protestant Internationalism

"Protestant internationalism" is an emerging scholarly conversation that provides contrast to World Christianity's focus on local actors. Moving beyond the transatlantic turn that dominated analyses in the 1980s and 1990s, Protestant internationalism highlights the ways in which American Christians have engaged with and shaped the modern world beyond the United States' national borders.[18] In this script, Americans arise as protagonists whose relationships, efforts, power, and Christian faith shape the world as they imagine it. Melani McAlister's recent book, *The Kingdom of God Has No Borders*, argues, "American evangelicals have operated in many registers, crossing borders as they created networks, constructing their sense of a multiracial faith community . . . intricately linked to the experiences and values of believers around the world."[19] What arises from Protestant internationalism is a robust picture of networks and imaginations, where American Christians have acted on the world—through intervention, advocacy, investment, mission, and charity—and been transformed in the process.

This literature also shares a geographical affinity with the literature of the "global war on Christians," as both highlight Christians in North Africa, the Middle East, and Eastern Europe as particular subjects of concern. Together, these geographical regions have typically been ancillary to the subfield of World Christianity, for they problematize the narrative of a growing and successful global Christian movement. These contrasts, however, are not merely geographical puzzle pieces that can be fastened together or acceptable differences explained by disparate data gathering. Rather, they often constitute distinct and isolated streams of scholarship and methodologies that rarely intersect, much less constructively inform one another. The need for constructive engagement across these literatures is evident from the complexity of the issues they address.

These dynamics are likewise evident in the case of the abducted girls from Chibok. The hashtag #BringBackOurGirls leveraged common religious sensibilities among Western Christians and humanitarians. As it spread beyond Nigeria, so too did questionable assumptions: who is the "us" implied by the "our"? As Sara Ahmed wrote, "'You' implicitly evokes a 'we,' a group of subjects who can identify themselves with the injured nation in this performance of personal injury."[20] While #BringBackOurGirls originated among a group of Nigerian activists, the meaning of the "our" necessarily shifted as the campaign moved across social media platforms. The girls' abduction and the viral global social media campaign that came from it are evidence of a powerful intersection of interests and causes. For some people, the Chibok raid was part of a generalized "war" against girls, children, or Black lives in general.[21] Many American Christians, however, also leveraged a common Christian identity, creating enduring transatlantic networks and often effectively lobbying on behalf of Nigerian Christians.[22] But even having quickly garnered the attention of the then–U.S. president and first lady, Barack and Michelle Obama (and the consequent addition of American military resources), the campaign struggled with achieving its actual aim of returning the abducted girls to their families. More than seven years after the attack at the school, more than 100 of the 276 girls remain missing.[23] Still, the role of Western Christian humanitarian organizations, nonprofits, and individuals remains relevant to understanding how the abductions became a global event and facilitated the complex international workings that secured the release of several dozen of the girls in the intervening years. Understanding how the Chibok girls became part of an Americanized Christian "we" or "our" can illumine dynamics of transnational affiliation among Christians and how these affiliations can have political, economic, and religious effects.

Toward a New Analysis

The global interconnectedness of Christian movements has gained increasing focus in the fields of American religious history and World Christianity. We posit that there are three broadly contrasting ways of imagining Christianity globally in current scholarship: one largely concerned with persecution, suffering, and martyrdom ("global war on Christians"); another with growth, creativity, and agency ("World Christianity"); and a third with the construction of globalized networks on the part of Americans ("Protestant internationalism"). Each of these fields of inquiry is also interdisciplinary, with historians, political scientists, ethnographers, sociologists, and theologians, among others, making important contributions to them. These literatures are largely isolated from one another and even analytically contradictory, but we contend that the theme of violence is an important *through line* across these relatively distinct fields of inquiry. That is, scholarship on World Christianity has very infrequently accounted for violence (either interreligious or intra-Christian), while those who argue that there is presently a global war on Christians see worldwide religious violence as a pervasive reality. Similarly, if Protestant internationalism primes how Americans have perceived and interacted with the world (including through politicized concepts such as international religious freedom), then it also tends to limit its analysis to the actions, beliefs, and ideologies held by Americans rather than those who are the subjects of their actions (which is more often the focus of the field of World Christianity). The contributors to this volume collectively indicate the need to establish analytical and methodological priorities within these areas of scholarship in order to avoid reifying the existing narratives within these fields of inquiry. They highlight the need to work in interdisciplinary ways to fully explore the complex issues surrounding violence, persecution, and religious identity and belief.

What we seek here is not merely rapprochement among these lines of inquiry, but generation: new analytical directions emerging from the intentional combination of narratives and literatures that have, heretofore, remained relatively isolated from one another. In *Global Visions of Violence*, we argue that violence creates a lens, a bridge, and a method for interdisciplinary collaboration that examines Christianity worldwide in the twentieth and twenty-first centuries. We want to ask how a renewed focus on agency might begin to shape how scholars of international religious freedom view Christians living in legally precarious contexts. How can an appreciation for the power dynamics within global Christian networks shift analyses of constraints and agency with respect to religious belief, identity, and practice? How does a renewed attention to the ways in which suffering inflicted on Christians by other Christians challenge the ecumenical ways in which the faith might be imagined within World Christian scholarship? The chapters in this volume provide an analytical through line that makes clear the pluriform ways in which violence has become a dynamic agent, exerting multidirectional change on diverse global Christian communities.

Crucial to this volume's efforts to integrate and intervene within these literatures is the contributors' careful and consistent attention to the issue of *agency*. Agency emerged as a category of analysis in the last quarter of the twentieth century, when it often served to capture a critique of structuralist accounts of societies.[24] In particular, the term was featured in analyses that considered how change comes about, especially revolutionary and transformational change. In one sense, the term carried the baggage of Western Enlightenment sensibilities, focusing on the role of individuals vis-à-vis perceived cultural systems. As such, it can presuppose a rational actor and often analytically prioritizes dissent. In this way, a "no" is more constitutive of agency than a "yes."[25] Many early theorists of the concept, however, also resisted this simplicity and frequently used the term to capture a dialectic between persons and their societies: social structures shape (and transform) individuals, who in turn shape (and change) the structures.[26] Attuning to agency frequently prioritizes a basic question of who has the power to act, in what contexts, and to what ends. That is, agency does not require or presuppose a lack of constraints in order to be consequential or analytically relevant.[27] Yet attending to the question of whose actions are believed to be of consequence in a given time and place can reveal the analytical priorities (and lacunae) of a scholarly field. It is clear that the three primary literatures that are most relevant to the topic under consideration here tend to configure agency in different and methodologically divergent ways. While the agents vary from chapter to chapter—ranging from globally concerned US Christian women (Hillary Kaell) to Mexican women seeking a means to address ubiquitous violence in their lives (Kingsbury), to Dalit Christians' ethics that seek to respond to the negative affect produced by caste-based violence (Boopalan)—the dynamic of violence and action is woven throughout the volume.

This Volume's Contributions

If violence is a thematic and analytical priority across the following chapters, what each contributor takes to be violence varies. Throughout this volume contributors grapple with different conceptualizations, perceptions, and imaginations of violence rather than a particular form of violence (such as war or ethnic conflict). Some chapters focus on globally imagined forms of suffering as a result of natural and human-caused disasters (John Corrigan and Kaell), and others examine contexts that are more often understood as religious persecution and martyrdom (Omri Elisha, Chow, Boopalan, and Lukasik). Still others include gender as the primary analytic (Kingsbury and Cabrita). Yet there are important intersections. Kaell notes how one woman's perception of humanitarian child sponsorship was folded into a broader sense of global Christian persecution, and Kwiyani, Boopalan, and Lukasik, respectively, show the complexities of contextual notions of race and caste across religious and national boundaries. What the chapters collectively demonstrate is that violence can be understood as pervasive, unequal, dynamic, and contextually variant while nevertheless exerting powerful influences on Christian identity, belief, and practice across multiple contexts.

Toward that end, *Global Visions of Violence* begins with a focus on the global entanglements of American Christianity. The opening section explores how contextual factors impact the global circulation of images, stories, and data of and about persecuted and suffering Christians (Corrigan). Editors and writers frame events, stories, and statistics within narratives that they hope resonate with or provoke their readers. Media have the power to create insiders and outsiders, depicting certain communities as a "global other" in need of humanitarian rescue or government intervention. But this focus on the agency of traditional media can also obscure other sources, uses, and effects of information. In this respect, particular religious actors play complex roles in shaping narratives of religious violence and persecution. Missionaries and their support letters sent to donors back home, foreign diplomats reporting on religious conflict, or nongovernmental organization (NGO) volunteers defending their mission abroad are all important conduits of information. The complex ways in which media and individuals raise funds, recruit volunteers, and maintain support provide a multilayered context for analyzing images of suffering and persecuted Christians (Kaell). Furthermore, it is common for humanitarian NGOs to curate images of passive victims abroad in need of rescue. Within certain theological understandings, however, Western Christians imbue persecuted Christians with extraordinary spiritual power, thereby creating the possibility of dynamic relationships (Elisha). The chapters in this section, therefore, consider the reciprocal ways in which Christians in contexts of persecution employ, ignore, or otherwise utilizes reports, statistics, or other forms of data and media in local contexts. These chapters explore the ways in which religious violence *created* networks and *curated* a global vision of violence.

From questions of moral and spiritual geographies, the volume moves toward bodies. Anti-Christian persecution literature and activism tend to focus on cases in which physical violence, imprisonment, and/or death are inflicted on individuals or communities due to their religious identity. In doing so, their analysis often foregrounds religious belief and identity to the near exclusion of other contextual factors. Additionally, religious persecution is sometimes only one type of violence that a community might experience. Gender-based violence, social structures that inflict unequal suffering, and intra-Christian persecution are also constitutive of the forms of violence that Christians create, perpetuate, and experience around the world. Two chapters prioritize the embodied experiences of women of color and how contexts of intra-Christian (Cabrita) and large-scale violence (Kingsbury) have shaped the creative expressions of Christian faith in colonial Swaziland and contemporary Mexico, respectively. Lukasik's chapter on Coptic Christian transnational networks locates religious identity within the racial politics of post-9/11 America, arguing that the "racialization of American Copts is a dual process oscillating between Christian kinship with white America and the optics of nonwhite suspicion." Taken together, these chapters challenge the ecumenical assumptions that undergird World Christianity scholarship, even as both illuminate different kinds of examples of Christians marginalizing other Christians.

Finally, the volume examines the communities formed in the midst of violence and persecution by focusing on three minoritized communities in World Christianity—African Christians in Malawi (Kwiyani), Dalits in India (Boopalan), and Chinese Christians (Chow). Religious identity and belief are often primed as explanatory factors in discussions of religious violence. Such prioritization, while relevant in some instances, might also obscure other contextual factors of identity, such as language, ethnicity, race, and socioeconomic status. Insufficient attention to these dimensions can paint an incomplete picture of local and regional conflicts. This section, therefore, explores the ways in which religious violence is not ethereal but rather inflicted on persons living in particular times and places, and how experiences and long historical contexts of persecution can themselves be important shapers of religious traditions. These contexts are chosen for their potential for wider insight but also for their prominence in narratives outside World Christianity. Kwiyani's chapter engages with literature and processes that have been central to scholarship in World Christianity: the development of independent Christian movements in sub-Saharan Africa. In focusing on Chilembwe's Uprising in early twentieth-century Malawi, Kwiyani not only analytically centers colonial violence but also questions the enduring ways in which Western Christianity continues to remain "[ambivalent] concerning issues involving slavery, colonialism, racism, and white supremacy."

In the case of Dalit Christianity, Boopalan perceptively draws our attention to the importance of affective forms of quotidian violence in maintaining the marginalization of historic caste divisions, the ways that these practices are reproduced within Indian diasporic communities, and how Christian faith can sustain a resistance to these practices. Finally, Chow engages in a digital ethnography of a controversial Chinese sect, showing how its members have responded to political persecution by developing creative global networks. These chapters treat these dynamics with insight and sensitivity, and their analyses show the gaps in viewing those who experience persecution as merely, or even primarily, as victims. They also highlight communal identity, the development of local traditions and ideologies, the pressure of cultural change, and the responses of Christians to contexts of persecution. The arguments developed by Kwiyani, Boopalan, and Chow challenge simplistic assumptions regarding those who experience persecution and offer important insights into the ways that such experiences have resulted in creativity, theological reflection, political action, and the development of digital and global networks. Diasporic networks of persecuted Christians demonstrate the creative ways in which they have used the theological, spiritual, and ritual resources of their traditions and denominations in order to form connections across geographical distances. These chapters challenge scholarship on Christian growth that has often left violence unaccounted for, while ignoring persecution narratives that can wield data and stories toward partisan ends.

Taken together, the disciplines and fields of scholarship represented in this volume bring necessary methodological and analytical resources for understanding violence with respect to Christianity worldwide. In assembling the contributors to this volume, we intentionally sought historians, anthropologists, theologians, and those trained within area studies in order to show the possibilities of simultaneous interventions within these fields. Furthermore, we also sought out scholars who were at different phases of their careers. This diversity also raises an editorial challenge: how to allow the chapters to cohere while preserving the disciplinary distinctiveness of the respective scholars? We contend that the chapters' analytical diversity creates new syntheses and suggests new directions for approaching religious persecution, violence, and Christianity in the modern world. Kwiyani and Boopalan write as theologians, respectively, of missions and ethics, though both demonstrate historical and ethnographic sensibilities. Similarly, other contributors who work ethnographically, such as Kaell, Kingsbury, Lukasik, and Chow, do so with a sensitivity to the beliefs and theologies of their interlocutors. Chapters that are more historical in nature, such as Corrigan's analysis of American Christians' efforts to quantify violence and suffering or Cabrita's description of the ways in which the field of African Christianity has served as a place of methodological marginalization and violence, are also historiographically conversant with literature that connects them with chapters elsewhere in the volume, such as literature on Protestant internationalism and World Christianity.

Alternative chapter configurations are possible or even desirable. We want readers to find resonances among these chapters—new assemblages of questions and issues that can further illumine these complex and dynamic contexts, lives, and issues. We hope, therefore, that this volume offers new methodological directions for pushing conversations forward, including within constructive and ongoing projects that seek justice, peace, and human rights among suffering Christians. Together, they gesture in new synthetic analytical directions, illuminating wide and often hidden landscapes that have been shaped by global visions of violence.

NOTES

1. Howard LaFranchi, "What Role for US in Efforts to Rescue Nigeria's Kidnapped Girls?," *Christian Science Monitor*, May 5, 2014, https://www.csmonitor.com/USA/Foreign -Policy/2014/0505/What-role-for-US-in-efforts-to-rescue-Nigeria-s-kidnapped-girls; Oren Dowell, "Terrorists Kidnap More Than 200 Nigerian Girls," *USA Today*, April 21, 2014, https://www.usatoday.com/story/news/world/2014/04/21/parents-234-girls-kidnapped -from-nigeria-school/7958307; David Smith and Harriet Sherwood, "Military Operation Launched to Locate Missing Nigerian Girls," *Guardian*, May 14, 2014, https://www .theguardian.com/world/2014/may/14/nigeria-launches-military-operation-to-find -kidnapped-girls.

2. Johnnie Moore, *The Martyr's Oath: Living for the Jesus They're Willing to Die For* (Carol Stream, IL: Tyndale House, 2018); John Allen Jr., *The Global War on Christians: Dispatches from the Front Lines of Anti-Christian Persecution* (New York: Image, 2013).

3. Naomi Haynes, "'Zambia Shall Be Saved!': Prosperity Gospel Politics in a Self-Proclaimed Christian Nation," *Nova Religio* 19, no. 1 (2014): 5–24; Ruth Maclean and Andrew Esiebo, "Eat, Pray, Live: The Lagos Megachurches Building Their Very Own Cities," *Guardian*, September 11, 2017, https://www.theguardian.com/cities/2017/sep/11/eat-pray-live-lagos -nigeria-megachurches-redemption-camp.

4. Chris Deliso, "Ecumenical US Conference Highlights Persecution of Christians," *Tablet*, December 5, 2017, https://www.thetablet.co.uk/news/8191/ecumenical-us-conference -highlights-persecution-of-christians-; Todd M. Johnson and Gina Zurlo, "Christian Martyrdom as a Pervasive Phenomenon," *Society* 51 (2014): 679–685; see also Pew Research Center, "Rising Restrictions on Religion—One-Third of the World's Population Experiences an Increase," August 9, 2011, https://www.pewforum.org/2011/08/09 /rising-restrictions-on-religion2/.

5. Allen, *Global War on Christians*.

6. Daniel Philpott and Timothy Samuel Shah, eds., *Under Caesar's Sword: How Christians Respond to Persecution* (Cambridge: Cambridge University Press, 2018).

7. Moore, *Martyr's Oath*, 13.

8. "World Watch List: Nigeria," Open Doors International, accessed July 2, 2021, https:// www.opendoorsusa.org/christian-persecution/world-watch-list/nigeria/.

9. U.S. Commission on International Religious Freedom, "Nigeria," *USCIRF Annual Report 2021*, 3, accessed July 2, 2021, https://www.uscirf.gov/sites/default/files/2021-05/Nigeria %20Chapter%20AR2021.pdf.

10. Joe Parkinson and Drew Hinshaw, "Whispered Prayers, Hidden Bibles, Secretly Scribbled Verses: Inside the Resilient Faith of the #BringBackOurGirls Hostages," *Christianity Today*, June 21, 2020, https://www.christianitytoday.com/ct/2021/july-august/bring-back-our-girls-parkinson-hinshaw-nigeria-boko-haram.html.

11. Parkinson and Hinshaw, "Whispered Prayers."

12. Alan Anderson, *Spreading Fires: The Missionary Nature of Early Pentecostalism* (Maryknoll, NY: Orbis Books, 2007).

13. Andrew Walls, *The Missionary Movement in Christian History: Studies in the Transmission of the Faith* (Maryknoll, NY: Orbis Books, 1996); Dana L. Robert, "Shifting Southward: Global Christianity since 1945," *International Bulletin of Missionary Research* 24, no. 2 (2000): 50–58; Kenneth Scott Latourette, *A History of the Expansion of Christianity*, 7 vols. (New York: Harper and Brothers, 1937–1945); David B. Barrett, *Schism and Renewal in Africa: An Analysis of Six Thousand Contemporary Religious Movements* (Nairobi: Oxford University Press, 1970).

14. Philip Jenkins, *The Next Christendom: The Coming of Global Christianity* (New York: Oxford University Press, 2002).

15. Ruth Marshall, *Political Spiritualities: The Pentecostal Revolution in Nigeria* (Chicago: University of Chicago Press, 2009); Nimi Wariboko, *Nigerian Pentecostalism* (Rochester: University of Rochester Press, 2014).

16. Lamin O. Sanneh, *West African Christianity: The Religious Impact* (Maryknoll, NY: Orbis Books, 1983).

17. Richard Fox Young and Jonathan Seitz, eds., *Asia in the Making of Christianity: Conversion, Agency, and Indigeneity, 1600s to the Present* (Leiden: Brill, 2013); Stephen B. Bevans and Robert P. Schroeder, *Constants in Contexts: A Theology of Mission for Today* (Maryknoll, NY: Orbis Books, 2014); David J. Bosch, *Transforming Mission: Paradigm Shifts in Theology of Mission* (Maryknoll, NY: Orbis Books, 1991; reprint, 2011).

18. David Hollinger, *Protestants Abroad: How Missionaries Tried to Change the World but Changed America* (Princeton: Princeton University Press, 2017); Lauren Turek, "To Support a 'Brother in Christ': Evangelical Groups and U.S.-Guatemalan Relations during the Ríos Montt Regime," *Diplomatic History* 39, no. 4 (2015): 689–719; Robert Wuthnow, *Boundless Faith: The Global Outreach of American Churches* (Berkeley: University of California Press, 2010).

19. Melani McAlister, *The Kingdom of God Has No Borders: A Global History of American Evangelicals* (New York: Oxford University Press, 2018), 290.

20. Sara Ahmed, *The Cultural Politics of Emotion* (New York: Routledge, 2015), 2. See also Kathleen Stewart, *Ordinary Affects* (Durham, NC: Duke University Press, 2007); Lauren Berlant, *Cruel Optimism* (Durham, NC: Duke University Press, 2011).

21. Innocent Chiluwa and Presley Ifukor, "'War against Our Children': Stance and Evaluation in #BringBackOurGirls Campaign Discourse on Twitter and Facebook," *Discourse & Society* 26, no. 3 (2015): 267–296.

22. Sunday Oguntola, "Leah Sharibu Inspires Nigeria's Christians, Faces Execution by Boko Haram," *Christianity Today*, October 15, 2018, https://www.christianitytoday.com/news/2018/october/free-leah-sharibu-boko-haram-execution-dapchi-nigeria.html; Holly McKay, "Nigeria's Christian Community Slowly Being Erased as Militants Step up Vicious Killings, Kidnappings," *Fox News*, June 18, 2018, https://www.foxnews.com/faith-values/nigeria-christian-militants-isis-erased-killings-kidnappings. This is not to suggest, however, that non-faith-based organizations were not actively involved in

the #BringBackOurGirls and subsequent campaigns. See Adekalu Samuel Olutokunbo, Turiman Suandi, Oluwaseyitan Rotimi Cephas, and Irza Hanie Abu-Samah, "Bring Back Our Girls, Social Mobilization: Implications for Cross-Cultural Research," *Journal of Education and Practice* 6, no. 6 (2015): 64–75.

23. Timothy Obiezu, "More Than 100 Chibok Girls Still Missing Seven Years Later," *Voice of America*, April 15, 2021, https://www.voanews.com/africa/more-100-chibok-girls-still -missing-seven-years-later.

24. Laura Ahern, "Agency," *Journal of Linguistic Anthropology* 9, nos. 1–2 (1999): 12–15.

25. Saba Mahmood, *Politics of Piety: The Islamic Revival and the Feminist Subject* (Princeton: Princeton University Press, 2004).

26. Dennis Tedlock and Bruce Mannheim, eds., *The Dialogic Emergence of Culture* (Urbana: University of Illinois Press, 1995); Ilana Gershon, "Neoliberal Agency," *Current Anthropology* 52, no. 4 (2011): 537–555; Jean Comaroff and John Comaroff, "Millennial Capitalism: First Thoughts on a Second Coming," in *Millennial Capitalism and the Cultural of Neoliberalism*, ed. Jean Comaroff and John Comaroff (Durham, NC: Duke University Press, 2001), 1–56; Michel de Certeau, *The Practice of Everyday Life*, trans. Steven Rendall (Berkeley: University of California Press, 2011).

27. Jason Bruner, *Living Salvation in the East African Revival in Uganda* (Rochester: University of Rochester Press, 2017).

PART ONE

Geographies

What role have American Christians played in imagining, producing, and engaging with a "global" world? *Global*, in this sense, does not merely represent the scope or scale, but rather a sense of affiliation, connection, and exchange—a form of relationship with people who are otherwise separated by geography. Global can also mean the extent of imagined proximity. How does this work within and among Christian communities? What are the techniques, practices, and beliefs that sustain these connections, specifically among American Christians? The three chapters in Part I offer provocative and insightful analyses of these questions. They show the intertwining of quantification, imagination, practices of affiliation, and the cultivation of affect. These chapters also highlight how American Christians, as well as Christians elsewhere, combine these factors in new, and sometimes surprising, ways.

Statistical estimations have a long Christian history, going back at least to William Carey's plea to British evangelicals to support missionary efforts among the vast multitudes of unconverted peoples of the world. In Carey's *Enquiry*, statistics were meant to compel, to make clear the immense scope of Christians' obligations. These inclinations remain, and they have been fostered through missionary and media networks in the nineteenth and twentieth (and now, the twenty-first) centuries. John Corrigan's chapter shows how American Christians have used statistics to create affective connections with those separated by vast distances. Similarly, *Jesus Freaks*, the text with which Omri Elisha's chapter opens, itself begins with a statistic: 164,000 Christians were martyred in 1998 (the year prior to its publication), followed by the prediction that the following year the number would be 165,000. Faith-based humanitarian groups such as World Vision have likewise come to describe their work quantitatively. Even if child sponsorship programs, which foster a sense of personal connection between Western donors and (typically) non-Western recipients, remain some of the best-known forms of financial support, they are also clear to communicate the massive scale on which they are able to operate. As World Vision claims of its work in 2020, in the previous year they "assisted 78.2 million disaster survivors, refugees, and internally displaced people," and "helped to equip over 3.4 million kids through our child sponsorship program."[1]

These chapters are not just about the affective ties made possible by quantification. As both Elisha and Hillary Kaell show, these global relationships are also about practices: writing letters, reading world news, receiving personal updates, poring devotedly over testimonies, praying with pictures of foreign Christians and sponsored children, and so on. These practices sustain a sense of proximity in the midst of different forms of violence and suffering. If the chapters here engage with a range of violence—from natural disasters and famine to religious persecution and mass atrocities—they also explore how quantification, practices, beliefs, and assumptions work together among some American Christians to foster different forms of agency. This agency can take the forms of curating data to compel donations (Corrigan), by encountering the providential force of a martyr's testimony (Elisha), or even by claiming, as World Vision does, that they put "the power to choose a sponsor in the child's hands—affirming that kids living in extreme poverty are not passive recipients."[2] Collectively, these chapters clarify the work, relationships, and practices that contribute to American Christians' sustaining global obligations and commitments in light of the violence and suffering they see.

NOTES

1. World Vision, "Our Work," accessed May 20, 2022, https://www.worldvision.org/our
    -work.

2. "World Vision U.S. 2019 Annual Review," accessed May 20, 2022, https://s3.us-east-2
    .amazonaws.com/wvusstatic.com/2020/landing-pages/financial-accountability/pdfs
    /2019+Annual+Report+Brochure-F_updated-final.pdf.

1

Of Numbers and Subjects

Empathic Distance in the American Protestant Missionary Agenda

JOHN CORRIGAN

An international team of researchers, surveying incidences of religious intolerance worldwide, recently concluded that people with an interest in the problem "simply do not have time or inclination to read hundreds of pages of qualitative description and analysis." While noting that the categories that investigators invent as they order their data can be laced with assumptions about what, exactly, constitutes an act of religious persecution, the team's recommendation was pointed. They proposed that the way forward was through "quantifying persecution." Qualitative assessment mattered, but "quantitative studies," they advised, "can provide a wonderfully quick and insightful way to get a handle on the national, regional, and indeed global situation."[1]

Nineteenth-century American observers of the overseas missions scene would have agreed that numbers helped. But during that century and into the next, when the American Protestant denominations cranked up what over time would become an enormous machinery of overseas proselytization, the gold standard for understanding the plight of persecuted Christians was the dramatic tale of suffering. When missions organizations reported the situation overseas, it was the depiction of the travail of the brave child, the native pastor, or the faithful woman that broached the topic of overseas persecution to a domestic audience of potential donors and collaborators.

Stories of Christian heroism in China, Japan, Africa, South Asia, and the Pacific set the tone for the discussion of mission activity in far-off places. Sometimes the achievements of missionaries were defined by their successes in building infrastructure or in growing congregations: the opening of a school, the raising of a new church, the conversion of a village. Often, however, mission magazines and reports featured accounts of missionaries or members of their churches who suffered for their faith. Their predicaments were recounted in sanguine detail, accompanied by commentary that capitalized on the emotional impact of the story in the interest of garnering support for the mission enterprise.

Rarely did a year pass without sensational stories of persecution. The annals of American Protestant missionizing are replete with news about burnings, hackings, beatings, imprisonments, and beheadings. At times such persecutions were clustered around severe social disruptions or political turmoil, as in the case of the Boxer Rebellion in 1900. A Chinese revolt against Western intrusion, the rebellion targeted foreigners of all sorts, including traders and merchants, investors and missionaries. In the wake of such upheavals, the Protestant churches (alongside Roman Catholics) made urgent appeals to their American memberships to think about the suffering of Christians overseas and act in some way to address it. The victims of persecution, hailed as martyrs and upheld as Christian exemplars, proved inspiring figures for Christians back home.

Luella Miner's, *China's Book of Martyrs: A Record of Heroic Martyrdoms and Marvelous Deliverances during the Summer of 1900* (1903) represents the approach of most Protestant writing of the time about Christian persecution overseas. Once "the Boxer hordes broke loose" in China, there ensued terror and brutality, and such "indescribable cruelty during that summer of horror" that "it is impossible to express" it. Miner's witnesses repeatedly protested that "no words can tell the misery" that they endured, and Miner confessed that her book could "not tell in full the story of the faithful witness of China."[2] It was impossible to fully convey the content of distant suffering.

Miner nevertheless attempted to narrate victims' misery, in highly wrought descriptions of the tortures they endured, the executions, and the lasting emotional trauma. Like all persecution narratives that appeared in Protestant publications, she offered lengthy, point-by-point descriptions of the progress of torture, in each of her cases, that were "representative and typical" of the "bloody slaughter."[3] Miner arranged the terrible events, written pathetically, in geographical categories: Peking, T'ungchou, Pao Ting Fu, and Shansi, among others, all far-off places with strange names. While the literary critic Elaine Scarry argued in 1985 that "to have great pain is to have certainty; to hear that another person has pain is to have doubt,"[4] Miner effused her certainty about her own grasp of events in her hundreds of attempts to communicate a sense of her subjects' pain through her adjective-rich accounts of people on the other side of the globe, as in the following example:

> Dragging her out of the house to a tree in the yard, they held her as she stood, her baby in her arms, and saw her dear boy slowly stabbed to death. A cruel spear thrust through his back, then as he ran screaming round and round the tree, one after another cut at him with swords and spears. A wild thought came into the mind of the frenzied mother as she clasped her doomed baby close to her heart; perhaps she could save him from that

slow torment. With the strength of a maniac, she dashed the child against the tree killing him instantly. The boxers took their revenge by slowly doing the mother to death.[5]

Miner's style is characteristic of the prose of book and magazine writers who rehearsed for American readerships the pain of people in China in 1900, and in other places around the globe, during the nineteenth and twentieth centuries.[6] The pathos in the writing aimed to cultivate sympathy, a feeling often identified as a core Christian virtue in missionary publications until it was superseded in late twentieth-century missionary discourse by empathy.[7] Christian chroniclers of the pain of foreign others worked hard to inspire an emotional response, exploiting the ancient historical conventions of the prose genre of martyrology as well as leveraging innovations in publishing in service to their cause. As the technology of image reproduction advanced, editors supplemented texts with photographic images. Publications such as the *Christian and Missionary Alliance* and *Christian Herald*, beginning in the 1890s, increasingly ran photographs of foreigners in pain in an effort to relate misery that was beyond language. Presuming that pictures were worth thousands of words, magazines took images as points of departure and built stories around them. Such "spectacles of suffering" were braided with a commercial agenda to entertain a mass culture, and as such they relied, to a certain extent, on the capability of both images and prose to render people who lived far away as legible objects within that mass culture.[8]

The process, however, begat ironies. Photographs, in fact, could distance readers from the reality of persecution overseas as much as they prompted sympathy. Narrators such as Miner reached deep for the heartstrings of readers, and photographs may have assisted in cultivating fellow-feeling. But for Miner, the violence of persecution remained "impossible to express," and photographs of human ordeal, as historian Heather Curtis and others have argued, risked reinforcing a sense of difference and distance from the exotic object.[9] Photography could be as much an alienating medium as a familiarizing one through bringing into focus the strangeness of people on other continents.[10] Depicting distant suffering, in photographs or in prose, could be, as Scarry proposed, a prompt to doubt. That was especially the case given that Americans insistently closed their eyes to religious persecution in their own country, refusing to see the damage it wrought across a range of ongoing violent encounters between competing groups. The simple fact that foreigners experienced persecution and Americans (so they believed) did not was itself an estranging fact.[11]

Americans who followed the news about missionary activities in foreign lands experienced other uncertainties that could distance them from the people depicted in stories and photographs. While a story about torture and pictures of suffering might, in their own way, lead to a sense of distance from foreigners, American Protestants sometimes wondered as well whether emergent Christian communities overseas were comprised of people who were genuinely converted. From the early nineteenth century onward, Americans who were concerned with the organization of overseas missions remained troubled about locals who presented themselves as converted only in order to claim the membership benefits—such as rice—that the missionaries offered. A commentator in the *Wesleyan Methodist Magazine*, observing the Chinese scene, worried in 1852 that "the few converts come from the lowest and poorest class; and these, it seems, are often, bribed with a little rice,—so that they are frequently made mention of as 'rice Christians.'"[12] The term has remained ubiquitous in American missionary publications and is often discussed in scholarly literature.[13] It represents something of the ambivalence of Americans toward the missionary project, a cause for questioning it even as Americans pledged greater personal resources to its increase. Rice Christians were distant Christians in more ways than one.

Empathy

In 1817, the Congregationalist minister Lyman Beecher preached a sermon in Boston on the occasion of the ordination of five ministers who were to be commissioned for overseas duty as "missionaries to the heathen."[14] His view of the predicament of the heathen was severe. Beecher asked his auditors, "What need then of all this sympathy for the heathen?" Rejecting the argument that the heathen were "guileless children of our common father, all affectionately striving to please him," he inventoried twenty-three of their sins, from "murder" and "malignity" to being "inventors of evil things" and "without natural affection."[15] The heathen were a contradistinctive people. Beecher, intending to arm the young missionaries with realism in advance of their encounter with faraway populations, advised the forthright imposition of the biblical "code of laws" as a better course than sympathy.

In spite of Beecher's public notice of a breach between the New England soul and the heathen soul overseas, exponents of missions settled into the habit of recommending the cultivation of sympathy for the people they encountered in the mission field. But that sympathy remained tinctured with suspicion that the heathen was "not like us." Missions organizations could beg their readers for help "in producing a sympathy for the heathen," even while asserting that a "certain portion of the family of man, who worship idols" were bizarre figures of "moral degradation and mental imbecility."[16] The American Board of Commissioners of Foreign Missions congratulated themselves in 1868 that they "had awakened and cultivated a sympathy for the heathen." Other observers leveraged that insight in advocating a fiduciary outcome: "Again, this sympathy for the heathen should manifest itself in *giving*." A missionary could be eulogized for her "sympathy to the heathen, her skill in winning individuals to Christ." But American sympathy for peoples overseas did not fail to recognize *"the importance of informing ourselves respecting the actual condition of the heathen.*"[17] That is, how people over there were different.

Sympathy, a word for a feeling, appeared with increasing frequency in nineteenth-century American writing partly because Adam Smith had made it a keystone of his psychological investigations into morality, *The Theory of Moral Sentiments* (1759). Smith wrote that sympathy was imagining how others felt. Yet "we have no immediate experience of what other men feel." That meant that "we can form no idea of the manner in which they are affected, but by conceiving what we ourselves should feel in the like situation. Though our brother is on the rack, as long as we ourselves are at our ease, our senses will never inform us of what he suffers. They never did, and never can, carry us beyond our own person, and it is by the imagination only that we can form any conception of what are his sensations."[18] For Smith, sympathy was psychological bridgework that enabled what philosophers in general had called "moral sense." Smith's theory, over time spun in various directions by his interpreters, and often viewed as a development of similar theorizing by Jean-Jacques Rousseau, for the most part remained a way of thinking about both human difference and similarity.[19] One person remained different from another while imagining how another felt. There was a tension in Smith's influential theory about sympathy, and that tension remained in religious literature that addressed the business of missions.[20]

Smith's thinking came to America in conjunction with Scottish Common Sense Realism, with which it shared certain constructs. A medley of treatises by Thomas Reid, Dugald Stewart, Adam Ferguson and others, the Common Sense philosophy proved to be a key influence on the coalescing evangelical religion of the early Republic.[21] Smith's work especially was popular with the revolutionary era founders, and in the nineteenth century it eclipsed that of Reid on American library shelves. In the nineteenth century Smith's theories of economics and belief in sympathy as crucial to moral sense were broadly diffused in curricula, commentary, and academic treatises.[22]

The theory of sympathy that found currency in American Protestant writing underwrote a sense of difference from others alongside a feeling of intimate connection. It found good use in schematizations of the nature of the relationship of American Protestants to people in foreign, non-Christian places. It functioned well in depicting both the field experiences of overseas missionaries and the emotional cast of domestic patrons of religious missions. Jacques Derrida, writing of Rousseau's notion of sympathy in *Of Grammatology* (1967), proposed that sympathy, for Rousseau, necessitated "a certain distance." Analyzing "the paradox of the relation to the other" in Rousseau, Derrida argued that "there is no identification except in a certain non-identification," by which he meant that full identification with the other would foreclose the possibility of recognizing suffering as the suffering of the other.[23] The case was largely the same for Smith.[24] Sympathy required distance. The American Protestant imagination, as historian

David Morgan noted in analyzing nineteenth-century Protestant visual culture, was constituted in part by that complex notion of sympathy: "Deeply encoded in the life of fellow-feeling may reside an antipathy for those who are not like 'us.'" Sympathy, for all the sense of connection it offered, remained a potential means "to preserve difference."[25]

The engine of sympathy drove appeals of support for Protestant missionizing for decades and remains an important part of the rhetoric of twenty-first-century global Protestantism. But the paradoxical experience that was enunciated as sympathy eventually troubled Protestants, who wanted a cleaner, less ambiguous articulation of their felt connections to persons in distant places. In the latter part of the twentieth century, American Protestants accordingly expressed a preference for the term *empathy* in their descriptions of their missions activities. Indeed, *empathy* became the favorite term of human rights activists as well, and in the early twenty-first century it became such a popular topic of academic research and political discourse that it recently was described as "one of our culture's most ubiquitous sacred cows."[26]

Empathy replaced sympathy in most American Christian writing about missions and, especially, in accounts of persecution suffered by Christians. The Christian author of *Stories of Persecution* (2017) instructed the reader that "there's a fundamental difference between sympathy and empathy. Sympathy is acknowledging someone's pain. Empathy is allowing yourself to feel that pain. Sympathy looks at a person from a distance and says, 'Oh man, let me fix that. Empathy enters into the person's pain.'" When Christians pray for the persecuted, "we see them as 'other,' across the world, in situations we can't imagine and offer a quick prayer for THOSE people over THERE dealing with THAT." Empathy, however, "means we linger on the stories we hear."[27] Lingering presumably led to closing the distance with the distant sufferer.

Protestant writers who promoted empathy focused especially on the role of the missionary rather than on the experience of missions supporters on the home front. They distinguished "external" identification from "internal" identification with the other in an effort to explain the difference between sympathy and empathy. External identification with members of a host culture meant sharing in their everyday lives—in the material circumstances of their work and play—eating as they did, embracing the rhythms of their collective life, speaking and moving as they did, taking an active role in community activities, and learning and relaxing with locals. But "physical conformity, sometimes called 'outer identification,' should not be equated with 'inner identification,' the heartfelt empathy" of one God-given soul for another.[28] Writers agreed that true empathy as "inward identification is more difficult to obtain and superior to outward identification."[29] They conceptualized it as the complete closing of distance between the missionary and the local, a complete identification that finally crossed the space of "the last eighteen inches to the heart." But while such language became popular, there were people who wondered whether empathy was really any different from sympathy, internal identification was truly something different from external identification, and full identification with the other was, in fact, desirable. One veteran's pronouncement that missionaries like him "can never truly identify with the people in their host country" represented a sense of resignation on the part of some, even in the midst of feverish theorization of empathy as the answer, that distant suffering would always be distant.[30]

Just as significantly, critics questioned whether empathy, when recommended as the appropriate response to depictions of distant suffering, trampled on the subjectivities of those with whom it wished to attain union. Critics said that it objectified people. Dominick LaCapra, a historian of trauma, observed that some empathy, involving the illusion of a thoroughgoing identification between the observer and the sufferer, could manifest as "the unmediated fusion of self and other in which the otherness or the alterity of the other is not recognized and respected."[31] In other words, empathy could overplay its hand, and in the process lose the voice of the distant sufferer. Like sympathy, it played not only at objectifying the sufferer but also as making the sufferer disappear. Luc Boltanski, in *Distant Suffering*, made the point more precisely with regard to how people respond to media portrayals of human suffering that is geographically remote. Privileged Westerners, said Boltanski, prompted by media depictions of distant suffering, overidentify with the sufferers in a way that leads to a dismissal of their suffering as universal and thus unexceptional.[32] Such overidentification rendered subjects two-dimensional. The term *empathy* also attracted criticism that the personal disposition it signifies is biased, and at times even racist.[33]

American religious writers affirmed their goal of empathy with people in faraway places, and especially with those who experienced persecution as Christians. But some writers discovered that as much as they sought to cultivate empathy as union with the other, there remained a distance between observer and observed. There was always a danger of losing the subjectivity of the other, either through overidentification or lack of identification, both of which led to estrangement from the subject. Being too close was as problematic as being distant.

Statistics

Americans who concerned themselves with the treatment of Christians overseas increasingly turned to statistics as a means of understanding situations in distant places. The promotion of empathy—which was colored by a nagging suspicion that full identification was impossible and even, if so, maybe unadvisable—was joined to a growing program of data collection and statistical analysis.

The fascination with statistics did not emerge from a vacuum. Colonial-era revivalists had made conversion counts a key part of their promotional campaigns, and although the numbers sometimes failed to add up, the practice of head counting became customary. Enthusiasm for the conversion count translated into a broader field of accounting involving memberships, attendances, and charitable giving. American Protestants committed to the systematic recording of statistics about church membership during the period of the early Republic. Churches kept track of the local numbers and passed them on to regional associations or committees, and those organizations in turn consulted national bodies, which eventually aggregated the data and made it public.

Churches worked constantly to refine their censuses. Throughout the nineteenth and twentieth centuries their census taking improved in various ways, both in terms of the reliability of the count at the local level and the organization and interpretation of the data at the national level. But doubts and ambiguities remained. In its "Report on Statistics," the Presbyterian *Evangelical Repository* announced in 1873 that "statistical tables, in a new and improved form, have been received from each of the Presbyteries in the Church. Most of these tables have been prepared with care . . . still some of them are incomplete, and are not free from inaccuracies." Nevertheless, the report immediately added that the clerks of the church were to be commended for "the success they have attained in presenting the statistics of the Church, in a form so full and complete."[34] Exactly how an inaccurate and incomplete count could be full and complete is less important historically than the fact that statistics were collected as means to an end, not as an end in themselves. Power was in the picture of growth, in the numerical evidence of successfully competing against other denominations for members.

Data gathering continued among American Protestants throughout the twentieth century, alongside Roman Catholic census taking, which had a longer history, a more expansive administrative bureaucracy, and greater experience in the field. Eventually, Protestant efforts coalesced in several ambitious projects that have been foundational for the current Protestant interest in global numbers. The most important of those projects was the 1982 *World Christian Encyclopedia* (*WCE*), the creation of David B. Barrett (1927–2011), whose work, according to one disciple, "fundamentally changed the conception of religion in the modern world."[35] Barrett, an Englishman and missionary in Africa who eventually held the title of Research Professor of Missiometrics at Pat Robertson's Regent University in Virginia, gathered 1,000 pages of numbers bearing on Christian denominations worldwide.[36] His *Encyclopedia* served as a resource for researchers interested in global religious demography, but additionally it modeled a certain kind of census taking for other aspiring religious demographers and, most important, prompted a reassessment of the value of censuses to the promotions of Christian missions worldwide. Gordon-Conwell Theological

Seminary in Massachusetts subsequently invested in producing new iterations of the *Encyclopedia*, publishing updated figures, offering fresh demographic categories, and developing informants through the World Christian Database (WCD). The WCD became a full-blown global census, not only of Christianity but of other religions as well. It subsequently became known as the World Religion Database or (WRD).[37]

While some people embraced the vision offered by the WCD, critics reproved it as biased, ambiguous, and inaccurate, and the WRD inherited some of that criticism.[38] But the publication of the *WCE* and the subsequent regular censuses produced at Gordon-Conwell, among other census projects, built strong momentum for an across-the-board investment by Protestants in statistics.

As Christians were enthusiastically embracing the census as a tool that they believed could advance their project of World Christianity, human rights causes were doing the same. Like American Christian mission organizations, human rights organizations had relied heavily on narrations of the suffering of persons. The human rights movement built cases for reform based on the testimonials of witnesses who related their experiences, and especially their suffering, in public displays that appealed affectively to auditors. First-person accounts of detention and torture, of witnessing brutality, executions, and disappearances, became the truth that grounded reports of human rights violations. Truth was an affectual truth, as stories rich in feeling made their way from the mouths of witnesses to the ears of people distal to the suffering itself. The media were especially important in this process, as conveyors not only of words but also of images and sounds that contributed to the testimony's credibility.[39]

However, human rights organizations also collected data on abuses around the world and increasingly deployed that data in reports and articles alongside images of suffering others. In the early 1990s scholars began advocating for an awareness of "of how statistical methods and the statistical profession can contribute to the advancement of human rights for all."[40] That enterprise grew over time and finally received an official imprimatur in 2014, when the United Nations Office of Human Rights urged that organizations leverage the "data revolution" in their campaigns against human rights abuses. According to the UN, "The realisation of human rights correlates with the availability of sound official statistics" so that "the dissemination of relevant statistical information is essential." Moreover, the place of statisticians as well as the work they undertook were themselves a matter of concern, so that "the rights of statisticians themselves, who sometimes have to fear for their security in doing their work, is vital."[41] Human rights organizations and Protestant denominations eventually joined forces in their efforts to count global incidences of persecution.

The turn to numbers took place throughout the Protestant missionary nexus. A leader in that venture was Ed Stetzer, the executive director of the Billy Graham Center for Evangelism. Stetzer affirmed that "in our complex religious landscape, quantifying solid research on evangelicals is essential," which is "why you should use stats in ministry." Stetzer beseeched evangelicals to recognize that "statistics help teach people," that "statistics help leaders make strategic decisions," and, most important, that "statistics help define reality." Numbers were good. "Have you ever heard the statement, 'facts are our friends'? It's true. Statistics can be our friends in helping us determine reality."[42]

Evangelicals' experimentations with statistics, however, prompted a biting response from academic sociologists, historians, and statisticians. The sociologist Christian Smith, himself a Wheaton graduate, summarized that criticism in "Evangelicals Behaving Badly with Statistics" (2007), in which he asked, "Why do evangelicals recurrently abuse statistics?" He surmised, "They are usually trying desperately to attract people's attention and raise people's concern in order to mobilize resources and action for some cause." Their use of statistics in trying to advance those causes sometimes amounted to a "misuse of statistics" that was "alarmist," "preposterous," and "inexcusable."[43]

Massification and Mediality

What was the reality that Ed Stetzer's statistics determined? How did he imagine tables of numbers would "define reality" in a certain way that would advantage evangelicals? How would a collection of numbers reinforce the effort to confront global persecution? There are two interrelated answers to that broad question.

The first way in which statistics abetted Protestant causes was through the obvious direct advantages arising from the systematic surveillance of persecution. That surveillance took the form of quantification. Protestant organizations and researchers, in collaboration with some Roman Catholic interests, became particularly concerned with the worldwide persecution of Christians and undertook to document it, not only through detailed reports of individual incidences but also through the gathering of quantitative data. The Dutch-founded organization Open Doors (whose slogan was "Serving Persecuted Christians Worldwide"), which was created in 1955 and subsequently established a major office in California, took the lead in presenting numbers that evidenced severe persecution of Christians, overwhelmingly in places where Muslims and atheist governments prevailed. Through the late twentieth and early twenty-first centuries, Open Doors published its annual *World Watch List* (*WWL*), which rank-ordered the worst offenders. In 2020, the list calculated that 260 million Christians lived under regimes that persecuted them and listed those nations in order of the severity of the persecution. The top five were North Korea, Afghanistan, Somalia, Libya, and Pakistan.[44] The list was created using a scoring system that defined the reality of persecution in its own way: "the *WWL* methodology has opted for a theological rather than a sociological definition" of persecution.[45]

Problems with scoring, data collection, and analysis haunted the *WWL*. The project nevertheless for both Protestant and Catholic denominations served for decades as a model of the application of statistics to the "definition of reality." Setting aside criticisms of the *WWL* that echoed those made of the *WCE* (for example, the criticism that "most of the martyrs suffer and die anonymously, unknown and forgotten. Nobody can report on them, nor give any figures"[46]), projects such as Under Caesar's Sword: Christian Response to Persecution encouraged the presentation of statistics, emphasizing that "reports including the use of rankings are especially effective."[47]

In the run-up to the U.S. passage of the International Religious Freedom Act in 1998, advocates for the legislation made a strong effort to supplement their archive of individuals' stories of personal suffering with quantifications of persecution drawn from Open Doors and other organizations. Some writers built their own statistical platforms out of personal travel, communications with global churches, and the analysis of field reports. One such entrepreneur, Paul Marshall, author of the widely read *Their Blood Cries Out* (1997), led with quantification on the jacket copy: "Today more than 200 million Christians around the world suffer imprisonment, abuse and even death because of their faith. Yet most Americans never hear their stories. In *Their Blood Cries Out*, Paul Marshall reveals the reality of this present-day persecution."[48] Boldly rounding out Barrett's statistical tables "to the nearest ten million," Marshall blended quantitative and qualitative data in defining the persecution of Christians as a worldwide problem.[49] Other American writers followed his lead and likewise made statistics a key part of their efforts to stir up interest in the predicaments of Christians overseas. Some, such as John L. Allen Jr., drew explicitly on the Gordon-Conwell data, lacing it throughout his book while also appealing to other data (e.g., "national statistics," "statistics maintained by the Church in Brazil," "Vatican statistics," "statistics maintained by the Coptic church").[50]

The turn to statistics among those who sought relief for persecuted Christians overseas affected the conversation about how Americans were to feel about those distant Christians. Some organizations, including those adopting a statistical approach, voiced concerns (while still defending their use of data tables and rankings). David Curry, the CEO of Open Doors USA, published a letter to his followers in 2019 urging them to consider that "the rankings and the numbers are important. But please remember that these numbers represent real people and every data point represents Christians, like you and me."[51] It was an issue that at least one promoter of statistical research had recognized previously, when Barrett's *World Christian Encyclopedia* had first appeared. Reaching for a defense of Barrett's census, the writer protested, perhaps too much, that "most of us will more likely have the feeling of being submerged rather than of appearing in the statistical tables. It is not so much the humanized and compassionate interpretation given to the statistics (p. 41) but rather the large number of photographs that remind us all that the *Encyclopedia* is about human beings, not mere cyphers or figures."[52] Photographs, said some people, connected overseas subjects emotionally to their American observers because photographs brought humanity to abstract tables of figures. (But *did* they?)[53]

The lure of numbers—the "seductions of quantification"[54]—remained powerful in part because statistical information had its own quasi-religious pull, which overlapped with a mystical Protestant notion of the worldwide "family of Christians."[55] The power of statistics was alluring: "Statistics offer a kind of gnosis, a mystic transcendence of individuality, a tasting of the forbidden fruit of knowledge . . . a mystic insight into the state of the universe. This new kind of knowledge—knowledge that absolves individuals from the claims of *deixis*, of existing at one place and in one moment—is of course none other than information. Information is knowledge with the human body taken out of it."[56] Thus, statistics themselves did, in fact, "define reality." Their purpose was to "'measure the world but, in practice, create the world they are measuring.'"[57]

The second way in which statistics—as based on the various censuses undertaken by Christian groups—reinforced the effort to prompt Americans to engage with the issue of global persecution was through their role in cultivating empathy. The process by which that took place was complicated, counterintuitive, and perhaps unwitting. It involved, first of all, the confounding fact that the global aggregation of data "caused singularities to disappear."[58] That is, statistics, when taken as "commonsense or 'truth,'"[59] objectified people. Equally problematic, as Jean-Paul Sartre once observed, was the seeming singularity of statistics itself as a form of expression; in Sartre's words, "Statistics can never be dialectics."[60] If Sartre was right, the "definition of reality" that is redolent in statistical tables might be difficult to reconcile with other realities, including those depicted in qualitative data such as eyewitness testimonies to persecution. The religious studies scholar Charles Mabee, commenting even more severely on the objectifying power of statistics, wrote, "Statistics are utilized in the modern world as a way of imposing a restricted one-way view of reality. If truth is relational in nature, then truth has no opportunity for manifestation in a society that is grounded in statistics."[61]

More to the point, statistics objectified people and rendered them distant. That process of objectification was part of the broader cultural development of massification, which profoundly changed public life in the modern era. The philosopher Ortega y Gasset in 1932 proposed that "mass man" was a distinguishing feature of modernity. In so doing, he drew on Søren Kierkegaard and Friedrich Nietzsche and anticipated Hannah Arendt, whose study of totalitarianism historically referenced deindividualization within the structureless mass society.[62] In the mid-twentieth century, a group of Columbia University faculty, including Paul Lazarsfeld, Robert Merton, and Harold Lasswell, extended thinking about massification into the study of how mass media functioned to progressively erase individuality, causing difference to disappear into social homogeneity.[63] For

Frankfurt School "culture industry" critics such as Theodor Adorno and Max Horkheimer, mass-produced media abetted the coalescence of mass consciousness and the passive consumption of capitalist values.[64] Massification as a conceptualization of mass society shaped by mass media was central to Boltanski's thinking about how the dramatization of distant suffering in human rights campaigns risked the "massification of a collection of unfortunates who are not there in person," and, accordingly, risked erasing them as subjects by inserting distance between them and well-wishing observers.[65]

Statistics massify. A modern census is an exemplary instancing of the process of massification. It is an instrument of massification. A census of religious persecution, with its rankings of offender nations, typically represents an effort to inspire empathy. Yet it abstracts subjects into tables reifying the "mass human." Censuses themselves do not constitute a distinct medium. But, like lists of any sort, they manifest "mediality." A census, and more specifically a list such as a ranked ordering of persecuting nations, is a "medial format."[66] It is a medial formatting of suffering—abstracting and quantifying that suffering—with important consequences for empathy.

Recall that for LaCapra, empathy requires a certain amount of distance from the subject. LaCapra called that distance "empathic unsettlement."[67] That term referred to an observer empathically engaging a victim's trauma while maintaining awareness of difference from the victim. As articulated by LaCapra, it is a concept that is useful in understanding American Protestant efforts to raise empathy for Christians overseas. On the one hand, a census about religious persecution holds the victim at a distance. The massification of subjects, who are quantitatively represented in a census, disembodies them and, in so doing, opens a space between them and the observer. At the same time, narratives about the suffering of subjects aim at closing that space, cultivating empathy for the pain they experience. The two approaches work together. Empathy is possible only when one does not completely identify with the subject.

It is unlikely that American Protestants were philosophically concerned that their empathy was bringing them too close to their observed victim subjects and so turned energetically to statistics and lists in the late twentieth century because they saw that as a means to prevent overidentification with victims. But their embrace of censuses and rankings made it possible for them to construct a program of consciousness regarding overseas others that urged identification with persecuted Christians at the same time that it fostered an awareness of difference. Unwittingly, Protestant missionary organizations and their allies strengthened the process by which they imagined themselves stepping out of their American shoes into the shoes of Christians overseas even as they retained a keen sense of the separateness of America from those other places.

In the end, the combination of emotional narratives and statistical rankings worked together to keep the balance between identification with others and recognition of difference that writers from Nietzsche to LaCapra have argued are necessary ingredients for empathy. It also ensured that American Protestants would be able to continue speaking from a platform built on American exceptionalism. In their empathizing they remained aware of the distance between America and other parts of the world. They remained invested in belief in a God-given destiny of America that deeply informs their sense of the nation and their commitment to the global projection of their American way of life. That notion of American exceptionalism has been ingrained in much of American Protestant writing about missions, and about global religious freedom. The language is unmistakable in the National Association of Evangelicals' "Statement of Conscience" (1996), a foundational document protesting the global persecution of Christians, and it appears in much other writing—some Protestant, some Catholic—by those who have concerned themselves with that problem.[68] The distance was always there in some form, and it happened that the embrace of statistics as a leg of the campaign against persecution of Christians pronounced it more clearly and worked to keep it there.

NOTES

1. Mauro Gatti, Pasquale Annicchino, Judd Birdsall, Valeria Fabretti, and Marco Ventura, "Quantifying Persecution: Developing an International Law-Based Measurement of Freedom of Religion or Belief," *Review of Faith and International Affairs* 17 (2019): 93, 87, 94.

2. Luella Miner, *China's Book of Martyrs: A Record of Heroic Martyrdoms and Marvelous Deliverances during the Summer of 1900* (Cincinnati: Jennings and Pye, 1903), 20, 141, 389, 290.

3. Miner, *China's Book of Martyrs*, 5, 190.

4. Elaine Scarry, *The Body in Pain: The Making and Unmaking of the World* (New York: Oxford University Press, 1985), 7.

5. Scarry, *Body in Pain*, 327.

6. A similar account of the 1900 persecution in China is E. H. Edwards, *The Reign of Terror in the Western Hills, or Stories of the Persecution of Chinese Christians in Shansi in 1900, Reprinted from the Shanghai Mercury* (Shanghai: Printed at the *Shanghai Mercury*, 1901). Other examples among thousands are R. Grundemann, "Missions: A Story of Persecution in the South," *Independent*, January 11, 1883, 7; "The Christian Martyrs in Uganda," *Christian Union*, October 7, 1886, 26; A. J. Gordon, "Martyr-Seed and Martyr-Fruit in Africa," *Baptist Missionary Magazine*, February 1889, 43–45; "The Martyr Church of Madagascar," *Scribner's Monthly*, April 1871, 639–646; P. E. Price, "The Persecution in China," *Christian Observer*, January 23, 1901, 7–8. As historians have noted, such accounts typically describe in graphic detail the acts of physical violence against Christians.

7. Sympathy remained an important virtue but Christian missions narrators came to prefer empathy, theorizing that it was a deeper, "internal" identification with local hosts, as opposed to the "external" identification that characterized sympathy. See the discussion that follows.

8. Historian Heather Curtis writes: "The front page of the *Christian and Missionary Alliance* for May 12, 1900, for example, featured a display of 'Famine's Ravages in India' by

Marcus Fuller that included photographs of emaciated children; a pile of gaunt, dead 'bodies ready for burning'; and (on the second page) a prostrate, skeletal form stretched out on a pallet 'starved to death.' Accompanying these images was a caption that explained their purpose: 'These pictures just received from Mr. Fuller present the awful need of famine stricken India *as no words could plead*'" ("Depicting Distant Suffering: Evangelicals and the Politics of Pictorial Humanitarianism in the Age of American Empire,'" *Material Religion* 8, no. 2 [2012]: 165, emphasis mine).

9. Curtis emphasizes how photographs of suffering persons overseas, published in magazines to evoke sympathy, distanced American readers from those persons because the latter appeared to be powerless and helpless, people without agency; this was a strangeness to Americans certain of their own agency and power ("Depicting Distant Suffering," 177–178). Dennis Kennedy discusses the "contradictory effects" of the image of suffering as used by humanitarian groups, noting that "on one hand, it facilitates principled action and consciousness raising. On the other, it can discard that which is most human about the victim: autonomy, dignity, and context" ("Selling the Distant Other: Humanitarianism and Imagery: Ethical Dilemmas of Humanitarian Action," *Journal of Humanitarian Assistance* 28 [2009]: 1–25). Judith Lichtenberg, in discussing humanitarian outreach to the distant needy, concludes that "other people's suffering is almost always abstract" ("Absence and the Unfond Heart: Why People Are Less Giving Than They Might Be," in *The Ethics of Assistance: Morality and the Distant Needy*, ed. Deen K. Chatterjee [New York: Cambridge University Press, 2004]: 82–87).

10. There is an extensive literature on the capability of photography to "make strange" its subjects. See Simon Watney, "Making Strange: The Shattered Mirror," in *Thinking about Photography*, ed. Victor Burgin (London: Macmillan, 1982), 154–176. For Watney, photography offered a fresh view of the familiar by making it strange. But photographs can distance the viewer from subjects presented as anonymous at the same time that they evoke a sense of intimacy with the subject. For a discussion of that process with regard to a collection of World War II photographs see Moira McIver, *Memory, Memorial* (Belfast: Artefact, 1997). For a discussion of how photography makes strange the inhabitants of "other places" see Catherine Palmer and J.-A. Lester, "Stalking the Cannibals: Photographic Behavior on the Sepik River," *Tourist Studies* 7 (2007): 83–106; Caroline Scarles, "The Photographed Other: Interplays of Agency in Tourist Photography in Cisco, Peru," *Annals of Tourism Research* 39 (2012): 928–950; Keith Hollingshead, "Surveillance of the Worlds of Tourism: Foucault and the Eye of Power," *Tourism Management* 20 (1999): 7–23; Erik Cohen, Yeshayahu Nir, and Uri Aklmagor, "Stranger-Local Interaction in Photography," *Annals of Tourism Research* 19 (1992): 213–233.

11. John Corrigan, *Religious Intolerance, America, and the World: A History of Remembering and Forgetting* (Chicago: University of Chicago Press, 2020); John Corrigan and Lynn Neal, *Religious Intolerance in America: A Documentary History*, 2nd ed. (Chapel Hill: University of North Carolina Press, 2020).

12. Peter Kruse, "Miscellaneous Communications. Proposed Wesleyan Mission to China," *Wesleyan Methodist Magazine*, vol. 2: *1833–1854* (London: John Mason, 1854), 955.

13. See, for example, Sahoo Sarbeswar, *Pentecostalism and the Politics of Conversion in India* (Cambridge: Cambridge University Press, 2018).

14. Lyman Beecher, *The Bible a Code of Laws* (Andover: Flagg and Gould, 1818).

15. Beecher, *The Bible a Code of Laws*, 47, 49.

16. "American Board of Missions," *Missionary Herald*, February 1828, 60; "Sympathy for the Heathen," *Baptist Missionary Magazine*, May 1842, 131.

17. "Miscellaneous: Monthly Concert," *Religious Intelligencer*, September 5, 1835, 210; H. C. DuBose, "Home and Foreign," *Christian Observer*, November 20, 1895, 6; "Sympathy for the Heathen," 131.

18. Adam Smith, *The Theory of Moral Sentiments* (London: T. Cadell, 1767), part I, sect. I, chap. I, p. 2.

19. Pierre Force, "Rousseau and Smith: On Sympathy as a First Principle," in *Thinking with Rousseau: From Machiavelli to Schmitt*, eds. Helena Rosenblatt and Paul Schweigert (New York: Cambridge University Press, 2017), 115–131.

20. Smith stressed the context of sympathy, holding that one sympathizes with the circumstances of another. It is "the situation which excites it" (*Theory of Moral Sentiments*, 7). Among the many recent scholarly analyses of sympathy in Smith's work are Jack Russell Weinstein, "Sympathy, Difference, and Education: Social Unity in the Work of Adam Smith," *Economics and Philosophy* 22 (2006): 79–111; Nava Ashraf, Colin F. Camerer, and George Loewenstein, "Adam Smith, Behavioral Economist," *Journal of Economic Perspectives* 19 (2005): 131–145; Bence Nanay, "Adam Smith's Concept of Sympathy and Its Contemporary Interpretations," *Essays on the Philosophy of Adam Smith: The Adam Smith Review* 5 (2010): 85–105; Geoffrey Sayre-McCord, "Hume and Smith on Sympathy, Approbation, and Moral Judgment," in *Sympathy: A History*, ed. Eric Schlesser (New York: Oxford University Press, 2015), 208–246.

21. George Marsden's influential analyses, *The Evangelical Mind and the New School Presbyterian Experience* (New Haven: Yale University Press, 1970), and *Fundamentalism and American Culture* (New York: Oxford University Press, 1982), were part of a cluster of historical studies that includes Sydney E. Ahlstrom, "The Scottish Philosophy and American Theology," *Church History* 24 (1955): 257–272; Theodore Dwight Bozeman, *Protestants in an Age of Science: The Baconian Ideal and Antebellum American Religious Thought* (Chapel Hill: University of North Carolina Press, 1977); E. Brooks Holifield, *The Gentlemen Theologians: American Theology in Southern Culture 1795–1860* (Durham, NC: Duke University Press, 1978); and Mark A. Noll, "Common Sense Traditions and American Evangelical Thought," *American Quarterly* 37 (1985): 216–238. A related discussion of Smith's theory of sympathy that addresses its strong influence on the nineteenth-century realist novel can be found in Rae Greiner, "Sympathy Time: Adam Smith, George Eliot, and the Realist Novel," *Narrative* 17 (2009): 291–311.

22. Samuel Fleischacker, "Adam Smith's Reception among the American Founders, 1776–1790," *William and Mary Quarterly* 59 (2002): 897–924.

23. Jacques Derrida, *Of Grammatology*, trans. Gayatri Chakravorty Spivak (Baltimore: Johns Hopkins University Press, 2016), 207.

24. Sean Gaston, "The Impossibility of Sympathy," *Eighteenth Century* 51 (2010): 129–152.

25. David Morgan, "The Look of Sympathy: Religion, Visual Culture, and the Social Life of Feeling," *Material Religion* 5 (2009): 136, 137.

26. Jennifer Senior, "Have a Heart, But Be Careful Not to Lose Your Head," *New York Times*, December 7, 2016, C4; Mark Honigsbaum, "Barack Obama and the Empathy Deficit," *Guardian*, January 4, 2013, https://www.theguardian.com/science/2013/jan/04/barack -obama-empathy-deficit; Roman Kznaric, *Empathy: Why It Matters and How to Get It* (New York: TarcherPerigee, 2014).

27. Joshua Pease, "The One Thing the Persecuted Church Doesn't Need from You," *Open Doors*, May 30, 2017, https://www.opendoorsusa.org/christian-persecution/stories/one -thing-persecuted-church-doesnt-need/.

28. Gailyn Van Rheenen, *Missions: Biblical Foundations and Contemporary Strategies* (Grand Rapids, MI: Zondervan, 2014), 72.

29. Tom Steffen and Lois McKinney Douglas, *Encountering Missionary Life and Work: Preparing for Intercultural Ministry* (Grand Rapids, MI: Baker Academic, 2008).

30. Karl Dahlfred, "Why Missionaries Can Never Go Home Again," *Gleanings from the Field: A Missionary Blog*, November 25, 2014, https://www.dahlfred.com/index.php/blogs /gleanings-from-the-field/747-why-missionaries-can-never-go-home-again.

31. Dominick LaCapra, *Writing History, Writing Trauma* (Baltimore: Johns Hopkins University Press, 2001), 27.

32. Luc Boltanski, *Distant Suffering: Morality, Media, and Politics* (New York: Cambridge University Press, 1999).

33. Paul Bloom, *Against Empathy: The Case for Rational Compassion* (New York: Ecco, 2016).

34. "Report on Statistics," *Evangelical Repository* 12 (June 1873): 170.

35. Gina A. Zurlo, "The Legacy of David B. Barrett," *International Bulletin of Mission Research* 42 (2017): 29.

36. David B. Barrett, *World Christian Encyclopedia: A Comparative Study of Churches and Religions in the Modern World, 1900–2000* (New York: Oxford University Press, 1982). The fact that the historical coverage advertised in the title of the encyclopedia reached eighteen years beyond the publication date suggests the prescriptive agenda of "Great Commission" evangelizing that informed the project.

37. World Religion Database, accessed February 15, 2020, https://worldreligiondatabase .org/wrd/#/homepage/wrd-main-page. The site is not free, although access is possible through institutions of higher education that subscribe to it.

38. One of the criticisms of the *WCE* was that its category of "crypto-Christians" (sometimes mentioned as "secret believers") was questionable. Critics wondered how such "secret believers" were counted if their belief was not public. Jan Jongeneel questioned the category of "crypto-Christians" in the *WCE* while judging that "the *WCE* has a missionary/missiological view," an implicit problem as far as its reliability ("David Barrett's *World Christian Encyclopedia*," *Exchange* 30, no. 4 [2001]: 375). Christopher Brennan expanded on that criticism: "David Barrett and his colleagues have taken their own basic assumptions and measured the world's people (Christian and non-Christian alike) against those standards, regardless of whether or not those measures are accepted or normative" ("Rearranging Their Prejudices: The *World Christian Encyclopedia* as a Case Study of Bias in Reference Books," *American Theological Library Association Summary of Proceedings* 57 [2003]: 54). Mark Noll, noting strengths and weaknesses in the *Encyclopedia*, criticized it for its construction of a category, "Great Commission Christians," as well as its questionable counts in some geographical areas ("Review: *World Christian Encyclopedia*," *Church History* 71 [2002]: 448–454). Similar criticisms can be found in Michael J. McClymond, "Making Sense of the Census: What 1,999,563,838 Christians Might Mean for the Study of Religion," *Journal of the American Academy of Religion* 70, no. 4 (2002): 875–890. A review essay notes various shortcomings but concludes that the *Encyclopedia* is a useful tool (Becky Hsu, Amy Reynolds, Conrad Hackett, and James Gibbon, "Estimating the Religious Composition of All Nations: An Empirical Assessment of the World Christian Database," *Journal for the Scientific Study of Religion* 47 [2008]: 678–693). See also the chapter "'The Actual Arithmetic': A Survey of Contemporary Global Evangelicalism," in Mark Hutchinson and John Wolfe, *A Short History of Global Evangelicalism* (New York: Cambridge University Press, 2012), 209–243. For a sample of the tables offered in the *WCE*, see David B.

Barrett and Todd M. Johnson, "Annual Statistical Tables on Global Mission: 2002," *International Bulletin of Missionary Research* 26 (2002): 22–44. Critics did not raise the broader question about the epistemology of the census and its role in abstracting and objectivizing populations.

39. Mark Philip Bradley, *The World Reimagined* (New York: Cambridge University Press, 2016), 137–148.

40. Thomas B. Jabine and Richard B. Claude, *Human Rights and Statistics: Getting the Record Straight* (Philadelphia: University of Pennsylvania Press, 1992), xii.

41. United Nations Office of the High Commissioner for Human Rights, "Official Statistics and Human Rights: 'Statistics Matter for Human Rights and Human Rights Matter for Statistics,'" United Nations, 2014, https://www.ohchr.org/Documents/Issues/HRIndicators/StatisticsAndHumanRights.pdf.

42. Ed Stetzer, "Why You Should Use Stats in Ministry," *Exchange*, July 27, 2016, https://www.christianitytoday.com/edstetzer/2016/july/how-to-use-stats.html; and Ed Stetzer, "Defining Evangelicals in Research," National Association of Evangelicals, Winter 2017–2018, https://www.nae.net/defining-evangelicals-research/.

43. Christian Smith, "Evangelicals Behaving Badly with Statistics," *Books and Culture* 13 (2007): 11.

44. Open Doors, "Open Doors World Watch List 2022: The Fifty Countries Where It Is Most Dangerous to Follow Jesus," accessed May 20, 2022, https://www.opendoorsusa.org/christian-persecution/world-watch-list/.

45. Open Doors, "How the Scoring Works," 2018, https://www.opendoorsusa.org/christian-persecution/world-watch-list/about-the-ranking/.

46. Manfred Seitz ("Das Martyrium in der evangelischen Theologie," [2006]), quoted in Christof Sauer, "Researching Persecution and Martyrdom," *International Journal of Religious Freedom* 1 (2008): 45.

47. "In Response to Persecution: Findings of the *Under Caesar's Sword* Project on Global Christian Communities," University of Notre Dame, 2020, https://ucs.nd.edu/report/.

48. Paul Marshall with Lela Gilbert, *Their Blood Cries Out: The Untold Story of Persecution against Christians in the Modern World* (Dallas: Word Publishing, 1997); Nina Shea, *In the Lion's Den* (Nashville: B and H Publishing, 1997).

49. Marshall and Gilbert, *Their Blood Cries Out*, 319n4.

50. John L. Allen, *The Global War on Christians: Dispatches from the Front Lines of Anti-Christian Persecution* (New York: Image, 2013), 42–43, 206, 94, 96, 121.

51. David Curry, "A Letter from David Curry, CEO," *World Watch List 2019*, Open Doors, accessed May 20, 2022, https://revelation-now.org/wp-content/uploads/WWL2019_Full Booklet-1.pdf.

52. Frans J. Verstraelen, "Calculation and Surprise in the *World Christian Encyclopedia*," *Missiology: An International Review* 12, no. 1 (1984): 61.

53. Some writers recommitted to a basic strategy of relating the kind of stories that had garnered attention in previous decades See, for example, Paul Marshall, Lela Gilbert, and Nina Shea, *Persecuted: The Global Assault on Christians* (Nashville: Thomas Nelson, 2013).

54. Sally Engle Merry, *The Seductions of Quantification: Measuring Human Rights, Gender, Violence, and Sex Trafficking* (Chicago: University of Chicago Press, 2016).

55. The term has been in constant use among Protestant missionary concerns for over two centuries. The *Andover Review* commentary on the activities of the American Board of Commissioners of Foreign Missions in 1885 asserted the organization's commitment to "THE SPREAD OF THE GOSPEL and THE CONVERSION OF THE WORLD," a project that "has already begun to unite, the affections, prayers, and labors of the great family of Christians" (*Andover Review* 4 [1885]: 356).

56. John Durham Peters, "Information: Notes toward a Critical History," *Journal of Communication Inquiry* 12, no. 2 (1988): 15.

57. Merry, *Seductions of Quantification*, 21.

58. Alain Desrosières, *The Politics of Large Numbers: A History of Statistical Reasoning*, trans. Camille Naish (Cambridge, MA: Harvard University Press, 1998), 72. Here Desrosières is specifically discussing averages, but this point about statistical reasoning is made throughout the book.

59. I take this phrasing from Amanda Walker Johnson, "Objectifying Measures: Mapping the Terrain of Statistical Discourse in the Hegemony and Racial Politics of High Stakes Testing," PhD diss., University of Texas at Austin, 2004, 11.

60. Quoted in Walter Garrison Runciman, *The Social Animal* (Ann Arbor: University of Michigan Press, 2000), 101. Jacques Ellul articulated that idea more precisely: "Statistics is necessarily a univocal method that expresses an aspect of reality which is uncombinable with any other (except other statistics)" (quoted in Charles Mabee, *Reading Sacred Texts through American Eyes* [Macon, GA: Mercer University Press, 1991], 79).

61. In Mabee, *Reading Sacred Texts*, 79.

62. Ortega y Gasset, *The Revolt of the Masses* (New York: W. W. Norton, 1932); Hannah Arendt, *The Origins of Totalitarianism* (New York: Harcourt, Brace, 1951).

63. Wilbur Schramm collected foundational essays in the field in *The Process and Effects of Mass Communication* (Urbana: University of Illinois Press, 1954).

64. A key essay from 1944 is Max Horkheimer and Theodor W. Adorno, "The Culture Industry: Enlightenment as Mass Deception," in *Dialectic of Enlightenment*, trans. John Cumming (New York: Herder and Herder, 1972), 94–137. See also the collection of Theodor W. Adorno's essays in *The Culture Industry: Selected Essays on Mass Culture*, ed. J. M. Bernstein (London: Routledge, 2001).

65. Boltanski, *Distant Suffering*, 13.

66. Liam Cole Young, "'What's in a List?' Cultural Techniques, Logistics, Poesis," PhD diss., University of Western Ontario, 2014, 31.

67. LaCapra discusses "empathic unsettlement" throughout *Writing History, Writing Trauma*.

68. National Association of Evangelicals (NAE), "Statement of Conscience of the National Association of Evangelicals Concerning Worldwide Religious Persecution, January 23, 1996," PCA Historical Center, accessed February 17, 2020, http://pcahistory.org/pca/studies/3-476.html. With regard to the exceptionalist aspect of the NAE statement, and similar American initiatives, see Corrigan, *Religious Intolerance*.

2

Saved by a Martyr

Media, Suffering, and Power in Evangelical Internationalism

OMRI ELISHA

The lobby of Calvary Chapel buzzed with eager crowds huddled around merchandise tables. A conference sponsored by the Voice of the Martyrs (VOM) in 2012 was well underway, and with a fifteen-minute break between speakers, those who were not lined up at the espresso bar rushed to examine the latest media products related to Christian persecution. While picking up fact sheets, newsletters, and pamphlets, attendees sorted through items that were for sale, including inspirational books and DVDs, commemorative wristbands and t-shirts, and tote bags that read, "I Smuggled A Bible . . . Ask Me How." Entitled "Bound With Them," the conference drew hundreds of people to this Pennsylvania church to learn about "the persecuted church," in the hopes of deepening their spiritual ties with those who suffer.

A young woman to my left held up a copy of *Jesus Freaks*, a collection of stories of Christian martyrs past and present marketed to' young adults. She opened the book to a specific page and showed it to a friend who had accompanied her to the conference, pointing emphatically. "This one here is my favorite testimony. I became a Christian after reading this woman's story." She handed the book to her friend. "It had such an amazing effect on me. That's why I come to these conferences. I was saved by a martyr!"

VOM is a nondenominational, nonprofit organization that works on behalf of Christians who have been identified as victims of religious persecution, communal violence, and state oppression, mostly in majority non-Christian societies. Their mission is described as "serving the persecuted church through practical and spiritual assistance while leading Christians in the free world into fellowship with them." In what follows, I examine the latter aspect of VOM's mandate—the domestic agenda to lead Western Christians, especially evangelical Protestants, into "fellowship" with foreign believers who have been coded as living martyrs. Considering a variety of texts and images, communiqués, commercial products, and live programs, along with observations from field-work in a white, middle-class, evangelical community, I look at how VOM products and projects address as well as implicate churchgoing evangelicals.

I argue that VOM, which is a key player in the Christian antipersecution movement, invites Westerners to share the mantle of martyrdom by urging them to engage in purposeful acts of religious mediation, including the consumption and circulation of martyrological media. By *mediation* I refer to the connective cultural work achieved by material channels—including embodied, textual, and technological practices—in which religious precepts, sensations, and relationships are generated, transmitted, and transformed. It is the process in which social realties are constructed from the material worlds in which human beings are embedded.[1] Although it is not a term often used by evangelicals, mediation is crucial to how they envision their specialized agency in the world, as "witnesses to the faith." It is the very essence of what God has commissioned them to do. VOM programs actively encourage believers to experience, reproduce, and disseminate a variety of texts, images, and objects that reference the extreme suffering and moral virtues of Christian martyrs (from the Greek *martur*, meaning "witness"), whose stories register as radical testimonies of spiritual triumph and vehicles for the proliferation of religious ideology.[2]

I argue that media centered on the persecuted church draw moral force from self-referential qualities inherent in how they are meant to be received and used. Social practices associated with these media accentuate their status *as* media; they become "hyper-apparent."[3] While they are made to address pressing humanitarian and political concerns of global Christians, VOM media, in in their capacity to be knowingly consumed, distributed, and shared, are endowed with significance beyond mere representation. My brief opening vignette about the young woman is illustrative insofar as what appears to have contributed to her being "saved" (however she meant this exactly) was not the martyr in question so much as the martyr's *story* and its material medium: that is, the book she was now eagerly urging her friend to buy.

Furthermore, in the process of promoting martyrological and missiological themes, VOM media products and events reinforce a tendency among Western evangelicals to compare themselves, often wistfully, to foreign Christians in regions where churches are oppressed. While tales of victimization evoke horror and grief, persecution is portrayed as a gift that brings believers closer to God, generating extraordinary acts of courage and perseverance in the face of death, especially among non-Western evangelists. In valorizing a particular model of suffering in this way, the casting of foreign Christians as martyrs assigns meaning to their misery and inspires evangelicals with an admiration verging on jealous longing.

Of course, American evangelicalism is hardly free of its own "persecution complexes."[4] Conservative evangelicals in the United States are known to regard themselves as a religious minority that is "under siege," citing such impositions as constitutional limits on religious expression and the so-called War on Christmas, or the specter of homegrown Islamic extremism. Yet this embattled consciousness exists alongside an internal and largely self-critical discourse fixated on the belief that while foreign brethren are suffering at the "front lines" of persecution, churchgoers here are more likely to take their freedoms for granted and fall short of the life-altering sacrifices befitting an authentic faith. As one megachurch pastor once told me: "We all continue to struggle with what it means to really follow Christ in a comfortable culture where you can't get martyred anymore."[5]

In light of such yearnings, VOM offers up the stories, images, and bodies of persecuted Christians and portable media produced by, about, and for them as resources for reflexive contemplation and religious action. Although VOM relies on financial donations, its public solicitations are rarely direct appeals for money. Supporters are encouraged to sign up for free publications and email alerts, participate in letter-writing campaigns and conferences, and purchase media such as DVDs, graphic novels, and persecution "Action Packs." Taken together, these practices are framed as means of embodying a global spirit of communion between believers in the "free world" and the persecuted church through developing participatory networks of volunteerism, communication, and evangelism and mobilizing patterns of consumption and circulation oriented around a missional paradigm.[6]

Along with humanitarian services, VOM programs and products recruit mission-minded Christians as self-conscious agents of mediation to join the ranks of exemplary martyrs and missionaries in turning private devotions into public declarations. By symbolically linking Christianized geopolitics of crisis to the metaphysics of sanctification, antipersecution activism relies on cultural forms that promise to mediate bonds of transcendental connectedness between otherwise diffuse and disconnected Christians, rallying them around "persecution" as a wellspring of world-historical agency.

As American evangelicals approach the particular landscape of pain that is the persecuted church, they encounter new ways of identifying vicariously with the "predetermined agony" of religious martyrs and anticipate a role alongside them in a drama of cosmic proportions, through which they "seek in part to extend themselves as subjects."[7] Yet insofar as this depends on the mobilization of Western political and economic resources that are intended to *relieve* the pain and suffering of foreign Christians, the fight against persecution reinforces boundaries of differentiation between those who must endure suffering and those who assume the power to stop it. These cultural practices thus shed light on the "enchanted internationalism" of contemporary evangelical engagement, with its complex neocolonial fantasies and fears.[8] They also point to the fact that we cannot fully assess the cultural politics of the persecuted church without also considering the rather intricate question of exactly who is saving whom.

Martyrs and Mediation

The Voice of the Martyrs was founded in 1967 (originally as Jesus to the Communist World) by Romanian minister Richard Wurmbrand and his wife, Sabina. Wurmbrand's memoir, *Tortured for Christ*, which recounts his years of imprisonment by communist authorities, is still widely read and distributed among VOM subscribers and participating churches. On the strength of his testimony and public advocacy—he once removed his shirt before a Senate subcommittee to reveal his torture scars—Wurmbrand embodied the style and tone of Christian antipersecution activism in the climate of the Cold War.[9] VOM's focus eventually expanded to include human rights work on behalf of Christian minorities in Islamist as well as communist states, especially in the so-called 10/40 Window, which includes North Africa, the Middle East, and Asia.

Headquartered in Bartlesville, Oklahoma, VOM's humanitarian relief and advocacy efforts are not unlike those of secular NGOs such as Amnesty International or Human Rights Watch, including fact-finding expeditions, political lobbying, and publicity campaigns in support of political prisoners. However, VOM clearly distinguishes itself from its secular counterparts by working exclusively on behalf of Christians. Addressing the audience at Calvary Chapel in 2012, VOM board member Mark Shumaker explained, "We don't let ourselves get off track by helping people who aren't persecuted Christians." The organization's objectives are explicitly evangelistic: "to encourage and empower Christians to fulfill the Great Commission in areas of the world where they are persecuted for sharing the gospel of Jesus Christ," and "to equip persecuted Christians to love and win to Christ those who are opposed to the gospel." With the aim of advancing global Christianity, VOM invests resources and partners with international missionary agencies to support everything from Bible translations and schools to medical missions, missionary aviation programs, and "Bible smuggling."

Donors are encouraged to support these commitments as humanitarian projects, and even more as strategies of ministering to the global Body of Christ and winning converts. Ironically, the more intense the persecution they report, the more evangelicals are convinced their efforts are bearing fruit. The mantle of suffering is both lamented and cherished because oppression and victory are both intertwined and inevitable. If the righteous suffer, it is because they prevail.

Although its aims are clearly evangelistic, the antipersecution movement achieved much of its political legitimacy by capitalizing on its affinities with related causes and US foreign policy concerns. The lobbying efforts of conservative evangelicals were crucial to the passage, for example, of the International

Religious Freedom Act in 1998 and the Trafficking Victims Protection Act of 2000, as well as the 2004 US-brokered Sudanese peace deal.[10] Although this lobbying indicated a style of "humanitarian and social justice activism that ultimately transcended a focus on Christians-first,"[11] the persecuted church continued to serve nonetheless as a keystone of conservative Christian identity politics and became a rallying symbol that "now so dominates the representation of the global South that even very traditional Christian programs for feeding the hungry or providing jobs have frequently been reframed in those terms."[12]

In the midst of it all, the figure of the martyr remains paramount, crystallizing scriptural, historical, moral, and affective resonances beyond the politicization of suffering. Just as it was in late antiquity, martyrology is vital to the construction of modern Christian personhood and collective memory.[13] Antipersecution activists reinforce the idea that believers share an inalienable responsibility to sense the urgency and immediacy of Christian martyrdom as a universal phenomenon, which is neither confined to bygone eras of church history nor limited to distant conflict zones. VOM programs and media campaigns promote vigilance and participation, not only by encouraging the faithful to consume images and stories of virtuous suffering but also by implicating them in everyday acts of entextualization and circulation. Interactive media and mediated presences are idealized in and of themselves. They are empowered rather than diminished by their status as conspicuous or "hyper-apparent" media.[14] Rather than hidden carriers of signification, these textual, sensory, and digital channels of sacred communication are devotional forms whose very material and social functionality are vital to the larger story they tell and the work of sanctification that they enable.

Suffering in Circulation

A featured story in the July 2012 VOM newsletter was entitled "Witness Protection in Nigeria." It began as follows: "Your church probably doesn't have armed guards at the gate, checking each vehicle as it enters the parking lot. In fact, your church probably doesn't have gates at all." The article went on to describe a church in northern Nigeria, where "churches without guards or gates are easy targets for the Islamist Boko Haram terrorists." It continued, "The Voice of the Martyrs helps protect God's witnesses in Nigeria by providing tools for evangelism, support for Christian workers and medical care for those injured in attacks." An accompanying photograph showed a young Nigerian evangelist who was severely beaten by a mob on his way to a revival. His leg was "shattered," it reads, but "his faith remains intact." On the adjacent page was a photo of doctors operating on a heavily bandaged leg, their hands and surgical instruments speckled with blood.

VOM's free monthly newsletter is a full-color, glossy periodical that reaches roughly a half million subscribers, with additional content published online.

Each issue features an array of "heartbreaking" stories accompanied by evocative images, regional updates, and missionary reports. Graphic photographs and narratives are presented as snippets of raw, unadulterated truth, but the medium of their representation is far from incidental. As a material, textual artifact, the newsletter is more than a source of information; it is a means of witnessing to readers and inviting them to become witnesses themselves. Indeed, like most VOM media, the newsletters are self-referential in terms of their value for purposes of testimony, evangelism, and activism. They interpellate readers as potential collaborators, advocates, and evangelists as well as consumers, encouraging them to not only internalize stories and images of persecution but also to participate in their active circulation through a range of corresponding practices, from participating in letter-writing campaigns to hosting events where VOM materials are sold or freely distributed.

VOM newsletters are often organized around general themes, with provocative titles such as "Somalia: Where Christians Are Hunted," or "The Rising Threat of Islam." Yet much of the content tends to be stories about particular communities and individuals, whose names are sometimes changed and faces obscured and whose lives are presented as object lessons in virtuous suffering under harrowing or precarious circumstances. Including adults and children, the living and the dead, they are not always described explicitly as "martyrs," nor do they necessarily conform to a uniform idea of what that term should mean. Some face oppression for refusing to renounce their faith and others for covert activities, such as convening illegal "house churches." Collectively, however, their stories reinforce the overlying theological message that personal experiences of violence, terror, loss, and anguish in the name of Jesus Christ are ultimately affirmations of God's love because they advance a biblical master narrative in which triumph is born of sacrifice, even as Christians fight to alleviate the punishing burdens of martyrdom. Those who need to be rescued from suffering are sanctified by it.

Photographs in VOM newsletters portray non-Western Christians engaged in familiar activities, such as performing daily tasks, attending services, reading and teaching from the Bible, praying intensely, or simply smiling for the camera. Yet they are also captured in moments of pain and distress over the death and imprisonment of loved ones or shown displaying gruesome scars and amputations. Such images complicate the element of familiarity by highlighting extreme conditions that most Western subscribers are unlikely to ever experience firsthand as well as their exceptionality as models of sacrifice, perseverance, and grace (in some cases, even forgiving their assailants). Such exceptional qualities, which have long been associated with venerated martyrs in church history, are read as indicative of an extraordinary capacity to surrender oneself to the will of God, yielding to divine agency when the agency of the individual appears most vulnerable.[15]

The cover of the January 2011 VOM newsletter featured a particularly evocative and unsettling image. It was a tight close-up of an Indonesian woman named Yubelina, whose face was horribly disfigured by severe burns suffered in what is described as an attack on her village by Muslims. Her skin is raw, scarred, and peeling. One of her eyes is little more than a gaping wound. The camera spares nothing of the details of her damaged visage. Yet what commands the viewer's attention is the expression on her face. She is smiling brilliantly, seemingly in the midst of laughter. Her bright teeth illuminate the frame. Her good eye seizes hold of the viewer, almost playfully.

The cover drew strong reactions from subscribers, including criticism. Some readers found it gruesome and sensationalist and worried about its effect on children. Others responded positively, extolling Yubelina for exceptional virtues in spite of unfathomable pain. An independent Christian blogger, whose comments were reposted on VOM's *Persecution Blog*, wrote, "Yubelina has figured out where her identity lies. . . . [She] is beautiful. I guarantee she has a joy, a contentment, that no name-brand, trendy clothing; no perfect haircut & makeup; no flawless skin or toned body can bring. . . . I want to be beautiful like that. I want my face to shine like Moses, because I have been in the presence of God." On VOM's Facebook page, comments posted alongside the image voiced similar sentiments: "The obvious suffering this beautiful woman has endured and the fact that she smiles so joyfully because of Jesus light and love! [*sic*] I use it to remind me of how fortunate I am and how far I have to go with my struggles of contentment and joy." Another user added: "She is beautiful!! . . . She inspires me to go beyond my discouragement and continue to reach out to others with God's love." One more comment worth quoting emphasized, "And to think that there are people who complain about their satellite tv going out!"

Such responses point to complex structures of feeling in which images of the suffering other become vehicles for introspective commentary attending a Western gaze.[16] By providing fodder for comparative self-reflection, illustrations of the persecuted church highlight the virtues of distant and disadvantaged Christians who are to be emulated more than pitied. But how can they be emulated? When the ravages of embodied suffering as a consequence of one's faith are far from commonplace, how does one become "bound with them"? I argue that for a segment of American evangelicals, the answer lies less in their own direct claims of domestic persecution and more in the availability of alternative avenues of witness, that is, alternative modes of advocacy and declaration that sacralize violent persecution while seeking to prevent it.

VOM newsletters provide such avenues. They are multifaceted visual and discursive texts that serve simultaneously as ready-made objects of circulation, as are supplemental materials that are advertised within. Each newsletter includes inserts for special offers such as free "prayer cards" and color-coded "persecution maps," as well as cardstock order forms for various other media products. These include books such as *Jesus Freaks* and *Foxe: Voice of the Martyrs* (a leather-bound "updated" version of Foxe's *Book of Martyrs*) and popular animated films such as *Jesus: He Lived Among Us* and the DVD series *The Torchlighters: Heroes of the Faith*. Church leaders and subscribers are encouraged to "purchase multiple copies for your church's youth group or for your grandchildren." An ad for *Jesus: He Lived Among Us* reads: "Our persecuted brothers and sisters are witnessing, and we should be, too. That's why we want to offer you one of the most effective evangelism tools that our field workers use. . . . You can order the DVDs in packs of 5 for $10 or 20 for $20."

VOM subscribers may also purchase "Prison Letter Writing Kits," complete with detailed "prisoner profiles" and instructions (e.g., omit negative comments about foreign governments) or VOM "Action Packs"—large sealable plastic bags for packing donations such as soap, school supplies, blankets, and clothes, to be sent to countries abroad so that "our brothers and sisters know that Christians in the West have not forgotten them." This program once included "Colombia Parachute Packs," which were aerially deployed from a Cessna by a missionary aviator over areas controlled by FARC guerrillas. The parachutes contained Bibles, copies of James Dobson's *When God Doesn't Make Sense*, and shortwave radios pretuned to Christian radio stations. Promotional materials emphasized the risk involved—"I've been shot at a few times," the pilot explains—and also the rewards, in stories of guerrillas renouncing violence after reading Bibles that parachuted from the sky. Images of white American teenagers posing enthusiastically with the parachute bundles they made reinforced the joys of participation: "All you need is a pair of scissors and a willing heart!"

Such programs validate the role of everyday church communities and families in the aspirations of evangelical internationalism and the importance of mediating practices in solidifying global affinities. Beyond the valorization of suffering, they define the persecuted church as a framework of action and intercession, in practical and metaphysical terms, which is further reinforced through VOM's regional conferences.

Bound with Them

Each year VOM holds dozens of regional conferences at local churches across the country to enhance public awareness and solicit support. Featured speakers are often missionaries, public activists, foreign pastors, and trauma survivors, whose impassioned multimedia presentations include statistical charts and maps along with photographs and video clips of everything from scenes of worship in Chinese "house churches" to images of Coptic Christians being beaten in the streets of Cairo. Virtually every speaker I have seen emphasized the bonds that Western believers are meant to share with persecuted Christians. They stressed the importance of information and vigilance and of reexamining one's priorities relative to the demands of radical faith. One speaker at the Calvary Chapel conference encouraged churchgoers to make a daily habit of praying for Christians who live "in the places where our clothes are made."

The prevailing mode of address at these conferences verges on homiletic, as speakers prick the conscience of middle-class churchgoers and call them out of their "comfort zones." Darcie Gill, one of VOM's active speakers, told an audience in 2012 that despite oppression, Christian churches in "hostile areas" are growing more rapidly than in the West, where churches struggle to stay relevant. Addressing the same group, American missionary Gracia Burnham, who was once held hostage by Muslim guerrillas in the Philippines for over a year with her husband Martin (who was killed during a military rescue), spoke of her ordeal as an experience that tested and renewed her faith. She urged believers to confront their fears, embrace the meaning of sacrifice, and accept their responsibilities to the persecuted church. "We must be bound with them," she said, "as if their pain was in our own bodies." Conservative religious activist Faith McDonnell, speaking at an event in 2000 (see below), hit a similar tone: "To help martyrs who are losing their lives, we need to be willing to put our own lifestyles to death."

Often the most forceful and anticipated speakers at VOM conferences are foreign non-Western Christians with direct experience of violence and trauma. Having endured great trials and personal losses, these presenters embody the persecuted church in all its tortured glory and alterity. More than victims, they appear as emboldened witnesses whose stories and native expertise endow them with a sanctifying aura as well as the authority to explain political and social dynamics in their home countries; be it a Nigerian man analyzing Boko Haram's connections to Islamic extremism, an Iraqi ex-patriot explaining that "there are no moderate Muslims" and denouncing ISIS as "a plan of Satan," or a church pastor from China describing government harassment and imprisonment. Representatives from Muslim societies, such as Iranian televangelist Hormoz Shariat and Pakistani author Daniel Scot, serve as inside interpreters of Islam, confirming negative stereotypes about Islamic doctrine and selling books about the Qur'an and how to evangelize Muslims.

As mediated spaces of live encounter, where racially and ethnically coded others become physically present as spiritual kin, the conferences are known to have a profound impact. One volunteer organizer explained to me in an interview that American Christians often initially react with shock and skepticism, "bewilderment that this could actually be true." But coming face to face with survivors, he explained, they can no longer deny the truth. Disbelief is replaced by righteous indignation and renewed commitment. "The idea is not to shock, but to move people to action and get them past the denial stage. Even Christ told Thomas to probe his wounds so that he might believe, which resulted in Thomas going off and evangelizing large parts of India!"

The comparison with "doubting Thomas," whose faith was won by a direct physical encounter with the resurrected Christ, reveals the extent to which former victims of persecution are venerated in the eyes of Western Christians. Their testimonies are sacred narratives—ritualized intersections of temporal suffering and spiritual salvation. They are the martyrs who have not died, speaking on behalf of the living and the dead. Pain, hardship, and perseverance become indices of higher virtue, born of a charismatic and seemingly exceptional capacity to embody the frailties and limitations of human existence while simultaneously transcending them.

I observed a striking example of the effect of such speakers in 2000, at a VOM conference hosted by Eternal Vine Church, an affluent suburban megachurch in Knoxville, Tennessee, where I was doing fieldwork. Pastor Glen, the church's director of missions, organized the event because he felt his congregants needed a deeper appreciation of what it means to be "World Christians," as opposed to "Sunday morning Christians" who write yearly checks for missionaries but rarely invest more of themselves. Speakers included political activists Faith McDonnell of the Institute on Religion and Democracy and Paul Marshall of the Hudson Institute, as well as a Christian Kurd from Iraq, a young Sudanese man described as a "redeemed slave," a middle-aged Vietnamese expatriate who lost her family as a child, and two American teenagers, Shellie Adams and Crystal Woodman, both survivors of recent school shootings (the latter at Columbine High School), which many churchgoers felt were motivated in part by anti-Christian bigotry.

The emotional presentations by Adams and Woodman, who spoke at length about how the shootings impacted their faith, were highlighted by memories of slain friends (including one, Cassie Bernall, who was rumored to have affirmed her faith before being shot at Columbine) and sober reflections on what it means to give one's life over to God. Shellie Adams in particular urged listeners to understand that "God wants us to give up the American dream," because "comfortable Christianity is not at all biblical." Her words hit home for the crowd of roughly 500 people, which did not surprise Pastor Glen because, as he told me, "that's what they relate to." What he felt was more significant was how moved many churchgoers said they were by the international presenters: "They would tell me, 'Thank you for doing this!' They were surprised that they enjoyed it. They were surprised that they would enjoy hearing about Iraq and Sudan, even as hard as the stories were. The realization came to them that, 'I needed this. I needed this.'"

Indeed, the most talked-about part of the conference in the days after the event was not the two school-shooting survivors (who drew the largest audience) but the Vietnamese woman, whom I will call "Anna." Speaking in a heavily accented but commanding voice, Anna talked about the loss and devastation of her childhood as a Christian in Vietnam, including family members murdered and homes destroyed. She sang church hymns in English and Vietnamese. While showing pictures of suitcases full of smuggled Bibles, she described the dangerous work that she and others were doing on behalf of Vietnamese Christians in rural villages like her own. The congregation hung on her every word, many in tears.

A week later the senior pastor of Eternal Vine dedicated a portion of his Sunday sermon to Anna, recalling her unbreakable and defiant spirit and singling her out as someone who knows how to serve God unconditionally. Later, in a small-group Bible study, a man in his thirties named Todd said he was so moved by Anna's testimony that he felt ashamed about not doing more for God in his own life. Others in the group sympathized but warned Todd against being led by guilt or comparing himself to others. A friend pointed out that despite the extreme circumstances of Anna's life, the only real difference between her and Todd was that Anna accepted God's plan for her whereas Todd, a gainfully employed father of two, could not accept that God was using him for different but no less important purposes, such as raising godly children.

Expressions of admiration along with self-doubt in response to testimonies of distant suffering are common among white, middle-class evangelicals, who tend to "idealize global South believers as 'closer' to that longed-for numinous faith."[17] The wounds and deprivations of foreign Christians who are oppressed by "wicked" ideologies and unsullied by material comforts and securities are interpreted as indelible marks of spiritual authenticity. They inspire a kind of agonized ethical contemplation on the part of Westerners who are eager to be saved from themselves. At the same time, they reinforce perceptions of sinister cultural and geopolitical forces that threaten global Christian ascendancy.

VOM conferences are thus more than venues for simply sharing images and stories, soliciting donations, and signing petitions. They are sites for ritually reimagining ethnic and national boundaries in service of an invigorated Christian universalism predicated on the virtues of suffering. Yet they also reaffirm the urgency of humanitarian, political, and even military interventions and the loci of power from which such interventions are expected to emerge. While the activism of global South Christians is "deeply engaged with a multitude of global networks" and continues to influence much in the way of evangelical internationalism, there remains the sense in which it is the economic and political resources of the Western "free world" that ultimately make the important difference between life and death.[18] For American evangelicals, being "saved by a martyr" cannot be disentangled from the modern imperative to overcome suffering and save those who cannot save themselves from becoming martyred in the first place.

Conclusion

As the conference at Calvary Chapel came to a close, a short video was shown with footage from an unidentified village in East Asia. Local converts are seen greeting missionaries who had delivered new Bibles, the materiality of which becomes paramount as villagers weep with joy, clutching, caressing, and even smelling the books, perhaps for the first time. What struck me as significant about the video was not just the moving scene it captured but also its status as a visual testimony whose very existence was seen as proof of God's work and whose subjects seemed to embody that ideal union of innocence and pathos. If the video served its purpose, members of the audience would undoubtedly tell their friends about it. They may even have felt a tinge of envy in being reminded, perhaps for the first time, what it is supposed to feel like to carry God's Word in your own hands.

Religion scholar David Morgan has argued that "media are not delivery devices but the generation of experiences, forms of shared consciousness, communion, or community that allow people to assemble meanings that articulate and extend their relations to one another."[19] By framing my analysis in terms of mediation, I aim to extend this conceptualization beyond tangible media per se and account for multiple avenues of participation and experience. Across the full array of products and program—books, newsletters, animated films, letter-writing campaigns, prayer cards, "Action Packs," conferences, and a wide range of novelty merchandise, such as nylon Bible sleeves with "This Book Is Illegal in 52 Countries" printed on the flaps—the mediating practices promoted by VOM facilitate the linking of evangelicals to idealized networks of communication, commemoration, and commitment, beyond their immediate circumstances. They present diverse modes of religious action and affinity in a compelling aura of sanctification, inviting good Christians to take the steps necessary to feel like better ones.

The antipersecution movement as a whole, moreover, is a fertile source of cultural forms that address and mobilize one of Christianity's deeper theological mysteries going back to the passion of Christ: the relationship between vulnerability and power. Organizations such as VOM operate on the premise that "mission and persecution are inseparable," which entails viewing suffering and agency, trauma and triumph, as one and the same.[20] It is noteworthy in this regard that the organization is called the *Voice* of the Martyrs, and not (for example) the *blood* of the martyrs. To the extent that evangelical mediations of the persecuted church valorize tales of redemptive sacrifice, they are at the same time clarion calls for advocacy and intervention, particularly on the part of Western powers. This not only reinforces the movement's humanitarian aspect—that is, the alleviation of human (Christian) suffering—but it does so in ways that keep it anchored to a particular "logic of neo-colonial benevolence" whereby certain types of religious and cultural difference are valued above others and modernity's victims are set apart from its villains.[21] For American evangelicals, the persecuted church is a global union in which to locate themselves and a standard against which to measure themselves. It is also an ideological framework for recognizing and exercising the power to determine what it means to suffer and decide whose suffering has the right to be redeemed.

NOTES

1. Angela Zito, "Religion Is Media," *Revealer*, April 16, 2018, https://therevealer.org/religion -is-media/.

2. Elizabeth Castelli, *Martyrdom and Memory: Early Christian Culture Making* (New York: Columbia University Press, 2004).

3. Birgit Meyer, "Mediation and Immediacy: Sensational Forms, Semiotic Ideologies, and the Question of the Medium," *Social Anthropology* 19, no. 1 (2011): 23–39.

4. Elizabeth Castelli, "Persecution Complexes: Identity Politics and the 'War on Christians,'" *differences: A Journal of Feminist Cultural Studies* 18, no. 5 (2007): 152–180.

5. Quoted in Omri Elisha, *Moral Ambition: Mobilization and Social Outreach in Evangelical Megachurches* (Berkeley: University of California Press, 2011), 129.

6. Simon Coleman, *The Globalisation of Charismatic Christianity: Spreading the Gospel of Prosperity* (Cambridge: Cambridge University Press, 2000).

7. Talal Asad, *Formations of the Secular: Christianity, Islam, Modernity* (Stanford: Stanford University Press, 2003), 78.

8. Melani McAlister, "What Is Your Heart For?: Affect and Internationalism in the Evangelical Public Sphere," *American Literary History* 20, no. 4 (2008): 870–895.

9. Melani McAlister, "The Persecuted Body: Evangelical Internationalism, Islam, and the Politics of Fear," in *Facing Fear: The History of an Emotion in Global Perspective*, ed. M. Laffan and M. Weiss (Princeton: University of Princeton Press, 2012), 133–161.

10. Allen D. Hertzke, *Freeing God's Children: The Unlikely Alliance for Global Human Rights* (Lanham, MD: Rowman and Littlefield, 2004).

11. McAlister, "Persecuted Body," 161.

12. Elizabeth Castelli, "Praying for the Persecuted Church: US Christian Activism in the Global Arena," *Journal of Human Rights* 4 (2005): 1–31; McAlister, "Persecuted Body," 153.

13. Castelli, *Martyrdom and Memory.*

14. Meyer, "Mediation and Immediacy"; Martijn Oosterbaan, "Virtually Global: Online Evangelical Cartography," *Social Anthropology* 19, no. 1 (2011): 56–73.

15. Lacey Baldwin Smith, *Fools, Martyrs, Traitors: The Story of Martyrdom in the Western World* (New York: Alfred A. Knopf, 1997).

16. Heather Curtis, "Depicting Distant Suffering: Evangelicals and the Politics of Pictorial Humanitarianism in the Age of American Empire," *Material Religion* 8, no. 2 (2012): 153–182.

17. McAlister, "What Is Your Heart For?," 883.

18. Swartz, "Global Reflex"; McAlister, "What Is Your Heart For?," 888.

19. David Morgan, *Key Words in Religion, Media and Culture* (New York: Routledge, 2008), 7.

20. Glenn M. Penner, *In the Shadow of the Cross: A Biblical Theology of Persecution & Discipleship* (Bartlesville, OK: Living Sacrifice Books, 2004), 119.

21. McAlister, "What Is Your Heart For?," 887.

3

American Theodicy

Human Nature and Natural Disaster

HILLARY KAELL

Bonnie and I were chopping vegetables for lunch in her suburban home out-side Kansas City while the television perched on a nearby countertop cycled through scenes of collapsed buildings and landslides in free-fall. The death toll was rising, the CNN announcer intoned over clips of people pressing rags to their mouths to block the dust as they sifted through the rubble. It was already being called the worst disaster on record in Nepal. Bonnie switched off the television. "That's what I was telling you, Hillary," she said, setting out the plates for lunch. "I listen to world news so I can get more of what's going on in places but then it drags you right down. There's just so much negativity you can handle." Since I was there to chat about the child she sponsors, I asked her about the materials she accessed through the sponsorship organization. Did she feel the same way about their depictions of dire poverty or disasters, which often covered the same events as CNN? "But it's different," Bonnie replied, "because at least I'm *interacting*. It's not like suddenly [their problems] will be solved but somebody out there is thinking about them, prays [for] them, and cares about them."

As many studies have noted, both humanitarian organizations and media outlets pitch global connections in the superlative of emergency relief and disas-ter news. Scholars of globalization remark that these communications—in both their tone and their frequency—often create a sense of uncontrollable global cri-sis.[1] Experts also tell us that this sense of "negativity," as Bonnie put it, leads to what in the 1980s was dubbed *compassion fatigue* after military jargon. People become worn out and so they tune out.[2] Yet what Bonnie expressed to me was that the same information might have vastly different capacities to call forth connection. When it derives from Christian sources, the news can prompt what she views as generative activities, which are characterized by focused giving and prayer. Yet when CNN covers the same story, it may "drag" her into despair or apathy instead. Such subtle differences are crucial if we are to understand how globally minded Christians hear news from abroad and feel its effects. It also reminds us that there is no simple equation that accounts for donor apathy. In fact, in the 1990s, at the very moment when critics warned most emphatically about compassion fatigue, United Nations Development Program surveys showed no downward turn in public opinion about foreign aid. Instead, there were significant upticks in aid directed to refugee and disaster relief.[3] The Christian child sponsorship organizations I study also grew enormously in this period.

Sponsorship is a popular fundraising tool in Europe and North America, and it refers, at the most basic level, to the systematic (usually monthly) support of an individual abroad with some communication between donors and recipients. From its inception, the model was tied to human suffering and insecurity. The American Board of Commissioners for Foreign Missions pitched the first sponsorship plans to U.S. donors in 1816, citing the many children left "friendless" in Bombay after they came to the city with families fleeing floods, famine, and other disasters and their parents "not infrequently" died.[4] A century later, sponsorship made the transition from missionary fundraising to World War I relief. During the war, it was used by dozens of early humanitarian organizations including the American Red Cross and Near East Relief.[5] This transition cemented the broad versatility of sponsorship beyond missionary circles. The nature of relief organizations' work also amplified sponsorship programs' focus on children in extreme distress, which carried over as fledgling nongovernmental organizations (NGOs) adopted it after World War II.

Sponsorship spread in the 1950s as a broad-based fundraising tool for humanitarian campaigns. It was part of the general proliferation of U.S. voluntary organizations working overseas; more than 200 were established in the four years after World War II alone.[6] More specific to U.S. Protestantism, emerging parachurch organizations revitalized sponsorship even as the denominational missionary boards that once used it declined. The best-known example is World Vision, which grew out of evangelical networks coalescing around Youth With a Mission and Billy Graham in the 1940s.[7] Christian Children's Fund (CCF) is another key example. Founded in 1938 by a liberal Presbyterian pastor, it appealed to mainline Protestants and, in the 1950s, was the largest U.S. Christian organization of its type. In many respects, CCF was heir to the pan-Christian fundraising that Heather Curtis has traced at the *Christian Herald* a generation before. (In fact, some of CCF's most successful 1950s campaigns were partnerships with the *Herald*, which ran short-term sponsorship plans as early as the Indian famine of 1900).[8]

Parachurch organizations such as World Vision and CCF leveraged sponsorship to access larger donor markets and fuel ambitious programs for rapid growth.[9] While missionary plans had included from a few hundred to a few thousand children at most, these new plans scaled up to support tens of thousands of children by the early 1960s (and hundreds of thousands by the 1980s). This growth brings us back to disaster: mid-century plans grew their donor base in part because they stoked a sense of urgency in the midst of disasters, notably in their appeals concerning war in the 1950s (mainly in Korea) and then natural events, such as cyclones (Bangladesh in 1970), earthquakes (Nicaragua in 1972), and drought-related famine (Ethiopia in 1984). The Ethiopian famine was a notable windfall: World Vision, which today is the largest Christian organization that uses sponsorship, saw its income jump 80 percent that year.[10]

The tight link between disasters and the success of sponsorship organizations remains. In her study of World Vision (WV), sociologist Susan McDonic noted that the international WV partnership circulates fast-breaking information about disasters, "which then is funnelled to the wider press and media associations . . . [allowing WV] to speak authoritatively about situations that are emerging and/or have erupted." World Vision's website promises "the most up-to-date information on emergencies, events and issues from around the globe" and, during McDonic's fieldwork, the organization was mentioned in the North American press an average of 150 times a day. She argues that by offering "the press first-hand accounts from the areas where disaster strikes, footage and pictures," World Vision promotes itself and makes its subsequent pitches to prospective sponsors more credible.[11] Although many of the larger organizations, including World Vision, have changed their marketing strategies since the early 2000s to focus on hopeful, happy children, disasters remain integral insofar as the same organizations still issue regular calls for emergency relief donations, beyond each sponsor's regular monthly contribution.

At a more existential level, the close relationship of sponsorship to disaster also prompts certain questions. What interests me here is how U.S. donors, like Bonnie, relate what they hear about global poverty and disasters to their belief that humanity is connected in basic terms via its shared relation to a single Creator—and, potentially, Destroyer. What is the space between a sense of existential security and chaos? How do sponsors grapple with persistent threats to human flourishing? These issues are extremely complex since the U.S. Christians with whom I worked credit their God as the only certain power in this world yet refuse the idea that He is capable of perpetrating such injustice. Herein lies a central problem of Christian theodicy.

To explore this topic, I draw on my five-year (2012–2017) study of Christian child sponsorship in the United States, which combined historical and ethnographic work. Here I focus on my conversations with child sponsors, including 196 hours of tape from discussions with 118 child sponsors. The people on whom I focus most closely in this chapter were Protestant supporters of Compassion International, an evangelical organization based in Colorado Springs, and Catholic supporters of Unbound, a liberal, lay Catholic organization in Kansas City.[12] I also worked with Protestants (including those whom scholars would dub liberal or mainline) who supported World Vision and ChildFund (formerly CCF).

Demographically, the people whose interviews I recorded were largely consistent with organizational estimates of the average sponsor; most were married, nearly all self-identified as white and Christian, and most went to church; three quarters were women. Their ages ranged from thirty to eighty-seven; among my Catholic interviewees the average age was sixty-five and among evangelicals it was fifty-five.[13]

This chapter focuses less on the official scripts that sponsorship organizations introduce or that priests, pastors, and other institutional bodies promote. There are, of course, massive amounts of literature produced for Christians about how to understand suffering and evil in the world. Instead, I draw on my conversations with sponsors to explore their grassroots theologies. These are generally ideas in the making rather than coherent pronouncements, and they may draw on more top-down conceptions but are rarely identical to them. One aspect that readers might consider pertains to how our conversations complicate the discourse related to "religious persecution." These popular campaigns, which most sponsors knew of and many supported, tend to reify the "religious" by downplaying contextual factors, such as poverty, war, or natural disasters; Christians may suffer in either case, but when that suffering is called "religious" it is prioritized as *Christian* suffering par excellence. Nonetheless, I found that the sponsors with whom I worked generally integrated a broad cross-section of concerns into their discussions about, and prayers for, suffering abroad. Though they rarely referred to this suffering as "Christian" per se, thy nearly all assumed that the faraway families and communities they supported through sponsorship were, in fact, Christians in distress. Many sponsors also linked their concern about foreign suffering to their own experiences, albeit with caveats.[14] In sum, this chapter teases out how U.S. Christians parse various forms of violence and injustice as they trace the contours of God's global projects.

The Security and Insecurity of Global Connection

I asked every sponsor with whom I spoke whether they felt the world was becoming more connected. Every one of them agreed—but they drew different conclusions about the results. Did connection lead to greater understanding and equality? Or did they lead to greater disunity and violence? Quite a few sponsors explicitly told me they felt either optimistic or pessimistic about the state of the world. Among Catholics and liberal Protestants, about 20 percent fell into either category, skewing slightly more toward the optimistic.[15] Among those who declared themselves pessimistic, most answers were either a resigned recognition that humans have always been cruel to each other and always will be; a feeling that things were actually worsening since there no longer seemed to be clearly defined global "good guys" and "bad guys"; or a concern about growing terrorism, especially in the Middle East.[16] The specter of Muslim violence haunted these discussions and many people explicitly mentioned Islam, but only one person among my Catholic and liberal Protestant interlocutors blamed the religion tout court. Nearly everyone else raised the issue to clarify that "real" Muslims were against violence.[17] By contrast, sponsors who chose to support Compassion, a more conservative evangelical organization, clearly swung onto the side of pessimism: almost 40 percent stated they were pessimistic about the world; a bit under 20 percent were optimistic. And nearly three quarters of the pessimists unhesitatingly pointed to Islam as the culprit.[18]

A fair minority of the Compassion sponsors whom I got to know, especially those with less education and affiliations with fundamentalist-leaning churches, offered a clash of civilizations model to explain this outlook. "You're not just dealing with a different religion [in Islam] but a whole *mindset* that is completely the opposite of the Christian one," said Carol, a secretary in western Massachusetts who self-defines as a Bible-believing Christian. Writing of domestic U.S. politics, Lauren Berlant remarks that intimacy is a powerful affective tool because it resides in familiarity and optimism while also cohering around concerns about threats to the world it seeks to sustain.[19] Globalization creates possibilities for new intimacies, but it also magnifies potential threats. Most sponsors quite handily identified the intimate "we," which encompassed their families and friends, Christians around the world (including the sponsored child), often extended to Americans in the United States as a whole (at least in the abstract), and sometimes included Canadians and others who seemed culturally and racially familiar (comments likely spurred by my presence). While not all respondents focused on Islam, those who named what was emphatically *not* part of the "we" *always* did. No other group was singled out this way in global terms.

Many sponsors, including Carol, talked about being scared, or even "terrified," of threats associated with Islam, primarily violence against the "we"—that is, targeting Americans (9/11 came up often) and Christians in the Middle East (televised killings by ISIS had made a recent and indelible impression).[20] They viewed Americans and Christians overseas as united by this common threat. It is a new pattern with older roots. Though Islam was rarely mentioned in evangelical sponsorship materials from the 1950s and 1960s, when it did come up, Muslims were blamed for being "aggressive" missionaries for their own religion as well as stubborn and fanatical—as evidenced by how many times they prayed each day or how the women refused to talk with Christian missionaries.[21] And yet contemporary sponsors are, above all, globally minded, which means that one cannot simply shut oneself off to others: one must try to engage them. Carol followed her previous comment with another one, speaking in the personal register even though she had never been abroad: "You go into these countries and whether they're Muslim or some other religion, you go to China you have their gods, and the thing is, my prayer would be that they realize that God is God and not Allah and not whoever they are over—you know, the Chinese ones and stuff like that. That, you know, not just that family [I am sponsoring] but that the country itself would realize that God is God." In responses like this one, "Muslims" (and Chinese "gods") are kept vague, as are the big dreams associated with their conversion. Ultimately, whole countries might come to realize that "God is God," as Carol put it.[22]

About a quarter of the liberal Protestants with whom I spoke and almost as many Catholics blamed the United States itself for stoking global insecurity. About 10 percent blamed the U.S. government for wars abroad and another 10 percent said that foreign people had legitimate reasons to distrust Americans. These respondents were all optimistic that the one-to-one charity associated with sponsorship could make amends. Their responses echo decades of American strategies in the world—one thinks of President Dwight Eisenhower's call for "People to People" diplomacy whereby pen pals or the Peace Corps would bring "regular" Americans into friendships with people abroad.[23] In the hands of politicians, these messages tend to efface larger questions about the structures that create and sustain global inequality.[24] Sponsors, like most Americans, contribute to those systems through mechanisms such as paying taxes and making investments, benefiting from white privilege and consuming the lion's share of the world's resources. Some of them addressed the issue directly, describing how they felt impotent in the face of structures that seemed so large as to defy clear understanding. Rather than focus on threats from without—Islam, terrorism, disasters—these sponsors viewed themselves as deeply enmeshed in threats to world prosperity. Barbara, an unmarried accountant in her late fifties, put it this way: "Pretty much the U.S. is in a state of permanent warfare. So what's the countervailing force? I can do nothing about the politics of my country. Really I cannot. That's a done deal but I *can* do something about that [child, Jimmy]. For me [sponsorship] is a political action. It's not how Jimmy's family thinks about it but for me it's a political act . . . For me this is my social justice political act. Just trying to nurture one little being."

Barbara lives in Kansas City, where she cares for her aging parents and is deeply involved in her Catholic parish as well as liberal Catholic organizations that promote social justice. She is passionate and educated, and she makes time to consume international news. Barbara was one of the few sponsors I met who drew a structural link between wealth in the United States and poverty elsewhere by, as Susan Sontag put it, mapping American privilege onto the same map as other people's suffering.[25] "We also take resources from other countries for our own use, like, since we consume most everything—right?—on the planet," Barbara told me. Other respondents did talk about curbing personal consumption in the West. A few also discussed the unethical practices of U.S. corporations, but they rarely saw these entities as "American" per se; rather, they viewed the U.S. government and people as generous and some corporations (run by certain Americans) as greedy. Only Barb insisted that the U.S. government's militarism and economic policies was a source of global unrest—and therefore that the American people who elected those leaders were enmeshed in threats to global prosperity.

Human Nature and Natural Disaster

Writing during the 1980s AIDS crisis in New York, with news reports about the recent Ethiopian famine on her mind, Susan Sontag noted how people in Western countries persistently reproduced a nature-culture divide in which calamities that ravaged poor countries were seen as "natural" whereas those in the West were understood as culture-making "world events." "Part of the self-definition of Europe and the neo-European countries," she wrote, "is that it, the First World, is where major calamities are history-making, transformative, while in poor, African or Asian countries they are part of a cycle, and therefore something like an aspect of nature."[26]

In fact, most of the U.S. Christians I got to know recognized "natural" disasters as part of the fabric of American life, especially if they came from regions hit by annual tornados or hurricanes. However, they did tend to divide disasters in the West into *either* natural or human-made (the latter being "world events" in Sontag's terms, such as 9/11 or the failed response after Hurricane Katrina). By contrast, when they discussed poor countries they persistently grouped *all* disasters into a seemingly endless, and therefore natural, cycle. The twin natures at stake were earthly elements, for example an earthquake or tsunami, and also human nature, which produced a parade of bad dictators and the like. Nearly every sponsor told me that humans have free will, are greedy by nature, and do bad things as a result. By a wide margin, sponsors blamed global inequality partly or wholly on the ways in which corrupt elites or government officials in the child's country of origin, giving into this base nature, diverted aid money and resources for personal gain. These responses echoed classic Christian theology, in which the vocabulary and emphasis reflected sponsors' upbringings and orientations; Catholics talked about free will, mainline Protestants talked about human tendencies, and evangelicals talked about inherent sinfulness.[27]

All the sponsors I got to know agreed on one major point: God did not target *particular* individuals to suffer. This was no book of Job—at least where the sponsored child and his family was concerned. My interlocutors often referred to poverty as an accident of birth; they had happened to be born in the United States and the sponsored child had not. Yet this idea prompted discomfort. After all, did God not choose where each one of us would be born? The resulting existential problem became even more intractable when the conversation turned to natural disasters, as it often did, which sponsors knew often deepen poverty and increase the unjust allocation of resources. As the term *natural* suggests, hurricanes or earthquakes are not caused by human action: the implication is that God is therefore responsible.

Western Christians have long believed that natural disasters carried a deeper message from God. This idea was standard before the Enlightenment and remained so, at least among Christian child sponsors, until the early twentieth century.[28] In previous periods, sponsorship promoters therefore suggested that natural disasters and war had the positive effect of creating orphans who, having been violently ripped from everything they knew, would be open to hearing Christian truth.[29] By contrast, the contemporary sponsors I got to know strongly emphasized that God abhorred seeing anyone suffer and did not *cause* natural disasters. At the same time, most of them also told me that God did *allow* these crises to happen.[30] Larger-scale surveys have noted similar responses following natural disasters in the United States. Among committed Christians, surviving such a disaster generally deepens a positive view of God and pushes people to find alternatives to blaming God for negative outcomes.[31] In our conversations, I heard Christian sponsors reasoning about similar ideas in greater detail.

Most often, sponsors suggested that God allowed poverty in general, including disasters that might deepen that poverty, to encourage Christians to realize their utter dependence on God. "For people that are having all their financial needs taken care of, it might be harder for them to realize that they need God too. And we all do," said Sue, a forty-seven-year-old who attends an evangelical Lutheran church in Massachusetts with her husband, Ted. She paused and continued, "I think for one thing, God allows trials in people's lives to draw them [closer] and make them stronger, to learn important lessons in life. . . . Destruction, you know, [like] earthquakes in India and other places and we've had our share of hurricanes and everything and floodings and everything [in America]." Sue continued in a personal register: "Disaster sometimes can bring brokenness, because we literally lost everything [in a hurricane] when we were growing up as kids. The family unit, it's almost like everybody's off busy-busy-busy and nobody knows their neighbor anymore and then it brings us together too."[32]

Sue knows something about surviving chaos. The hurricane ripped apart her home and, shortly after, as a teenager, she became an alcoholic. As a result, she and Ted have lived with a sense of impending disaster for decades; they chose not to have children because of her volatility. Now sober for five years, Sue feels a sense of relative peace. Along with Ted, she plans their budget carefully each month in order to sponsor three girls in Latin America. Sue does not equate her alcoholism—which she sees as a personal failing—with natural disaster. But in either case, she views God as allowing chaos in order to achieve greater ends. "I believe destruction . . . can bring blessings," she repeated. "And I don't believe that God wants people to necessarily to *stay poor.* That's why he has given people like me [the means] to help other people who are poor." In Sue's view, God also sent people to lift her up when she was "broken" by the hurricane and then by her alcoholism. Now, she believes, God is using her—because of her good fortune at being from the United States—to help other Christians who need spiritual and material stability in turbulent times.

Sociological and psychological surveys of U.S. Christians that ask about natural disasters are heavily biased toward Protestants. If Catholics are included, little distinction is made between responses from Christians of different backgrounds.[33] Yet in my conversations, at least, Catholics offered the most richly varied set of responses. Like their Protestant counterparts, Catholics pointed out that everyone had to bear physical suffering, whether it was "hunger or cancer," and struggle with spiritual consequences such as greed, envy, or ingratitude. The Catholics with whom I spoke were also much more likely to view the poor in other countries as already spiritually rich compared to Americans, usually because they were pictured as closer to the earth and to their families and therefore better able to recognize their dependence on God's natural processes—the food culled from the land and the joy that came from family. A large minority of Catholics also turned to the afterlife to reframe material poverty as potentially leading to spiritual wealth. John, a middle-aged Catholic sponsor in upstate New York, put it nicely: "God allows poverty to happen and I think that He sees the bigger picture, one that we don't see and that being, if heaven is eternal then our lives are very short. Just a tiny grain of sand. . . . And I think that if we really could stand back and see the large, the big picture, maybe those of us that think we're living in non-poverty would see it differently."[34]

No Protestant sponsor I got to know discussed the afterlife or eternity. As Sue demonstrated, they were future oriented insofar as they believed God uses brokenness for "good" ends that only become apparent later on. What sponsors agreed on, however, was that poverty elsewhere should move U.S. Christians to act.

Acting in the World through Prayer

For most globally minded Christians, giving and praying are interrelated ways to act in the world. Both provide ways of interacting, as Bonnie put it at the start of the chapter. As might be expected, prayer came up often with evangelical sponsors, however many mainline Protestants and Catholics (including Bonnie) also told me that prayer was an essential part of what they "gave" abroad. Natural disasters are fundamental in this respect because nearly every sponsor told me that, regardless of whether they prayed on a regular basis, the child and their family became the focus of their prayers in two main circumstances: when the child wrote about a specific need and when the sponsor heard news coverage of a disaster in the child's region. Generally, this kind of reporting was the *only* way sponsors heard about the child's country outside sponsorship materials since, as scholars of media note, European and North American media usually reports on the Global South, which is deemed "foreign" and thus of less interest to viewers, exclusively through the prism of fast-breaking disasters.[35]

Because so many sponsors told me they followed the news about the places where they supported children, at first I was surprised at how little most of them knew. This realization initially struck me as I was speaking with Melissa, an evangelical woman in her early thirties who worked as a nurse and had a child the same age as my daughter. As we commiserated about juggling parenting and work, she told me that she carved out some time for herself each night. "I'm an avid fan of [ABC] *World News Tonight* with David Muir. I love him. He just delivers it," she said. "And I watch it very closely for Ecuador and trying to keep tabs on it." Melissa has sponsored children in Ecuador with Compassion since she was a teenager. When I met her, she was supporting a boy named Jorge. Besides *World News Tonight*, Melissa pays attention to stories about Ecuador on her Facebook newsfeed and then follows up by reading online content from CNN. "Has there been a moment when you've seen something about Ecuador that's made you think?" I asked her. Melissa responded:

M: Yeah, when there were earthquakes and flooding and it was very scary and we got an email from Compassion saying we—you know, "We're trying to get in contact . . ." And it was a really long time before I heard—I mean weeks . . . it took a really, really long time to hear that [Jorge] was okay.

H: And in that period did you find you were focusing your prayers more or—?

A: Absolutely. Yeah—and not just him, but for him and his community. . . . [I]t really kind of hit close to home. So I found myself praying for Jorge . . . praying for strength for him and for them—not by name, you know, but for the victims.

H: . . . Are there other things [on the news] that you find yourself focused on in connection with [Jorge]?

A: Like I said, I keep up on news about ISIS and I heard about some kind of religious segregation. It was outside of Ecuador, you know, where people were targeted for being Christians and obviously in that area of the world—

H: Wait, sorry, I lost you. You mean it was near—near Ecuador?

A: Yeah, but—yeah, the surrounding areas. And, you know, I remember doing some of my own little research seeing if it was affecting [Jorge's family's] area, which I didn't find anything saying it was. But, you know, just you hear of all that religious persecution and things that it can be very dangerous to be an active Christian in some of those countries.

H: But do you get the sense that Ecuador is a Christian country or—I don't know if Compassion talks about that in their materials.

A: They'll send a little bit of demographic information of the country but I think there's a lot of Muslims and Buddhists also in that area.

Some sponsors were very well informed, of course. But Melissa was also not unique in her stated interest in foreign news yet strangely inaccurate conception of Ecuador. Like many sponsors, she gleans her news from mainstream and Christian sources (in her case, usually through Facebook). Both channels of information focus on natural disasters in the Global South, while the latter also emphasizes Christian persecution at the hands of religious "others," mainly Muslims.[36] Melissa is also not alone in conflating these two presumed threats to Christian well-being in poor countries to create an image of victimized life under duress. In this respect, it is notable that nearly every sponsor with whom I spoke assumed that the child's family was Christian. In fact they were usually right, at least at Unbound and Compassion,[37] but the point is that this assumption means that any threat described in sponsorship materials related to poverty or disasters is understood to put *Christian* families at risk. It is not a leap for U.S. sponsors who follow news about "persecution" to superimpose multiple levels of insecurity into a single picture of Christians abroad as always under threat.

While such assumptions came up in my conversations with all types of sponsors, it was most prevalent among evangelicals like Melissa; in fact, 17 percent of the evangelical sponsors with whom I spoke told me that concern about "religious persecution" was the *primary* reason they felt connected to Christians around the world.[38] Some of this focus is undoubtedly due to the strong Anglo-evangelical interest in "persecuted" Christians over the past two decades, but it may be exacerbated in this case because none of the countries where sponsors support children are majority evangelical. Regardless of the actual politics in each country, born-again Christians can therefore always be viewed as potentially at risk from a powerful majority religion that is "other." By contrast, U.S. Catholics were aware that many of the countries where they supported children, including Ecuador, were Catholic-majority places. It was one reason why they were often drawn to help them in the first place. As a result, Catholic sponsors were much more likely to distinguish between natural disaster/economic poverty and religious persecution, which they talked about almost exclusively in the context of Middle East Christians living in Muslim-majority places.

At a more basic level, inaccuracies also persist because sponsorship subtly discourages detailed information. What I mean is that sponsorship attempts to create kin-like relations that reflect back to U.S. Christians what is presumed to be shared at the most basic level: the hurts, loves, and aspirations that come with being part of a human family. Providing too many local details can muddy these waters. Sponsors never told me so explicitly, but they did often say that they learned "just enough to verify it is a very poor country," as another woman at Melissa's church put it. They wanted just enough specific information to be assured that Christian people and organizations were "very poor" and were getting the support they needed. They also wanted basic amounts of information to better focus their prayers. To return to the theme of this section, Christians

understand sponsorship as fostering resilience through relationships—a goal
that requires prayers (and letters) alongside monetary donations and development work.[39]

Not surprisingly, evangelical organizations have been particularly active in
producing materials to encourage their donors to use sponsorship as a launching pad for global prayer. For example, in 1989, Paul Borthwick, an evangelical
pastor in Massachusetts, wrote an article in *World Vision Magazine* about how to
pray in "an ever-widening circle" by launching "brief prayer arrows" across the
world.[40] Borthwick and his wife began this process each week with letters from
Oyie Kimasisa, a child they sponsored in Kenya. In studying those letters, they
discerned what they understood to be needs (some of which the boy probably
stated and others that he did not). They began their prayers with those specific
needs, while letting God guide their imaginations further based on what they
knew from media reports, including World Vision's newsletters. This made their
prayers "larger" as they prayed for "kings and all those in authority" (1 Tim. 2:2)
because, as Borthwick wrote, global leaders are often the key to successful Christian work abroad. Natural phenomena like sandstorms and plentiful ground
water were also a key feature of their prayers. Though Borthwick's article is somewhat outdated, I mention it here because I found similar patterns among sponsors as they scaled up from children's letters to "big," or more generalized, needs.
The opposite trajectory was also true, as Melissa demonstrated; at times sponsors begin with large-scale disastrous events on the news and then try to gain
more targeted information by scanning the child's letters and, in desperate
times, calling the sponsorship organization to pinpoint specific needs.

Prayer is pertinent to U.S. Catholic giving, too; sociological studies show that
Catholics rank intercessory prayer and material support as their top two priorities in global giving.[41] In contrast to evangelicals, however, a sizable minority of
Catholic sponsors told me they rarely pray extempore; instead, they follow the
cycle of prayers during Mass or use the rosary and prayer cards at home to
address God, Mary, and their favorite saints. Most did pray for the sponsored
child by name, at least on occasion, and they were likely to do so according to
what they sometimes called "a basket of intentions." This term refers to the practice of thinking of many names and keeping them in mind during a more general prayer, such as the Our Father. The "basket" becomes literal in parishes at
Lent and other times when those who are present may pass round a basket to
fill with strips of paper bearing the names of all who need prayer. These baskets—
both literal and metaphorical—gather familiar and foreign names. This pattern
of mingling prayers for self, family, and others was important across all my field
sites, whether Protestant or Catholic.

Bonnie, the Unbound sponsor mentioned at the outset, offers a sense of
these varied links. When she discussed praying for Julia's needs in Guatemala,
she continually returned to prayers she says on behalf of those closest to her.

Clinging precariously to the bottom rung of the middle class, she and her husband had bought a small suburban home outside Kansas City, where they raised their two kids. She taught Sunday school and did secretarial work in the parish while he worked for an electrical company. When he lost his job in 2010, they barely managed to keep their home. Her sister, who was not so lucky, has declared bankruptcy and now Bonnie supports her financially and through prayer. Another challenge concerns her daughter, who has been trying to get pregnant. As she discussed why Julia and her family were poor, Bonnie seamlessly overlapped one set of struggles onto another.

> I don't think God is saying, okay, you get to be poor, you get to be—I think there's blessings and all of that. . . . [And] I can't say that my sister who's now in bankruptcy is *not* blessed by the Lord . . . I mean, why is my daughter struggling and struggling to get pregnant? You can't look and say, I blame God. And you can't say, gosh, these people are awful and that's why it's bad for them. I think we need to work harder to find out what we can do to help people. And each person can do more. . . . I think you can find the Lord in all of those places of sadness or challenge.

Bonnie also describes another burden: loneliness. Her husband and adult children are no longer practicing Catholics and her mother, who had been her companion in matters of faith, died not long ago. She says the loneliness feels overwhelming at times. But Bonnie has a few spiritual guides, including a close friend who became a priest and then died suddenly when they were in their mid-thirties. His favorite saying was, "We're only but a prayer apart." "That's how I think of the world too," Bonnie tells me. She gestures at the large world map pinned to her wall. It has been there for years.

> It is a sense that we are all here together [in the world]. We really are. So I may not specifically say, okay, now I'm going to pray for Julia, I just feel she's within me. And if I'm deepening my spiritual life, if I'm getting closer to the Lord, they're all coming with me. And I think that helps me because like I said, I'm kind of the loner that still goes to Mass. . . . I was thinking of my mom and sometimes I felt that loneliness but then that sense of we are, in spirit, we are just only but a prayer apart. 'Cause [Julia] is in my heart and I'm in her heart so we—we, spiritually, already have met. We have met. I'm not a traveler . . . I hate traveling. I will never be going to Guatemala!

While telling me about Julia's family, Bonnie says that we must always "be aware of the fact that their experiences are not ours." It's the kind of message Unbound hopes its sponsors will assimilate. Nevertheless, based on Julia's letters, Bonnie feels that they do share a similar worldview, not least because Julia, who is now entering her teens, seems to share what Bonnie views as a Catholic sensibility of gratitude and activism. For Bonnie, prayers are essential in this regard. They are one way she can do more for the welfare of all those she holds in her heart. They are also a way to make sure the people who are not present with her at Mass—her family, who refuses to attend, and Julia, who is far away—are still "coming with" Bonnie as she moves through this life and, perhaps, into the next one. That's being only a prayer apart.

To Dwell within Suffering

When sponsors discuss the places where they support a child—places very few of them have been or will ever go—they often talk about human nature and natural disaster. Human sins, including government corruption, sow the seeds of poverty. Disasters deepen it. For sponsors, these twin factors are "natural" insofar as they operate at a level that far exceeds the discrete actions of sponsored children and their families and they seem to drive an endless cycle that keeps the majority of the world poor. For two centuries, sponsorship organizations have built their fundraising model on sometimes sensationalist reports about these twin forces. Perhaps counterintuitively to outsiders, the Christians who have responded to these appeals are, in fact, quite optimistic about how to perceive them. It does not mean that they are necessarily optimistic about the state of the world generally—some are and some are not—but they are certainly hopeful that sponsorship is an effective way to intervene in such cycles by nurturing "one little being," as Barbara put it.

This chapter identifies a few key patterns in terms of how contemporary sponsors understand the suffering of (what they often identify as) Christian families abroad. First, sponsors tend to access their news from mainstream and Christian sources; they choose when to tune in and when to turn off these various streams of information in order to glean just what they feel they need to spur a sense of connection. It means that they often view themselves as people who follow current events and research foreign news even if some of them are uninformed or incorrect about the places they support. Second, sponsors come to grips with natural disasters, and the suffering they cause, by viewing their God as *allowing* but not *activating* these events. Usually, they say God allows disasters or poverty to encourage people to realize their dependence on Him. Third, sponsors do recognize that human nature (sin) and natural disasters plague the United States, but with respect to poor countries they tend to group these two categories together to fuel a sense of constant crisis. However, we should not assume that they view "home" as always comforting and "away" as always threatening. Many of the sponsors I got to know had lived through death and abuse, depression and loneliness. They usually identify these threats to flourishing as a common human condition—which also leaves room for hope. This connection between struggles at home and abroad is most tangible during prayer, as sponsors audibly mingle petitions for themselves, their families, and faraway others.

These ideas help complicate what some scholars of globalization have noted about unpredictable events. In times of crisis, writes anthropologist Thomas Hylland Eriksen, most Western people blame processes on a higher scale ("government") or withdraw to trust only first-hand experience and face-to-face acquaintances.[42] To some degree the U.S. Christians with whom I worked are committed to being globally minded, as donors at least, so they do not simply fall back on what they know first-hand. They may blame larger human organizations, and thus humanity's fallible nature, but they also understand themselves to have a direct link to "the top," which is God. The result is a viewpoint that sees suffering as a mystery and nevertheless solidifies God's presence. Their answers recall Leibniz's classic mediations on the problem of theodicy: what may appear to us as evils in the present are in fact doing good from God's broader perspective.[43]

Read alongside the other chapters in this volume, my discussion here shows how sponsors talk about suffering in ways that complicate the discourse related to "international religious freedom" or "religious persecution," even as some of them consume this media and support these campaigns. Sponsors are also concerned about Christian suffering and well-being in the communities they support, but they integrate many contextual factors, such as poverty, war, or natural disasters when they imagine Christians elsewhere in distress. Further, their sense of connection to a "global church," though it may be sparked by reports of suffering, is rooted in an optimistic certainty that all Christians have something in common—a shared relation to an ultimately loving God.

NOTES

1. Barbara Adam and Chris Groves, *Future Matters: Action, Knowledge, Ethics* (Leiden: Brill, 2007); Zygmunt Bauman, *Globalisation: The Human Consequences* (Cambridge: Polity Press, 1998); Ulrich Beck, *Risk Society: Towards a New Modernity* (London: Sage, 1992); Nauja Kleist and Stef Jansen, "Introduction: Hope over Time—Crisis, Immobility and Future-Making," *History and Anthropology* 27, no. 4 (2016): 373–392.

2. Erica Burman, "Innocents Abroad: Western Fantasies of Childhood and the Iconography of Emergencies," *Disasters* 18, no. 3 (1994): 247; Susan D. Moeller, *Compassion Fatigue: How the Media Sell Disease, Famine, War and Death* (New York: Routledge, 1999); Alexander De Waal, *Famine Crimes: Politics & the Disaster Relief Industry in Africa* (Bloomington: Indiana University Press, 1997).

3. UNDP survey cited in Tara Linn Hefferan, "Deprofessionalizing Economic Development: Faith-based Development Alternatives through U.S.-Haiti Catholic Parish Twinning" (PhD diss., Michigan State University, 2006), 55–56.

4. "Thoughts on Various Methods of Advancing the Cause of Christ by Missionaries at Bombay," *Panoplist* 12, no.1 (January 1816): 34–39.

5. These two groups are notable as the first and second humanitarian organizations to be granted a charter by the U.S. Congress, in 1900 and 1919 respectively.

6. Sara Fieldston, *Raising the World: Child Welfare in the American Century* (Cambridge, MA: Harvard University Press, 2015), 3.

7. More common language at the time was "nonsectarian" or "interdenominational." On parachurch organizing, see Robert Wuthnow, *The Restructuring of American Religion: Society and Faith since World War II* (Princeton: Princeton University Press, 1990), 71–132; and Robert Wuthnow, *Boundless Faith: The Global Outreach of American Churches* (Berkeley: University of California Press, 2009), 239. See also David P. King, *God's Internationalists: World Vision and the Age of Evangelical Humanitarianism* (Philadelphia: University of Pennsylvania Press, 2019), 67–118.

8. Heather Curtis, *Holy Humanitarians: American Evangelicals and Global Aid* (Cambridge, MA: Harvard University Press, 2018), 153. On the 1950s campaigns, see J. Calvitt Clarke to F. H. Faber, 15 March 1956, Folder 8, Box IB22, ChildFund Archives, Richmond, VA.

9. These organizations scaled up quickly because they were ecumenical in their fund-raising and also in the field, where they partnered with a broad subset of established missionaries. Organizations matched donors with children who were already in missionary-run orphanages or schools, sending monthly transfer payments for each child who was sponsored. This system differed from nineteenth-century sponsorship plans run by missionary boards because it did not require that these organizations build their own infrastructure and it was not limited by the number of children missionaries in one denomination could handle at any given time. Thus mid-twentieth-century organizations accessed an essentially limitless "supply" of children to fulfill donor demand. The system's drawback was that at times organizations were only dimly aware of conditions in the institutions they supported. Changes since the 1970s have greatly improved communication and accountability.

10. David P. King, "The New Internationalists: World Vision and the Revival of American Evangelical Humanitarianism, 1950–2010," *Religions* 3, no. 4 (2012): 933, 937.

11. Susan McDonic, "Witnessing, Work and Worship: World Vision and the Negotiation of Faith, Development, and Culture" (PhD diss., Duke University, 2004), 117.

12. The Compassion sponsors with whom I worked most closely attended an Evangelical Free Church of America and a Presbyterian (PCUSA) church that was effectively non-denominational evangelical. I met these sponsors through their churches, after volunteering for sponsorship-related events. I conducted 12 interviews in Massachusetts, 13 in New Hampshire, and 8 in San Jose (where I also volunteered), for a total of 43 Compassion sponsors. The Unbound sponsors came from a variety of parishes and were nearly all 'cradle Catholics.' I met them thanks to Unbound, which sent out hundreds of letters on my behalf to sponsors in select parishes. I conducted 20 interviews in upstate New York and 19 in Kansas, interviewing a total of 52 Unbound sponsors (including spouses). Mainline Protestant sponsors were hardest to find, since they often supported organizations that were not explicitly religious. I found some through word of mouth, and a few more after I advertised in the *Christian Century* in 2015. I conducted 19 interviews (with 23 people), 8 of which were in person.

13. Rounding the numbers up or down, 87 percent of my interviewees were married or recently widowed; 90 percent had children (many grown); 75 percent were female; all self-identified as Christian and most went to church. My interviewees were somewhat more likely than organizational estimates to self-identify as white—all of my Protestant interviewees did so, along with 95 percent of Catholics. (Compassion and Unbound estimate that 85–90 percent of their sponsors are white). A main difference from

organizational averages concerned age: my interviewees were a decade older; Compassion's estimates put their average sponsor at 46 years old; at Unbound, it is 55 years old.

14. On resonances in the United Kingdom, see Frances Rabbitts, "Give and Take? Child Sponsors and the Ethics of Giving," in *Child Sponsorship: Exploring Pathways to a Brighter Future*, ed. Brad Watson and Matthew Clarke (New York: Palgrave Macmillan, 2014), 289.

15. My question about "connection" did not include the words "optimistic" or "pessimistic" but, since I was conducting open ended conversational interviews, my interlocutors were able to take their response where they wanted. Here, I am only counting those interviewees who explicitly self-identified as pessimistic (18 percent) or optimistic (21 percent).

16. Although only four individuals stated this directly, scholars argue that the post-Cold War world has seemed especially chaotic and bewildering in the face of the seemingly simple good/bad world of Cold War ideology. For example, Kleist and Jansen, "Introduction: Hope Over Time," 376.

17. Among Catholic and mainline respondents, 16 percent (n=12) talked about "terrorism," in the Middle East especially. Of these, two people blamed ISIS (implying Muslims) and one blamed Islam in general.

18. 39.5 percent (n=17) Compassion sponsors said they were pessimistic and 18.6 percent (n=8) said they were optimistic. In other words, about the same percentage were "optimistic" as their Catholic and mainline counterparts. The main difference lies in the fact that 60 percent of Catholic and mainline sponsors did not take a stand either way, compared to 40 percent of Compassion sponsors. In other words, evangelicals were more likely to swing onto the side of stated pessimism (which is not surprising, theologically speaking). They were also much more likely to point to "Islam" as the culprit: 30 percent (n=13) of my evangelical interlocutors did so. On a similar note about Islam, see Peter Ove, "Change a Life, Change Your Own: Child Sponsorship, the Discourse of Development, and the Production of Ethical Subjects" (PhD diss., University of British Columbia, 2013), 247–248.

19. Lauren Berlant, "Intimacy: A Special Issue," in *Intimacy*, ed. Lauren Berlant (Chicago: University of Chicago Press, 2000), 7.

20. Compassion sponsors raised these issues often. Only two connected this global breakdown with the End Times, although relevant theologies might certainly lead conservatives to be more pessimistic generally (see note 18). Some mainline Protestants (8 percent) and Catholics (12 percent) also talked about 9/11. On the importance of 9/11 for shattering American (including scholarly) assumptions about global connection, see Anna L. Tsing, *Friction: An Ethnography of Global Connection* (Princeton: Princeton University Press, 2005), 11.

21. I am thinking of the materials I surveyed at World Vision and Compassion. Some examples include: *A Call To Prayer* (Newsletter), 31 December 1959 and 15 January 1959, Ministries "Call To Prayer," Jan.–Dec. 1959, World Vision International Archives (WVIA), Monrovia, CA; *A Call To Prayer* (Newsletter), 15 July 1960, Ministries "Call To Prayer," Jan.–Dec. 1960, WVIA. On aggressive Muslim missionizing, see, for example, John T. Seamands, "Christianity's Answer to the Muslim Challenge," *WV Magazine*, May 1964, 6–7, accessed at Billy Graham Center Archives, Wheaton, IL.

22. Thomas Kidd, *American Christians and Islam: Evangelical Culture and Muslims from the Colonial Period to the Age of Terrorism* (Princeton: Princeton University Press, 2013).

23. Christina Klein, *Cold War Orientalism: Asia in the Middlebrow Imagination* (Berkeley: University of California Press, 2003), 49–56; Jonathan P. Herzog, *The Spiritual-Industrial Complex: America's Religious Battle against Communism in the Early Cold War* (New York: Oxford University Press, 2011), 78.

24. Lauren Berlant, "Introduction: Compassion (and Withholding)," in *Compassion: The Culture and Politics of an Emotion*, ed. Lauren Berlant (New York: Routledge, 2004), 3.

25. Susan Sontag, *Regarding the Pain of Others* (New York: Picador, 2004), 102.

26. Susan Sontag, *AIDS and Its Metaphors* (New York: Farrar, Straus and Giroux, 1989), 83–84.

27. Catholics discussed "free will" in nearly every interview. Of the few Protestants (n=4) who did so, half had grown up Catholic. Such linguistic cues might be worth exploring further. Other scholars have noted how evangelical leaders who engage with global issues (e.g., human trafficking) also blame corrupt foreign leadership for problems; for example, Todd M. Brenneman, *Homespun Gospel: The Triumph of Sentimentality in Contemporary American Evangelicalism* (New York: Oxford University Press, 2014), 139.

28. A small number (n=3) of highly conservative Protestant sponsors still said so. On this idea, see Jeanet Sinding Bentzen, "Acts of God? Religiosity and Natural Disasters Across Subnational World Districts," *Economic Journal* 129 (2019): 2295–2321.

29. For example, Address by Miss Classon in *Minutes of Public Meetings N.H. Br. Of W.B.M. Nov. 12 1872–Dec. 11 1883*, entry on July 9, 1874, folder 1, box 4, series 2, Women's Board of Missions Records (WBMR), The Burke Library Archives at Union Theological Seminary, New York, NY; James Smith, "Industrial Training in India," *Missionary Herald* 4 (April 1900): 168–172. On similar ideas among U.S. Catholics, see Fr. Paul de Fresonora, Letter extract in *Annals of the Holy Childhood* 111 (March 1873): 15–17, Special Collections, University of Notre Dame Archives (UNDA), South Bend, IN. Mid-century evangelicals also sometimes said Satan created devastating acts of nature (and disease) to cause human suffering. See, for example, Edmund Janss (dir., childcare ministries), *Manual for World Vision Superintendents* (World Vision International, 1975), 95–100, Folder 9: ORG/WVI 16 FY-74 Sponsorship Programs Manuals, Ed Janss, Central Records, Global Center, Los Angeles, WVIA, Monrovia, CA. Few contemporary sponsors mentioned Satan, and those who did emphasized how his attacks on *individuals* cause personal doubt and sin.

30. On this common distinction between "cause" and "allow," see Edward B. Davis, Cynthia N. Kimball, Jamie D. Aten, Benjamin Andrews, Daryl R. Van Tongeren, Joshua N. Hook, Don E. Davis, Pehr Granqvist, and Crystal L. Park, "Religious Meaning Making and Attachment in a Disaster Context: A Longitudinal Qualitative Study of Flood Survivors," *Journal of Positive Psychology* 14, no. 5 (2019): 665.

31. Davis et al.. "Religious Meaning Making"; Jamie D. Aten, Patrick R. Bennett, Peter C. Hill, Don Davis, and Joshua N. Hook, "Predictors of God Concept and God Control After Hurricane Katrina," *Psychology of Religion and Spirituality* 4, no. 3 (2012): 182–192; A. Taylor Newton and Daniel N. McIntosh, "Associations of General Religiousness and Specific Religious Beliefs with Coping Appraisals in Response to Hurricanes Katrina and Rita," *Mental Health, Religion & Culture* 12 (2009): 129–146; William C. Haynes, Daryl R. Van Tongeren, Jamie Alten, Edward B. Davis, Don E. Davis, Joshua N. Hook, David Boan, and Thomas Johnson, "The Meaning as a Buffer Hypothesis: Spiritual Meaning Attenuates the Effect of Disaster-Related Resource Loss on Posttraumatic Stress," *Psychology of Religion and Spirituality* 9, no. 4 (2017): 446–453. A few people in this study did note Satan's role (11 percent and 14 percent at different time intervals), which would undoubtedly be higher with samples of Pentecostals and Fundamentalist

Protestants, which were not strongly represented in my study (see Kidd, *American Christians and Islam*). By contrast, according to the studies mentioned previously, people in the United States with "negative religious coping" who "avoid" intimacy with God are more likely to interpret God's role negatively after natural disasters. Most psychology studies are strongly biased towards white women of college age, because of the sample sets. They also favor Protestants over Catholics, and ask about "God" rather than Jesus, Mary, and so forth, and thus give only a very basic sense of how people interact with a variety of other-than-human presences.

32. This is also relatively common reaction, for example in 53 percent of Katrina victims, according to Davis et al., "Religious Meaning Making," 665.

33. I am thinking especially of the many studies out of Wheaton College (see Berlant, "Introduction"). Typical is Bruce W. Smith, Kenneth I. Pargament, Curtis Brant, and Joan M. Oliver, "Noah Revisited: Religious Coping by Church Members and the Impact of the 1993 Midwest Flood," *Journal of Community Psychology* 28, no. 2 (2000): 176.

34. Nearly 20 percent of Catholics (n = 10) offered responses similar to John's, but not a single Protestant did so.

35. A classic early study is Johan Galtung and Mari Holmboe Ruge, "The Structure of Foreign News: The Presentation of Congo, Cuba and Cyprus crises in Four Norwegian Newspapers," *Journal of Peace Research* 2 (1965): 64–91.

36. Catholics were somewhat more likely to note that they received their foreign news from missionary priests who spoke in their parishes (these speakers did not emphasize Islam, it seems). Evangelicals were much more likely to refer to work by celebrity anti-Muslim writers like Nonie Darwish and Ayaan Hirsi Ali. For more on this phenomenon, see Melani McAlister, *The Kingdom of God Has No Borders: A Global History of American Evangelicals* (New York: Oxford University Press, 2018), 144–158.

37. Neither organization restricts its aid, but Unbound focuses on Catholic majority places and Compassion's program works through local evangelical and Pentecostal churches and schools. Christian parents are therefore most likely be aware of, and take part in, such programs due to their social networks and proximity (indeed, it is a Compassion requirement that children live within walking distance of its Christian service providers). I include Catholics as Christians, although Compassion does not (at least in terms of its service providers), which makes the question about whether children are Christian (and more specifically, "born again") rather delicate. Compassion does not gather statistics in this respect, but a number of the employees I interviewed did confirm a high probability of self-selection into the program by already Christian parents (e.g., Alistair Sim, program effectiveness research director, June 12, 2014; Mark Hanlon, senior vice president of global marketing and engagement, June 12, 2014).

38. For more on this trend among evangelicals, see Elizabeth Castelli, "Praying for the Persecuted Church: US Christian Activism in the Global Arena," *Journal of Human Rights* 4, no. 3 (2005): 321–51; McAlister, *Kingdom of God*, 159–174; Omri Elisha, "Saved by a Martyr: Evangelical Mediation, Sanctification, and the 'Persecuted Church,'" *Journal of the American Academy of Religion* 84, no. 4 (2016): 1056–1080; Wuthnow, *Boundless Faith*, 158–161.

39. I am making an argument that runs parallel to that of Kevin O'Neill, *Secure the Soul: Christian Piety and Gang Prevention in Guatemala* (Berkeley: University of California Press, 2015).

40. Paul Borthwick, "Sharpen Your Global Prayers," *WV Magazine*, August–September 1989, 10–11. Borthwick begins his prayers with "Oyie," but he is also inspired by thinking

about a missionary couple he supports in Mauritania, North Africa, whom I have not
mentioned.

41. Janet Kragt Bakker, *Sister Churches: American Congregations and their Partners Abroad*
(New York: Oxford University Press, 2014), 52.

42. Thomas Hylland Eriksen, *Overheating: An Anthropology of Accelerated Change* (London:
Pluto Press, 2016), 139–140.

43. Colin Campbell, *The Romantic Ethic and the Spirit of Modern Consumerism* (Oxford:
Alcuin Academics, 2005), 113–114.

PART TWO

Bodies

Accounts of persecution and martyrdom often appeal to religious or political identity as the motivating factor due to the visceral nature of violence. These stories, however, always emanate from and find credence within time and space, where violence, imprisonment, and death are inflicted against real people with physical bodies. Centering bodies in these analyses can illuminate the fact that causes and motivations for violence are often layered and complex. When individual religious adherents are understood with respect to their gendered bodies, one can see the intersecting forms of violence that can be inflicted, which cannot be reduced to religious identity alone.

The embodied experience of persecution reveals juxtapositions and contradictions, while generating new directions for analysis. In the case of American Coptic Christians, Candace Lukasik shows how they present American evangelicals with examples of the need for U.S. intervention abroad to protect their spiritual kin. Within the United States, however, Copts remain a racial other, lumped together with other religious and racial minorities. This juxtaposition—of spiritual kin and racial foreigner—reveals the complexity of persecution narratives in the United States. However, Lukasik reveals the ways in which the Copts are far from passive recipients, instead reimagining themselves as kin of the Religious Right, including reproducing persecution narratives within their own communities.

Gender-based violence, social structures that inflict disparate suffering, and intra-Christian persecution are also constitutive of the forms of violence that Christians can create, perpetuate, and experience around the world. The embodied experiences of women of color in contexts of intra-Christian (Joel Cabrita) and large-scale violence (Kate Kingsbury) have shaped the creative expressions of Christian faith in colonial Swaziland and contemporary Mexico. Taken together, these chapters challenge the ecumenical assumptions that undergird World Christianity scholarship, even as both illuminate different kinds of examples of Christians marginalizing other Christians. In both cases, this oppression led some Christians to form independent churches (Cabrita), and others to move beyond the apparent boundaries of Christianity altogether (Kingsbury). These analyses cut across the grain of wider scholarship and contribute to a full-orbed picture of violence within a global context. These chapters shatter stereotypes and flattened analyses to reveal the complex reality of violence at the grassroots level, where harm is inflicted on particular contexts and bodies.

4

Apartheid and World Christianity

How Violence Shaped Theories of "Indigenous" Religion in Twentieth-Century Africa

JOEL CABRITA

In 2017, in an introduction to an edited volume on "World Christianity," my coauthor and I argued that the focus on indigeneity in World Christianity was an ideological move born of the independence-era patriotic fever in Africa and elsewhere. The older (nineteenth-century) universalistic idea of World Christianity as a global ecumene that erased local cultural difference had, by the middle of the twentieth century, been superseded by different values: a commitment to cultural particularity and a celebration of Indigenous worldviews. Rather than the older belief that conversion entailed the creation of new Christian moderns—individuals who exemplified the supposedly universal values of "civilized" (read: Western European) societies—the feeling was now that Christianity could, and indeed *should*, take on the cultural and linguistic trappings of the society in which it found itself. We attributed this shift to the heady atmosphere of decolonization around the world, and especially in Africa, where many of the key proponents of the new style of World Christianity were located.[1]

However, in offering this narrative, my coauthor and I missed a vital component of the story: the significance of violence. Our rendering focused on the high-level narratives of elevated thinkers—all male and many within theology and religious studies departments or in prominent positions as missionaries and church leaders. We offered an account largely divorced from the mundane realities of day-to-day life, and we only very briefly touched on the considerable pressures of living according to the strictures, not only of race and class, but also of gender. To put it simply, what we neglected was that the individuals who crafted this new definition of World Christianity did so amid experiences of great suffering. Moreover, it was specifically the violence of the colonial encounter that caused many African intellectuals to craft newly indigenized theories of Christianity. World Christianity, in other words, cannot be considered independently of a chronology of violence; it is this painful history that directly gave rise to new arguments for what Christianity should look like in an Africa now independent of white rule.

Furthermore, while existing accounts, including my own, focused on male intellectuals, the truth is that there were also very many women, in Africa and elsewhere, who assumed responsibility for the work of reimagining World Christianity. That is why this chapter offers a brief glimpse into the life of Regina Gelana Twala, a South African–born Black woman whose life lived under apartheid and the indignities of a ruling white minority led her directly on a path from the older belief in Christian universalism—which appeared hopelessly hollow in the face of racial segregation—to a deliberate celebration of the Indigenous as a mode of resistance to white rule.

Twala's theorizing on Black-led Christianity should have established her as one of the preeminent scholars of religion in Africa. Instead, however, she was relegated to obscurity and her work on this topic was appropriated and eventually published by Bengt Sundkler, a European missionary-anthropologist who passed it off as his own. Instead of Twala being a famed name in the intellectual genealogy of World Christianity, it is Bengt Sundkler whom we remember as a pioneering giant of the field. This, then, is also an opportunity to reflect on the multilayered meanings of *violence*. As well as the racial and gendered violence of apartheid in Southern Africa, there is also the violence involved in the production of knowledge itself—the repressiveness of the Euro-American academy in privileging certain voices and silencing others. This chapter attempts to go some way toward redressing these issues by telling the intellectual history of World Christianity from the perspective of a Black woman who experienced firsthand the racial and gendered injustices that so significantly shaped her theological views.

Regina Gelana Twala and Christianity in Colonial South Africa

Regina Gelana Twala (nee Mazibuko) was born in 1908 at Indaleni Mission, Natal, South Africa (in isiZulu, the name is spelled "eNdaleni"). The mission was situated in the Midlands, a swathe of fertile-soiled hills extending into the interior of South Africa from the coastal city of Durban. It was the exceptional richness of the Midlands soils that would make the area such a sought-after prize for white farmers, thus signaling the demise of the economic fortunes of the region's Black residents. And there was no spot more fertile nor more scenic than the site of Indaleni Mission itself. Its small, white-washed buildings were erected in an almost impossibly bucolic location, as it was nestled in the green foothills of the massive Drakensberg Mountains at the base of eNdaleni Hill in a loop of the slow-flowing Ilovo River.

The mission had been founded in 1847 by British Methodist missionary James Allison. Allison had originally founded his mission in the nearby territory of Swaziland, but he experienced growing hostility from the-then Swazi monarch—who, like many other African hereditary rulers of the nineteenth century, was decidedly unsure about these new Christian proselytizers. Allison gathered together a small group of African converts and fled with them into neighboring Natal, which was then under British colonial rule.[2] Once the group arrived in Natal, the colonial state awarded Allison 6,000 acres of land for the mission, which he promptly named Indaleni, possibly after the thick forests that still grew in the area.[3] Within a year, a neatly laid-out village had emerged, which was identical to many other mission-run sites dotting the countryside of Natal in the nineteenth century. Within the green eNdaleni valley, Alison and his band of converts built sixty white-washed cottages, a chapel, and a school.

A community of prosperous isiZulu-speaking farmers, teachers, and crafts-people emerged. In common with other such settlements across Southern Africa, the mission's goal was to create a new community of Christian Africans. Detached from their older allegiances to tribe and chief and loyal to the new Christian God, these individuals were known as *amakholwa* (the believers). Indaleni's residents—including its first appointed Christian chief, Majozi, who operated in distinction to the region's hereditary "traditional" chiefs—were able to purchase small plots of land to farm. An individual's possession of property, as contrasted with the older African communal system of land ownership, was thought to be paramount in the formation of modern Christian identities.[4] Second only to individual land tenure and the renunciation of old loyalties to traditional chiefs, education sat at the heart of the mission's so-called civilizing enterprise. Within a few years a "Manual-Labour School" was established that taught converts basic literacy as well as construction and carpentry. All was directed toward the formation of new Africans: modern Christians adapted to Western ways and embracing the values of private entrepreneurship and individualism. The small community flourished. Allison approvingly observed: "The native Christians have been most industrious, besides cultivating their own gardens and building their own homes, they purchased poultry which they've now resold in [the nearby town of] Pietermaritzburg . . . our new congregation is now properly clothed in articles of British manufacture."[5] Fast-forwarding to the time of Regina's birth in 1908, half a century later, the mission had undergone a serious reversal of fortune. The rise of white commercial agriculture meant increasing pressure was put on eNdaleni, and other similar pockets of successful African Christian enterprise. White farmers viewed African agriculturalists as unwelcome competitors, naming them, moreover, as the reason why so many Africans were able to resist entering into the colonial labor economy. A raft of legislation was passed, including the 1913 Natives' Land Act, that largely denied Africans the possibility of economic independence or land ownership. In the famous words of Sol Plaatje, "Awakening on Friday morning, June 20, 1913, the South African native found himself a pariah in the land of his birth."[6]

The supposedly race-blind Christian universalism of the mid-nineteenth century was fast disappearing under pressure from white economic and political forces.[7] By the time Regina entered the missionary-run education system, this was truly the case. She would probably have enrolled in Indaleni's school around the age of six, in 1914, and have been educated there for a ten-year period, until she left the high school aged sixteen, in 1924. Her decade at the school would have sharply exposed Regina to the missionary truism of this period, that education for Black African girls should be "industrial" rather than "academic." School was thought to be a mechanism for preparing girls for lives of domestic service, both for white employers before marriage and for husbands after marriage. Missionaries of this period were complicit in this racist economic ideology; one European educationalist summarized Indaleni's goal in this way: "It will make the native girl more valuable to her community . . . [as she] will be able to keep her house better and be of service to white people."[8]

The events of the next decade of Regina's life further illustrate how the violence of both racism and patriarchy could intersect in South Africa. A whirlwind romance with one Percy Kumalo led to a quick marriage and her move to Johannesburg to be with her new husband, where she took a job teaching in a mission school (after eNdaleni, Regina had trained as a teacher at the American missionary-run Adams College). However, the marriage collapsed. Percy turned out to be a serial adulterer who eventually abandoned Regina. Yet according to the norms of the day, Black women were not meant to object to "a little philandering" from their husbands—this was the normal state of affairs—and they were considered to blame for the marriage breaking down if they did.[9]

Regina was shortly to find out just how hard it was for a Black woman to gain a divorce in 1930s South Africa, and how punishing the Christian community—both Black and white—were of divorced women. Regina was also bitterly disappointed in her white lawyer, H. M. Basner. He was ostensibly a famed liberal defender of African rights, but Regina felt he was not taking her case seriously enough. Her caustic take on her predicament was this: "I am a black woman, the curse of South Africa, and he is a white man, and of course a N—— has no feeling."[10] Eventually after two years of frustratingly slow legal process, she did succeed in gaining a divorce and soon married her second husband, Dan Twala.[11]

Regina's disillusionment with the myth of Christian universalism—the idea that "civilized," Westernized Blacks would receive treatment equal to that of whites in South Africa—would only grow as the years went on. After her marriage to Dan Twala, she decided to requalify as a social worker. She first took a diploma course at the newly opened Jan Hofmeyr School in Johannesburg and then enrolled at the University of the Witwatersrand, becoming the first Black woman to earn the new degree in Social Studies (including studying anthropology under the anthropologist Hilda Kuper of Swaziland, who was already famous).

But the experience was bittersweet. While in theory open to Black students, student life at Wits was horribly segregated, with Black students denied the use of common facilities and, perhaps most damagingly, not permitted to lodge close to the university because of urban segregation laws. As a result Regina had to undertake hours of travel every day on crowded trains to and from the university to her home with Dan Twala in the township of Orlando, twenty miles from Johannesburg. Her grades suffered as a result, something that her Orlando neighbor and classmate, Nelson Mandela, also attributed as the cause in his own failure at his law exams the following year.[12]

Around the time Regina graduated from Wits and started her new job at a social welfare center, the political situation in South Africa took a turn for the worse. The general election of May 1948 delivered a shock victory to the Afrikaner Nationalist Party. This party had run on a racist platform of apartheid—or "separate development" for South Africa's races; in reality, this meant far inferior "development" for all but the country's whites—and had deployed slogans such as "Swart Gevaar" ("Black Peril") to play to white South Africans' fears of extinction by a Black majority. Apartheid ideologues built on decades of prior legislation by intensifying the message that Africans belonged in rural "tribal" areas rather than cities. Fighting against the labor needs of city-based industry, Afrikaner fanatics argued that cities, with their supposedly Western ways, were alien and harmful environments for "tribal" Africans. The government removed tens of thousands from urban "blackspots"—cosmopolitan culturally influential neighborhoods like Sophiatown disappeared—and shunted the exiles into dusty, windswept flatlands far from the city. A flurry of legislation further undercut Africans' right to live in cities. Perhaps the most hated action was the government's introduction of the Pass Books a small identification document all Africans were to carry, ad without which they would be immediately ejected from the city.

As a Black woman resident in Johannesburg, Regina, of course, experienced the indignities of apartheid in a multitude of personal and painful ways. But one particular incident stands out. In 1949, she was being considered as the new director for the welfare center at which she worked, and by all accounts she was the best candidate. But the board—led by Violaine Junod, daughter of the famed Swiss missionary in South Africa, Henri-Alexandre Junod—delivered the shocking decision that in the present political climate, it would be too much of a liability to have a Black woman as director: "the Center's development would be affected." Regina resigned, disgusted at the hollowness of the Christian liberal tradition represented in Junod's betrayal.[13]

In 1951, Regina accepted a new post with South Africa's Council for Industrial and Scientific Research. This was a government-funded body that aimed to apply social scientific research to urban problems; it deployed Regina to the coastal Cape city of Port Elizabeth—more than a two-day journey by train from

Johannesburg—to conduct research into conditions of African housing in its large African township, New Brighton.[14] Port Elizabeth was Regina's crucible moment. After her humiliation at the hands of Christian liberal figures such as Junod, she arrived in Port Elizabeth well primed for political awakening.[15] By the early 1950s, the port city was one of the most radical environments in South Africa. Its long history of trade unionism, its liberal legacy of relatively relaxed segregation laws, and the dire living conditions in places like New Brighton all conspired to make it what the popular African magazine *Drum* called "a political time bomb."[16] Port Elizabeth was also one of the areas in which the African National Congress (ANC) was experiencing a major resurgence. After years of toothless gradualism and domination by older men who optimistically clung to ineffectual petitions and the chimera of reasoned debate with the government, the ANC had at last changed leadership. Young radicals such as Nelson Mandela demanded change now, and they devised concrete strategies to make it happen.

By 1952, Port Elizabeth had also become one of the hubs of the ANC-led Defiance Campaign. This was a nationwide mass action protest that recruited volunteers to defy apartheid laws with the aim of clogging up the judicial system by filling the prisons to capacity. "No bail, no defence, no fine" was the campaign's slogan. Over 8,000 people were arrested and imprisoned throughout 1952 for streaming into European-only postal offices and railways stations. The "Windy City," as the coastal Port Elizabeth was colloquially known, supplied more volunteers—tightly disciplined, carefully selected individuals—than anywhere else in the country.[17] Women—including Regina—became especially active in the city's campaign.[18] Yet Regina was just as preoccupied with the injustices of gender as she was of race. She became particularly outspoken on the issue of women's representation within the ANC, denouncing it a patriarchal organization that excluded women.[19] She is on record at the annual conference of the ANC in 1952, "strongly protesting" that "women have been used as tools to raise money without representation in Congress" (probably referring here to the "Shilling Campaign" run by female Congress members).[20] Her husband, Dan Twala, has a memory of a woman so outspoken that the men around were simultaneously attracted and repelled: "She was on fire, so that even the men were pulled around by her. Ah, she was very startling at that moment. She felt very strongly and she had an opinion that could not be defied. Even some of the men could not work with her because she was so straightforward."[21]

By the early 1950s, moreover, Regina had also discovered a new God. This was a deity who encouraged Black believers to take pride in their own cultural values and to critically interrogate the connection that Methodist missionaries at places like eNdaleni had drawn between Christianity and Western worldviews. It was during her brief time in Port Elizabeth that Regina started attending the religious services of Nicholas Bhengu, the wildly popular leader of the

Pentecostal Assemblies of God Church. By the 1950s, Bhengu was widely known as the South African "Billy Graham.. He had become famous throughout South Africa and internationally for his massive "Back to God" campaigns, whereby he would pitch a tent in a town, hold a series of revival meetings over the course of several weeks, and invite attendees to confess their sins and embrace Jesus Christ. In typical Pentecostal style, the services were famous for hardened criminals and drunkards tearfully giving up their old lives and turning to God. Supposedly services ended with "piles of knives, blackjacks, brass knuckles, stolen goods"—all tokens of the old life of sin—heaped at the altar.[22]

In part, we can understand Regina's admiration for Bhengu in intimate terms: her Pentecostal faith now became a way for her to bitterly criticize Dan Twala for his unfaithfulness to her (Regina, it turned out, had had bad luck in this, her second marriage, too). Bhengu was especially outspoken on the unraveling of "traditional" sexual mores and highly sympathetic to the predicament of women who found their husbands had strayed from them amid the supposed temptations of modern life in the city. Pentecostal-style Christianity, with its outspoken, uncompromising stance on adultery, became useful fodder for Regina use to attack Dan for his infidelities.[23]

But Bhengu's church also became a means for Regina to further express her sense that Africans should be independent of white influence—in this case, free to develop more culturally authentic ways of being Christian—for Bhengu was an ardent advocate of Black pride. This is not to say that he was explicitly political in orientation. He insisted that Christians "look to God" rather than attempt to reform the secular political system.[24] During the 1952 Defiance Campaign, Bhengu was criticized by many people for being a "sell-out" to the apartheid government and for not leveraging his enormous popularity in support of the political cause.[25] Bhengu was profoundly disturbed by the injustices of apartheid, something he vocally communicated to his huge numbers of followers. But rather than engaging in political protest, Bhengu's opinion was that a crucial part of the struggle involved strengthening the self-confidence and dignity of Africans. His sermons would often stress the African ancestry of Christianity, telling listeners gathered in his capacious revival tents that Christianity had been in Africa long before it arrived in Europe and that key biblical figures—Abraham, for example—had all sojourned in Africa.[26]

Regina's new commitment to African autonomy and Black cultural pride was soon severely tested. Her baptism by fire came on December 8, 1952, four days before her forty-fourth birthday. The protest held in Germiston Location, an African area in Johannesburg, was one of the final and most high-profile acts of Defiance during the entire campaign. Regina was one of fourteen African volunteers who took part in the protest that day in December. Wearing the black, green, and gold ribbons of the ANC, the protestors entered Germiston Location and were almost immediately met with "cheers and great excitement" and followed by a group of "about 1,000 singing Africans." More ominously, they were also trailed by uniformed police officers, both on foot and in police cars.[27]

Regina addressed the crowd in frank and personal terms. She spoke of her own many years of training as a social worker, and she expressed her profound disillusionment with the futility of "uplifting" Black life when faced with the brute reality of apartheid South Africa: "Most of the theories for solving the problems I learned at the university only work according to skin colour." Then, as Regina and her fellow protestors neared the exit, "squad cars raced up and encircled the crowd," screeching across the tar and blocking the road so they could not pass. The crowd started shouting "Afrika" and raising clenched fists—which would become the symbol of the antiapartheid resistance for the next forty years—as the protestors were bundled into cars and driven away for booking and processing.[28] Regina would spend some of 1953 in a bleak Johannesburg prison. Upon her release, she found herself not only with a criminal record but also without a job. She was immediately fired by the Research Council, and for the next year she struggled to find anyone who would employ her.[29] All the signs were that Regina was fast heading for more serious trouble. It was Dan's opinion that had she not left the country in 1954, she would have found herself imprisoned in 1956, when Mandela and other key ANC leadership were swooped up by the government in a catastrophic avalanche of arrests.

Not a moment too soon, Regina escaped to mountainous Swaziland, part of an ever-growing wave of Black exiles from apartheid South Africa who were crossing the border into the British Protectorate (her husband, Dan Twala, was also from Swaziland).[30] Regina had just received unexpected news: she had been awarded a prestigious four-year research fellowship by the Nuffield Foundation in the United Kingdom, an award that would affiliate her with the Institute for Social Research in South Africa and fund her to conduct ethnographic research on social conditions in Swaziland. In early 1954, at the personal invitation of the Swazi monarch, Sobhuza II, Regina left Johannesburg and moved to Swaziland.

Christianity and Intellectual Life in Swaziland

Intelligent, well-read, and intensely curious about the latest intellectual, cultural, and social trends, the Swazi king, Sobhuza II, was a frequent fixture in Johannesburg throughout the 1940s and 1950s. He could be seen, not only mingling with the cream of Black Johannesburg society at social hubs like the Bantu Men's Social Center, but also in attendance at a lively circuit of academic and intellectual events in the city, including anthropology seminars at Wits. He also subscribed to journals such as *Bantu Studies*, and he was close friends with the anthropologist Hilda Kuper, whom he had first welcomed to his country in the 1930s when she did her fieldwork in Swaziland, as well as with Kuper's mentor at the London School of Economics (LSE), Bronislaw Malinowski.[31]

Sobhuza's interest in anthropology was part of his lifelong quest for freedom from colonial violence for his emaSwati subjects. By the mid-1950s, fertile and mineral-rich Swaziland faced ominous forces threatening its very survival. From without, the threat was the same as it had been for the last half-century: a land-greedy Union of South Africa that wanted to amalgamate the tiny territory of Swaziland—one hundred miles long and only eighty miles wide—into its own borders.[32] Since his inauguration as paramount chief in 1921, aged only twenty-two, Sobhuza had devoted himself to blocking South African ambitions to cannibalize his country. A large part of this work was persuasion. Sobhuza skillfully and strategically invoked a supposedly superior British sense of justice to protect Swaziland against its vast and powerful neighbor. And after 1948, and the election of an avowedly racist government in South Africa, Sobhuza's chosen path was still diplomacy and deal brokering rather than outright opposition. It was for this reason that Sobhuza had sent word to his subjects in South Africa not to take part in the Defiance Campaign of 1952. He correctly foresaw that the campaign would not succeed and could only result in further oppression and even loss of life.[33]

Within Swaziland's border the threat was, of course, the British administration. Since the early years of the twentieth century, British colonial officials had worked hard to limit the scope and powers of the Indigenous monarchy. It was for this reason that Sobhuza's subjects were forbidden by Great Britain to address their monarch as "king," restricting the leader to the lesser rank of "paramount chief." Yet in recent years the stance of the British administration had changed. The period after World War II saw a shift in colonial policy, a greater interest in allying with Indigenous leaders in places like Swaziland, and a recognition that independence for its African colonies was surely on the horizon. It was a question of when, not if.

Skillfully responding to these political transformations, Sobhuza now doubled down on a strategy he had already been pursuing since the 1930s. This was to play the game of ethnic nationalism: to cast present-day Swaziland as a political entity that could lay claim to a long and glorious history, to play up the power of the monarchy as an ancient Indigenous institution, and to revive a range of cultural traditions presented by him and his council of elders as practiced since time immemorial. In this way, Sobhuza could bolster his argument for Swaziland's legitimacy as an independent nation-state of venerable and longstanding history—deserving of freedom from both British and South African interference—as well as pander to the British preference for dealing with "traditional" political authorities as part of their indirect rule policy.[34]

Swaziland's mood of neotraditionalism resonated with Regina's own changing political and intellectual views and her conviction that Africans should take great pride in their own cultural traditions. Once Regina moved to Swaziland, she continued to be involved in Bhengu's church: its Black pride message resonated well with Sobhuza's ethnic revival agenda of these years. In fact, it was Regina who first introduced Bhengu to Sobhuza and who helped him negotiate the expansion of his church into the country. It was no coincidence that the very first of Bhengu's Assemblies of God church was built in Kwaluseni, just around the corner from Regina's own home. Her daughter-in-law, Anne, told me that while the church was being constructed, Regina would host Sunday School in her front living room and play the piano for the children's songs.[35]

And if Port Elizabeth had brought Regina to Bhengu, it was Swaziland that now brought her to the Zionist churches. The Zionists were a loose federation of hundreds of evangelical churches, entirely African in leadership and membership, that had stemmed from a controversial faith-healing church in the American Midwest.[36] By the 1950s, though, the influence of the original Midwestern church was slight and Zionists were known as a thoroughly Africanized Christianity. Many Zionist prophets—as leaders of the movement were known—seamlessly incorporated Indigenous therapeutics with Christian faith healing, something that led European missionaries to denounce these believers as backsliding sinners.

Yet despite the many fingers pointed at them, Zionists grew exponentially across Southern Africa. These were the decades during which these churches mushroomed across the region, replicating in cramped meeting rooms in townships and increasingly visible gatherings in rural areas, praying on hillsides and baptizing in rivers. Their fusion of Christianity with Indigenous religion was welcomed by many African Christians who were tired of being lectured by missionaries for the supposed sin of syncretism. Not least due to the support of Sobhuza II, as well as the heavy footfall of migrant laborers between South Africa and Swaziland, Zionists became especially formidable in Swaziland. By the 1940s, Zionists accounted for half of all emaSwati Christians, and those numbers only continued to grow as the century progressed.[37]

The 1950s saw an already cozy relationship further ripen between Zionist churches and Sobhuza's nationalist maneuvering. The Zionists were as close to becoming a national church as possible. Zionist prophets argued that Sobhuza was divinely ordained, and they regularly lent their presence to key national rituals like the Incwala, an annual rain-making ceremony that took place over Christmas. Each December, snowy-garbed Zionist prophets lined up shoulder to shoulder in support of Sobhuza, standing alongside emaSwati warriors wearing feathery cloaks of cattle tails, their heads studded with gleaming black and white feathers. Zionist leaders used a biblical grammar of divinely ordained kingship to argue for Sobhuza's legitimacy. In 1956, a prominent Zionist published rousing praises of Sobhuza in the national newspaper, *Izwi lama Swazi*: "Sobhuza is like Solomon of old in wisdom and his grandfather, Mbandzeni I, compares with

Moses of old in Israel."[38] The queen mother—who co-ruled with Sobhuza and was an enormously powerful figure—had herself converted in the 1930s, after being healed of an eye ailment by one of the most famous Zionist healers in the country.[39]

Zionists, moreover, also gained standing in royal circles due to their ambivalent stance toward Western culture. While mission churches stressed book learning as part of the intertwined package of Christianity and "civilization," Zionists insisted that the only guidance for the people of God was the Bible and the Holy Spirit.[40] European missionaries in Swaziland strongly criticized Zionists as uneducated, faith-healing fanatics. But for Sobhuza, Zionists' reluctance to partake in the missionary educational enterprise was a welcome sign of their independence from Western influence. Zionists were even willing to sanction aspects of emaSwati's culture that European missionaries denounced as "satanic," including polygamy and the veneration of deceased ancestors, which was a widespread practice among emaSwati then and now. One prominent Zionist of the 1950s defended his church's adoption of Indigenous practices on the grounds of patriotism and national pride: "One was worried whether the customs of the Swazi were found so wanting that it became necessary for customs of other nations to be superimposed on Swazis."[41]

Regina was intensely interested in all this. To her, even more than Bhengu's church, perhaps, the Zionists seemed a compelling example of what a perfectly fused blend of African culture and Christianity might look like.[42] And living where she did in Kwaluseni—an African residential suburb of Manzini, one of the main cities in Swaziland—Regina could hardly have ignored them: one of the oldest and largest Zionist denominations in the country had its headquarters in the small town of Ludzeludze, just over the rise and down a gentle valley from Kwaluseni and within earshot of her own home (Zionists were a highly auditory church: weekends saw noisy night-long vigils punctuated with ecstatic prayers, babbling tongues, and shrieking exorcisms).[43] While she never became a Zionist herself, throughout all Regina's years in Swaziland there are many instances of her being closely allied with them. For example, in 1959 she persuaded senior Zionist officials to invite her own religious mentor and leader, Nicholas Bhengu, from South Africa to address them at their large Easter service, which was held in the very same valley where Sobhuza's Lobamba palace was situated.[44]

Another example of this close relationship was the help Regina gave to Zionist leaders as they worked to fulfill a decades-long dream that their many denominations would unite into a single national church. This was something that the Swazi monarch, Sobhuza, had identified as crucial to his push for self-rule. In reconciling the many squabbling denominations of Western missionaries, a single Swazi church—to be called Isonto ke Makrestu (Church of Christ)—would echo the unity of the emaSwati people themselves and form a strong foundation for impending nationhood and freedom from Britain. Prince

Madevu, the high-born royal architect of the single church idea, identified Regina's unique talents as a university-educated woman as strategic for the movement. At Madevu's request that she "edit and put into good English the constitution of Isonto ke Makrestu," she assisted in drawing up the constitution for this new national church.[45] In 1957, Regina was also considered as a candidate for the influential role of secretary for the League of Zionist Churches—the organization that worked for the creation of the single church—but this never came to pass. Women—in the 1950s as is still the case today—generally did not hold formal leadership positions within this patriarchal structure.[46]

In addition to this clerical assistance, Regina also wrote extensively about the Swazi Zionists: pages of perceptive ethnography grounded in her own personal experience of attending very many religious meetings. In 1958, the Swedish Lutheran church historian Bengt Sundkler became affiliated with Regina's own Institute for Social Research (ISR) in Durban, Natal.[47] Some ten years earlier, Sundkler had written the definitive ethnographic monograph on Zionist churches in South Africa, *Bantu Prophets in South Africa*.[48] His book—which was already famous by this decade—was a robust denunciation of the "syncretism" of independent churches. In this respect, Sundkler was evincing his ties to a prominent strand within his own Lutheran heritage—its commitment to a universalistic society of Christian moderns transcending race. As Sundkler put it, "the pull from this heathen heritage . . . constitutes an ever-present problem."[49] In a famous passage—using italics to underscore "the seriousness of the whole situation"— Sundkler concluded, "*The syncretistic sect becomes the bridge over which Africans are brought back to heathenism.*"[50]

However, by the late 1950s, Sundkler's views had radically changed. The altered political and theological climate of the 1950s (including the arrival of independence for Ghana in 1957, which Sundkler visited in that year) now pushed him toward a more celebratory stance on the African tradition that he had previously condemned. Thus, he was now seeking to update his book, not only by offering a more positive appraisal of the Zionists but also by including material on Swaziland, which had emerged as a major center of Zionism in the region.[51] But Sundkler was only in Southern Africa for six months, after which he had to return to his teaching duties at Uppsala University in Sweden. As he had done for first book, Sundkler hired a range of African researchers to do much of the work—mainly interviews with church leaders and accounts of religious services they had attended—that would go into the final product.[52] Already affiliated with the ISR and living in Swaziland, Regina would have seemed a natural choice as a contributor. Furthermore, by 1958, Regina's Nuffield funding was fast running out and she was looking for ways to make money.[53] But although there was a financial motivation for accepting the commission from Sundkler, there was also, of course, Regina's genuine commitment to an African religion free from

European influence. Thus, throughout the late 1950s, Regina attended numerous Zionist services and conducted interviews with prominent prophets, all at Sundkler's behest. There even seems to have been an ultimately abortive plan for Regina to assist Sundkler in making an ethnographic film on Swazi Zionists; she would have traveled with the film to Sweden and supplied "running commentary" on it during screenings.[54]

Regina's research notes for Sundkler—over twenty-five dense pages, which are preserved in his personal archives in Uppsala, Sweden—underscore her view of the Zionists as a thoroughly Africanized Christianity. Her case was meticulously made, comprising a body of work that Regina proudly confessed she had "done her best" with. She posted to Uppsala her neatly typed reports of the exact order of events in Zionist services in 1958 and 1959, explaining to Sundkler that she had conscientiously "tried to give a tidious [sic] account of all that happened because I feel that what I may leave out as unimportant may perhaps give you a useful clue."[55] Her careful footnotes cited recent local newspaper reports, added erudite elaborations on fine points of language and local botany, and comprehensively cited the work of other scholars of Swaziland, most of all Hilda Kuper. And due to Regina's high personal standing with the Zionists, she was also able to supply Sundkler with official minutes of executive meetings, a precious resource that I myself have used in my own writings on the topic of Zionism.[56] Sundkler must have been thrilled with this rich catch from this exceptionally accomplished researcher.

Regina's writings on this topic lucidly argued for Swazi Zionism as a form of Christianity wholly in keeping with African values. In late 1959, for example, she attended services run by a Zionist prophet in her own hometown of Kwaluseni. She transcribed and typed one of the Christian songs that was sung at these services, proclaiming it to be "very popular with the Zionists." Highlighting this song was Regina's way to draw Sundkler's attention to the distinctively African elements of Zionists' worship. The musical composition was a polemic against the European Christianity of the missionaries as well as a plea for unity among African churches, based on the unity they observed between the persons of the Trinity: "Jesus, united with Father and Spirit! They are united and love one another; They do not part. Well, whom do we copy?" Regina instructed Sundkler to "take note of the wording [of the song,] which brings out the clearly African concept." And it was not only the words of the song that communicated a proudly African Christianity independent of European influence, but also its specifically musical elements. As Regina told Sundkler, "Zionists say European composed songs are too dull and out of context with the feelings of the people of Africa." Along these lines, Regina added a small note to her research notes (handwritten in the margins, almost as an afterthought) informing Sundkler to "note that in tribal life, the songs are always accompanied by dancing or some other bodily movement or the swaying of the body, the characteristic which the Negroes of America took over with them[;] rhythm is in their veins. Western classics are not appreciated by our people."[57]

Bengt Sundkler's new book on Zionism in Swaziland and South Africa was itself only published more than fifteen years later as *Zulu Zion and Some Swazi Zionists* (1976). His chapter on Zionism was hailed as one of the most innovative and ground-breaking sections of the book.[58] Along with the second edition of *Bantu Prophets* (1958), *Zulu Zion* established Sundkler as one of the leading voices in the new field of World Christianity and a passionate advocate of the notion that true Christianity in Africa should be thoroughly indigenized. Despite the fact that Regina was his primary researcher in Swaziland, her contribution to his book went largely without mention, something that Sundkler had a habit of doing with respect to the work of his research assistants, including in previous books.[59] Yet a careful line-by-line reading of Sundkler's forty-page chapter on Swazi Zionism reveals a shocking and entirely unattributed reliance on Regina's material.

Sundkler's historical narrative of the growth of Zionism in Swaziland is constructed on factual data Regina supplied to him, all without acknowledgment. His presentation of rich primary material—songs, sermons and interviews— implies these were the fruit of his own personal efforts. Regina's rich ethnographic observations are presented from his perspective, drawing on the first person as if he was the one attending services rather than his assistant. Most of all, though, Sundkler repeatedly appropriated Regina's reports nearly word for word, passing her prose off as his own. Compare Regina's research report for Sundkler written in 1958 with the published text of *Zulu Zion*, which appeared in 1976:

> *Regina, sent to Sundkler in 1958*: A bell was rung, and that was a signal for all to find their staves and set out for Lobamba [Sobhuza's palace], then when the women began singing the congregation began marching in circles. The women with flags, emagosa, always led the way. This parade before the Church House is called kuhlehla, same term as used for warriors or age-groups when they dance or give a display before royalty.

> *Sundkler, published in 1976*: A bell was rung, the signal for all to find their "holy sticks" and to set out for Lobamba. The lady wardens (emagosa) bore flags and led the way. The women with sticks, while marching, would walk in circles, kuhlehla. This was the term used for warriors or age-groups when giving a dancing display before royalty.[60]

Regina would die in 1968, nearly ten years before Sundkler published his book and her unacknowledged research contained within it. I have found no correspondence that gives any indication of her feelings on Sundkler's use of her work nor any mention of it elsewhere in any records. Yet it seems painfully ironic that her ethnographic celebration of the Indigenous—Regina's chosen medium for articulating African autonomy—became another venue in which unequal racial power structures continued to silence her. But what we do know is this: Regina also put the research on Swazi Christianity she completed for Sundkler to work in other channels. She kept copies of everything she posted to him in Uppsala. This material she recycled into fodder for her weekly column in the country's national newspaper, the *Times of Swaziland*, a lively forum within which ideas about Swazi identity, race, and religion were read and much debated (she also reworked this material into her own—still sadly unpublished—book manuscript on Swazi religion and society in the 1960s).[61] Although her voice was nearly extinguished through the published work of white anthropologists, throughout the decade of the 1960s and even beyond, Regina Twala found other ways to make herself heard.

NOTES

1. Joel Cabrita and David Maxwell, "Relocating World Christianity," in *Relocating World Christianity*, ed. Joel Cabrita, David Maxwell, and Emma Wild-Wood (Leiden: Brill, 2017), 1–46.

2. Norman Etherington, "Mission Station Melting Pots as a Factor in the Rise of South African Black Nationalism," *International Journal of African Historical Studies* 9, no. 4 (1976): 600–601.

3. Dan Magaziner, *The Art of Life in South Africa* (Athens: Ohio University Press, 2016), 315n1.

4. Norman Etherington, *Peasants, Peasants and Politics in Southeast Africa, 1835–1880: African Christian Communities in Natal, Pondoland and Zululand* (London: Royal Historical Society, 1978), 122.

5. E. M. Preston-Whyte, "Land and Development at Indaleni: A Historical Perspective," *Development Southern Africa* 4, no. 3 (1987): 408.

6. Sol Plaatje, *Native Life in South Africa* (Northlands, South Africa: Picador Africa, 2007), 4.

7. See Richard Elphick, *The Equality of Believers: Protestant Missionaries and the Racial Politics of South Africa* (Charlottesville: University of Virginia Press, 2012).

8. *Natal Mercury*, June 1, 1926.

9. *Bantu World*, September 25, 1937.

10. Tim Couzens Papers, Greenside, Johannesburg (hereafter TCP), Regina to Dan, n.d. [August 1938].

11. TCP, Certificate of Non-Intervention in the Native Divorce Court, Case No. 48/46/1938, June 21, 1939.

12. Joel Cabrita, *Written Out: The Erasure of Regina Gelana Twala* (Athens: Ohio University Press, 2023), n.p.

13. Violaine Junod, "Entokozweni: Managing a Community Service in an Urban African Area," *Human Organization* 23, no. 1 (1964): 32–34.

14. Tom Lodge, *Black Politics in South Africa since 1945* (New York: Longman, 1983), 50.

15. Tim Couzens, interview with Dan Twala, July 26, 1979, Dube, Soweto, South Africa.

16. "The Eastern Province Is a Political Time Bomb," *Drum*, Oct. 1956.

17. Lodge, *Black Politics*, 42.

18. Gary Fred Baines, "New Brighton, Port Elizabeth, c. 1903–1953: A History of an Urban African Community" (PhD diss., University of Cape Town, 1994), 214.

19. Shireen Hassim, *The ANC Women's League: Sex, Gender and Politics* (Auckland Park, South Africa: Jacana, 2014).

20. *Drum*, February 1954, 10.

21. Interview with Dan Twala.

22. Anthony Balcomb, "From Apartheid to the New Dispensation: Evangelicals and the Democratization of South Africa," *Journal of Religion in Africa* 34, no. 1 (2004): 24; "No Room for Half a Million Christians," *Drum*, February 1956.

23. TCP, Dan to Regina, April 17, 1952.

24. Bhengu's *Back to God* magazine, 1958, cited in Balcomb, "From Apartheid to the New Dispensation," 24.

25. Balcomb, "From Apartheid to the New Dispensation," 25.

26. Balcomb, "From Apartheid to the New Dispensation," 23.

27. *Bantu World*, December 13, 1952; Wits Historical Papers, Advance Newspaper, CULL001, December 11, 1952.

28. *Bantu World*, January 31, 1953.

29. TCP, Director of the South African Council for Industrial and Science Research, PO Box 395, Visagie Street, Pretoria, to Mrs R. Twala, Atteridgeville, February 25, 1953.

30. "Duma Nokwe Interrogation," Wits Historical Papers, 1956 Treason Trial Papers, AD 1812, 2821. On South African exiles in Swaziland during this period, see Thula Simpson, "The Bay and the Ocean: A History of the ANC in Swaziland, 1960–1979," *African Historical Review* 41, no. 1 (2009), 90.

31. "Hilda Beemer/Matthews, African Fellows II," Miss H. Beemer to the International Institute of African Languages and Cultures, January 30, 1935, "First Report on Field Work," London School of Economics Archive, Malinowski 7/39.

32. Alan Booth, "Lord Selborne and the British Protectorates, 1908–1910," *Journal of African History* 10, no. 1 (1969): 137.

33. Hilda Kuper, *Sobhuza II, Ngwenyama and King of Swaziland: The Story of an Hereditary Ruler and His Country* (London: Duckworth, 1978), 191.

34. Hugh Macmillan, "Swaziland, Decolonization and the Triumph of Tradition," *Journal of Modern African Studies* 23, no. 4 (1985): 643–666; and Hugh Macmillan, "A Nation Divided: The Swazi in Swaziland and the Transvaal, 1865–1986," in *The Creation of Tribalism in Southern Africa*, ed. L. Vail (Berkeley: University of California Press, 1989), 289–323.

35. TCP, Nicholas Bhengu to Regina, April 28, 1960, interview with Mrs. Ndwandwe, Kwaluseni, Eswatini, July 10, 2018.

36. Joel Cabrita, *The People's Zion: Southern Africa, the USA and a Transatlantic Faith-Healing Movement* (Cambridge, MA: Harvard University Press, 2018).

37. Hilda Kuper, *The Uniform of Color: A Study of White-Black Relationships in Swaziland* (Johannesburg: University of Witwatersrand Press, 1947), 122.

38. *Izwi lama Swazi*, December 8, 1956, cited in Bengt Sundkler, *Zulu Zion and Some Swazi Zionists* (Oxford: Oxford University Press, 1976), 233.

39. Sundkler, *Zulu Zion*, 210.

40. Interview with Simon/Dabete Mavimbela, Mbabane, Eswatini, July 11, 2016.

41. "The Swazi National Council Challenges Statutory Marriage," June 18, 1959, Bengt Sundkler Papers, University of Uppsala (hereafter BSP), Box 92.

42. Interview with Dan Twala.

43. This was the Ekuphileni Church in Zion, founded by Stephen Mavimbela. Interview with Herbert Mavimbela, Ludzeludze, Eswatini, June 23, 2016.

44. Typewritten report, R. D. Twala, n.d. [approx. 1959], BSP, Box 110.

45. Typewritten report, R. D. Twala, n.d. [approx. 1959], BSP, Box 110.

46. Fiona Armitage, "The Zionist Movement in Swaziland: Origins and Bid for League Recognition, 1936–1958," Botswana History Workshop, August 1973, unpublished paper.

47. "Brief History of the Institute for Social Research, 1956–1965," University of KwaZulu-Natal Archives, Records of the Institute for Social Research (Durban, 1965), n.p.

48. Bengt Sundkler, *Bantu Prophets in South Africa* (London: Lutterworth Press, 1948).

49. Sundkler, *Bantu Prophets,* 237–240.

50. Sundkler, *Bantu Prophets,* 297.

51. Joel Cabrita, "Writing Apartheid: Ethnographic Collaborators and the Politics of Knowledge Production in Twentieth-Century South Africa," *American Historical Review* 125, no. 5 (2020): 1686.

52. Cabrita, "Writing Apartheid," 1678.

53. "Statement of Expenditure from 1st January 1958 to 30th June 1958: Nuffield Grant—Mrs Twala," KZN, Records of the Institute for Social Research.

54. Regina to Sundkler, no date (July or August 1958), BSP, Box 110.

55. R. D. Twala, "Saturday 26 July 1958, Lobamba Royal Kraal, Ibandla le League of African Churches," 6, BSP, Box 110.

56. R. D. Twala, "The New Baprofitha at Kwaluseni, Bremersdorp, Swaziland, October 1959," 6, BSP, Box 110.

57. R. D. Twala, "The New Baprofitha at Kwaluseni, Bremersdorp, Swaziland, October 1959," 9–10, BSP, Box 110.

58. See, for example, David Rycroft, "*Zulu Zion and Some Swazi Zionists* by Bengt Sundkler," *Bulletin of the School of Oriental and African Studies* 41, no. 1 (1978): 205–206; George Shepperson, "Review: Ethiopianism and Zionism in Southern Africa," *Journal of African History* 20, no. 1 (1979): 142–145.

59. Cabrita, "Writing Apartheid," 1681–1682.

60. R. D. Twala, "Saturday 26 July 1958, Lobamba Royal Kraal, Ibandla le League of African Churches," 1, BSP, Box 110. Sundkler, *Zulu Zion*, 230.

61. UCLA Archives, Hilda Kuper Papers, Box 19, Folder 2, untitled, undated manuscript by Regina Twala.

5

Danger, Distress, Disease, and Death

Santa Muerte and Her Female Followers

KATE KINGSBURY

Maria was twenty-one years old when she was kidnapped by the cartel five years ago. Her captors kept her locked up in a dark room and spent four days beating and raping her. Prior to her abduction, she had heard of Santa Muerte but was not a devotee. Maria's parents raised her as a Catholic, and she venerated La Virgen de Guadalupe. During those four days in captivity she turned to Santa Muerte, imploring her to let her live and promising the saint of death that she would get a tattoo of her should she help her escape. Shortly thereafter, while her captors were distracted, she freed herself and fled into the night. Her daughter was born nine months later.

"When I first saw [my daughter], I was afraid, I did not even want to see her. But something gripped me and I said, let me see her. All my fear melted away; she had my face and I knew that for some reason Santa Muerte had sent her to me." After giving birth, Maria purchased a black statue of the folk saint and embraced it as she prayed, "Please protect me; you freed me and now I will tattoo myself for you." She fulfilled her promise to Santa Muerte by tattooing the saint's image over the scars left from the beatings, in an act which she told me healed her and ensures that the saint continues to protect her. She became a fervent devotee, mounting an altar in her home. I asked Maria if women had a special relationship with the saint, given I had met twice as many women than men at the shrine where I was doing fieldwork. "She attracts women most of all because she is inside of us," she explained.

An analysis of the folk saint's female following is imperative for understanding changing patterns of religious belief and praxis—namely, how a shift from Marian veneration to Santa Muerte for some Mexican women correlates with increasing precarity for them in the postcolony. Moreover, we must recognize women's capacity for creating novel spiritual spaces of healing and empowerment to counter the dangers they face daily. Numerous Mexican women have found that the Virgin of Guadalupe can no longer offer them solace or protection and only death herself has the power to grant life. Nevertheless, women have not abandoned the Catholic contours of their faith. Instead of turning to the Virgin or St. Jude, the two most popular figures on the Mexican religious landscape, they have fashioned a new saint: the saint of death, Santa Muerte. If, as Maria explained, Santa Muerte is inside women, then she must be understood as a manifestation of their fears, desires, and responses to the world they inhabit.

In this chapter, I argue that an analysis of Santa Muerte devotion shows how Catholicism is morphing in new and unpredictable ways to contend with the dangers that many contemporary Mexicans—and especially Mexican women—face in the postcolony. I use this analysis to make three contributions to scholarly literatures on gender, violence, and Christianity. First, this work is in relation to existing scholarship in the subfields of World Christianity and the anthropology of Christianity that has frequently highlighted the essential role women have played in developing vernacular expressions of Christian faith in Latin America, sub-Saharan Africa, and Asia.[1] Much of this work, however, has focused on women's roles as missionary wives, missionaries, or Bible women, whereas my analysis of women and Santa Muerte highlights women's agency in innovating new forms of devotion and piety. Second, by centering my analysis on women who would largely also identify as Catholic, this chapter speaks to an overall bias toward Protestant forms of Christianity that predominate in the subfield of World Christianity.[2] Third, this chapter unquestionably demonstrates the essential contextual role of violence, including physical as well as unjust economic and social systems, when thinking about gender and agency with respect to new forms of religious life, spirituality, and faith. The chapter explores Santa Muerte worship by Mexican women in a space of death, danger, distress, and disease. I suggest that Santa Muerte has emerged as a unique form of World Christianity that women have choreographed to cope with the threat both of physical and of structural violence, which accounts for the saint's immense popularity among women.

Santa Muerte as a Religious Movement

Santa Muerte is the fastest growing new religious movement in the Americas, boasting 10 to 12 million followers, most of whom reside in Mexico, Central America, and the United States.[3] Santa Muerte is a Mexican female folk saint who personifies death and is at the fulcrum of a new popular form of folk Catholicism that is expanding rapidly across the Americas. In contrast to Catholic saints, who have been canonized by the church, folk saints are spirits of the deceased who have not obtained official recognition but are deemed holy by the local populace for their miracle-working powers.[4] Santa Muerte differs from other folk saints in that rather than being the spirit of a deceased Mexican woman, followers assert that she is the personification of death herself.[5]

The attributes of the folk saint and much of the religious praxis involved in her worship derive from Roman Catholicism. The saint, as Andrew Chesnut describes her, is connected to "the Christian concept of having a Holy Death, which involves dying amid one's loved ones with the proper prayers and ritual."[6] Devotees often plead with the saint to let them and their loved ones die of natural causes rather than violent ones, as a good death is seen as essential for crossing through purgatory and accessing heaven without impediments.[7] Akin to traditional saints and the Virginal advocations, the folk saint can be interpellated through prayer for protection, healing, and help. Santa Muerte also resembles the Virgin of Guadalupe in her iconography. She wears a long flowing mantle and dons a dress with a sash tied around her waist, but she also wields a scythe in her right hand. Like Marian advocations, she is said to be maternal, taking care of her devotees by rewarding them with generous miracles. But this is where the similarities end. Devotees imagine her as even more powerful than God himself, as only death is believed to be puissant enough to grant life. As such, a surplus of violence and death is causing what some would consider as conventional forms of Christianity to be relinquished.

Santa Muerte derives from a set of syncretic beliefs and practices that originate from Catholicism but also interweave influences from Indigenous religion, New Age faith, and Santeria.[8] There is no single Santa Muerte Church that could be an equivalent to the Catholic Church as the faith is loosely organized and "constructed in noncentralized ways from below."[9] Neither is there an official Santa Muerte clergy. Leaders of different groupings are not part of an overarching structure. They are mostly female and act in a laissez-faire manner. This absence of male intermediaries contrasts strongly with the patriarchal hierarchy of Roman Catholicism. There is no specific scriptural doctrine that devotees adhere to or behavioral rules and regulations that are enforced among practitioners.[10] Santa Muerte does not diminish the female gender as it is centered around a powerful female figure, which makes it appealing to women. Furthermore, it allows them to take their spiritual practices into their own hands from altars and chapels where they may autonomously perform and choreograph rites.

Despite diverging practices, there are certain ritualistic and liturgical commonalities shared by devotees.[11] Santa Muerte statues, votives, shrines, and altars are used in worship. Most devotees have a home altar, which may be ornate or consist of just a small statue or votive. Offerings on altars are often comprised of some of the following: flowers, alcohol, victuals, cigarettes, and glasses or bottles of water. Public shrines, which can accommodate many women, seem to have evolved from ever-expanding altars that originated in homes. This was the case for both Doña Queta and Doña Elena, who are discussed later in this chapter.

Just as death is said to judge no one, Santa Muerte is open to all petitions and can, therefore, be thought of as amoral—a stark contrast with the Virgin

Mary or canonized saints. She has a fierce, distinctive persona. The folk saint may be wrathful and vindictive, meting out punishment to the enemies of her devotees at their bequest. Devotees have described her as *una cabrona*, a battle-axe.[12] A female devotee in Oaxaca told me that she is *una chingona*, a term that may have vulgar connotations and means "bad-ass woman." Such terminology would never be used to describe the Virgin of Guadalupe, whose chasteness and "humble attitude" make her pure, according to devotees.[13] I suggest that her mul-tifaceted persona, which is doting yet dastardly, reflects the many sides of the Mexican women who are devoted to her, who, with maternal tenderness and fierceness, care for their families in a space of death and violence. The saint's ferocity speaks to the brutality and precarity of life in the postcolony, but also to the ways Mexican women have responded to it.

For many women, the Virgin of Guadalupe is no longer deemed powerful enough to aid them to overcome the many dangers they I encounter. Santa Muerte has emerged as a response to their need for spiritual succor given the context of violence. I heard countless stories such as the one Araceli narrated to me. She recalled that her sister had disappeared one night in July 2018. Though she feared for her sister's life, she did not pray to the Virgin of Guadalupe. Araceli did not believe the mild Marian advocation would be powerful enough to inter-cede for her sibling. Instead, she lit a votive and said a prayer to the saint of death. In venerating Santa Muerte, women create spiritual spaces to cope with the many daily difficulties they encounter, especially those related to violence and death. Their fears include the demise of loved ones and worries about their own security in a country where gendered violence is treated with impunity and narcoviolence abounds. But they also seek help in enduring the ramifications of structural violence, which include poverty, lack of sustenance, and minimal medical care, leading to frequent sickness and suffering. Nevertheless, to date no academic exploration of the importance of women in these developments has been undertaken.

Masculine Misconceptions of La Muerte

The Catholic Church has demonized devotion to death, decrying it as heretical and blasphemous.[14] They argue that worshiping a "fake" saint who represents death is a satanic perversion of Christian faith in Jesus, who gifted believers with eternal life. Mexican bishops, including the Archbishop of Oaxaca in Octo-ber 2013, threatened Catholics who worshipped Holy Death with excommunica-tion. Furthermore, in February 2016, on his first full day in Mexico as pontiff, the Argentine Pope Francis lambasted the folk saint of death as a macabre and dangerous symbol of narcoculture.[15]

The Mexican State has also deprecated Santa Muerte, associating venera-tion with drug cartels. The Mexican army, under the administration of Felipe

Calderon, destroyed scores of shrines dedicated to Santa Muerte in a futile act that failed to expunge drug-related crimes. In the media, devotees of death are depicted as dangerous Mexican men: drug dealers and murderers. The press refers to Santa Muerte as a "narcosaint" and the faith is often termed a "narco-cult." The cover of journalist Michael Deibert's book, *In the Shadow of Saint Death: The Gulf Cartel and the Price of America's Drug War in Mexico*, depicts an image of Santa Muerte praying over a handgun.[16]

Although some narcos venerate the saint, the majority of devotees are people who suffer from the violence that the narcos perpetrate and not perpetrators themselves. Many are also women. Santa Muerte's multifaceted persona reflects the many sides, needs, and experiences of Mexican women. An examination of how and why women venerate death reveals the precarious conditions they experience in the Mexican postcolony and how, in response, they reconstruct feminine spirituality, creating a new form of World Christianity.

Although the movement is perceived as violent, most followers turn to the folk saint to ward off violence and death. This shows that a normative definition of Christianity, as supposedly nonviolent, is operative in the perception of those outside the movement. My analysis, which demonstrates that Santa Muerte is not the narcocult it is frequently portrayed to be, speaks to the deeper-seated uses of violence in attempting to construct a normative definition of Christianity as something clearly distinct from Santa Muerte.

During ethnographic research, most devotees told me they considered themselves and the saint Catholic, making none of the distinctions that theologians and Catholic clergy might make between the Santa Muerte faith and Roman Catholicism. Many aspects of the Santa Muerte faith borrow from Catholic liturgy and praxis. On the first of the month most Santa Muerte chapels hold a rosary dedicated to the folk saint that mimics the Catholic ritual. Ceremonies I attended at several Santa Muerte shrines commenced with the Lord's Prayer. Votive candles to Santa Muerte that are sold in the many esoteric stores across the United States and Mexico frequently feature prayers on them with opening lines invoking Jesus Christ. When devotees pray they commonly commence by petitioning God and then supplicate the saint of death. Devotion transgresses, but also overlaps with, established doctrines and practices.

Santa Muerte devotion, therefore, can be understood to be one of the many variants of World Christianity. It is a response to the violence and death of the Mexican postcolony. Christianity, as it spread across the ecumene, has taken on myriad meanings and modes for those who practice it; much like Islam, it has "developed in manifold and sometimes incongruous ways."[17] Although theologians and clergy may believe that they are legitimized in labeling certain beliefs and practices as pure Catholicism versus impure or false forms, scholars of religion must recognize that there are many modes of Christianity and must not value any specific discourses or understandings of Christianity over others.

Perhaps ironically, many Christian scholars believe La Virgen de Guadalupe also arose from so-called impure forms of Indigenous religions. Many argue that the Aztec mother goddess Tontantzin-Cihuacóatel was worshipped at Tepeyac, where La Virgen appeared to Juan Diego. When seen in this light, Santa Muerte continues a longer story of Catholic hybridity.

Violence, Mortality, and Death Herself

Wide-scale violence has become a tragic quotidian reality for many Mexicans. In 2019, the Mexican murder rate reached an all-time high, with 35,000 confirmed murders. The 65,000 people who have vanished in the drug war since 2006 confirm the ineffectualness of President Andres Manuel Lopez Obrador's *abrazos no balazos* (hugs not bullets) policy toward narcos. Gendered violence in Mexico is distressingly ubiquitous, leading the country to be named one of the most dangerous for women. According to a Mexican nongovernmental organization (NGO), a woman is raped in Mexico every 18 seconds.[18] Government figures record that an average of ten women are murdered daily.[19] Mexican authorities have hazy definitions of femicide and allow it to be treated with leniency, which implies that the figures are no doubt much higher.[20] The number of femicides has grown 137 percent over the past five years. Yet perpetrators are frequently treated with impunity. The Femicide Observatory, a coalition of forty-three groups that document crimes affecting women, found that a mere 16 percent of female homicides in 2012 and 2013 were classified as femicides and only 1.6 percent resulted in convictions.[21]

Enraged by this pandemic of violence, women assembled across Mexico in March 2020 to protest femicide. Their actions were met with apathy from many government officials, including the president, Andres Manuel Lopez Obrador. Faced with such a surplus of death and violence, with little hope of support from state agencies and offices, women have taken to appealing to death itself for life. Gabriela told me that Santa Muerte "looks out for me like a mother." Gabriela began visiting the chapel because she feared for her life and believed the Virgin of Guadalupe would not be strong enough to defend her. Gabriela was afraid. She worked until late at night as a waitress in a neighborhood well known for its dangers. Through her friends she had heard of numerous recent femicides and rapes, and she knew that narcos were active in the area. Her fears became overwhelming after a close friend was killed, but she could not leave the area and her minimum-wage job because she had mouths to feed so she began lighting white candles, praying, and gifting fresh white flowers to her saint every first day of the month at the chapel. "The only thing I have ever asked for," she told me, "is protection."

Residing as a female scholar within the rural Oaxacan community where I studied Santa Muerte as a lived religion through participant observation, I was able to comprehend the cultural context from which she has emerged and what she represents to women. Unlike the women I came to know, I always had the luxury to take a plane and flee to a safer place. Yet there were moments during my fieldwork when I, too, feared for my own safety and even my life. One night I crashed my car on a pitch-black jungle road, close to the place where a woman had been murdered. I hid in the darkness and watched as SUVs drove by, as I had been warned that such vehicles are often driven by potentially dangerous men. I realized that if I were to pick one spiritual figure to protect me, to implore, it would not be the demure Virgin of Guadalupe—who, in her icons, always averts her eyes—but fierce Santa Muerte, whose defiant gaze, in all her imagery, meets me head-on. She always looks ready to fight to the death, if need be.

Women not only turn to Santa Muerte for protection against brutality but also for the injustices they encounter in everyday life, which result from unequal power relations. This often leads to structural violence. As defined by Johan Galtung, structural violence refers to the violence of injustice and inequity which is "embedded in ubiquitous social structures [and] normalized by stable institutions and regular experience."[22] It refers to an avoidable impairment of fundamental human needs, and situations wherein individuals are denied access to basic resources and services, such as access to proper health care. This results from what "political, economic, and institutional power does to people, and reciprocally, from how these forms of power themselves influence responses to social problems."[23] This indirect form of violence that takes the form of distress and injustice is known as "social suffering" and causes avoidable poverty, illness, injury, and even death.[24]

Many rural Oaxacans suffer from structural violence. One devotee of Santa Muerte told me that following a family tragedy she had only avoided a life on the streets with her children by the thinnest of margins. She attributed her prayers to Santa Muerte as helping her overcome the situation. One of Santa Muerte's important roles is in faith healing.[25] Given the lack of local medical care, which results in easily treatable health conditions failing to be resolved, this is not surprising. Many devotees turn to Santa Muerte for health issues, such as Carlita, who told me she had consulted a female *curandera* (healer) who worked with the saint of death to resolve recurrent headaches.

Such stories are by no means unique. In the town where the shrine at which my research was based, a government census recorded that 87.3 percent of the population live in poverty, with 56.6 percent of these people living in extreme poverty. Only 24.6 percent of people have access to running water, and 25 percent have no sewage drainage. Health care is available to a mere 40 percent of the population.[26] Even electricity is sparse. Doña Elena only had one weak light bulb and no running water in her windowless home, which was made of slats of wood and covered with a tin roof.

In February 2020, a hospital in the region made a public appeal for funds because it had not received medication for three months from the federal government for the children's cancer and leukemia ward. Over 350 sick children were at risk of relapse, and some of them died. With few options available to them, some mothers of these ailing children turned to Santa Muerte for support.

I frequently asked why so many women came to the shrine. Doña Elena told me, "She listens to us women more, because she is female and she has suffered the same difficulties." The saint is imagined as a like them woman, who takes on the roles they do and understands the injustices and difficulties they face. When faced with social suffering in the form of sickness in their families and inadequate nourishment, women, as heads of households, most often bear the brunt of danger, disease, and distress.

In Mexico, women have long been associated with death due to its linkages with childbirth, sexuality, passion, and liminality. Deceased female figures like la Llorona and Santa Muerte symbolically emphasize these cultural connections. Women are thus drawn to the female figure of deified death. Around her they have forged a spirituality that provides an arena to express their experiences of violence and construct responses to them. Santa Muerte not only reflects the realities women face but also provides a religious template for imagining an alternate reality devoid of danger—protected and safe under the saint's maternal watch.

On a practical level, death is women's work.[27] It is women who assemble and lead search parties for those who have disappeared.[28] It is also women who arrange funeral rites, by organizing *novenario* prayers for the deceased and purchasing and preparing food.[29] As Kirstin Norget has argued, the realm of popular religiosity provides cultural resources to "women and others who tend to be marginalised in the public sphere."[30] Funerals create opportunities for "female leadership . . . women create new social centers and shoulder new responsibilities for the guidance . . . of community social relations."[31] During funeral rites that take place in the domestic space, "men arrive at a house in time for a prayer session but never step foot inside the house, nor do they recite a single word of prayer. Instead they tend to stand in clusters outside the house, often drinking alcohol"[32]

Santa Muerte veneration has also become a realm of female leadership as most shrines have been established by women.[33] In Mexico, women have few spaces to speak out about their fears of violence and few means to cope with it. Pentecostalism, which offers some female uplift, remains a tiny religious minority community in contrast to its popularity in other neighboring countries. Through the establishment of shrines, however, female owners have accrued financial, spiritual, and social capital, which is often reinvested in the expansion of the shrines. These spaces can serve as community centers for women from across the region; their frequent visits to "speak"' to death herself are a means to deal with violence, bereavement, impoverishment, and sickness. Female followers of the female folk saint externalize their precarity to a saint they forge in their own image and whom they imagine as protecting them in a state where violence and death are commonplace and nobody else cares about their fate.

Judge, Jury, and Executioner

When faced with disasters, such as the murder or unexpected death of a family member, the formidable folk saint of death is perceived as a powerful resource. Santa Muerte is often depicted with the scales of justice in her hands, denoting her role in delivering justice to those who have suffered grievances. Devotees believe that the saint acts as judge, jury and executioner—vital roles given the state impunity toward murder and violence.

Zaniyah, a mother of three, related to me that she feared her husband's demise every day and prayed to the folk saint to keep him safe. With several children to take care of and no income of her own, his death would spell disaster. Her husband worked as a traveling salesman. She related how cartels frequently raid salesmen's vans, take the merchandise, and kill everyone in the vehicle. I asked why she turned to Santa Muerte. She replied: *"porque lo unico seguro que hay es la muerte"* (because the only thing that is certain is death). In the postcolony, women are constantly faced with the threat of death and violence, whether to themselves or to their loved ones, and they are well aware of the impunity.

The children are not exempt from violence, either. A conversation with Señora Xiadani, a devotee of death and grandmother to several children, was cut short when she told me she must hurry to pick up her granddaughter on time from school. If she did not, she explained, someone else might get there first. They might kidnap the girl and sell her into prostitution. Someone might rape and murder her. Or they might remove her liver, kidneys, eyes, and heart and sell them to rich white people for their child. The girl might disappear with no sign and no explanation why. Or her body might turn up a few weeks later and the police would turn a blind eye. Female life, in particular, she explained, "is not worth anything, except to those who make money from it."

Xiadani was a former Roman Catholic who had grown up venerating Guadalupe but no longer attended church and instead went to the Santa Muerte shrine to pray for the safety of her family. In her eyes, the saint is the most powerful of all and forcefully yet lovingly defends her devotees from evil and evildoers. In her description of the fiery but caring saint, she inadvertently manifested her own maternal ferocity, her determination, and her desire to protect her family from harm, confirming to me that women make the goddess of death in their own image.

Female Founders

Through the narratives of female shrine founders and devotees, I demonstrate how a surplus of death and violence is impelling religious innovation, and metamorphosing Christianity in new directions. Women have been founding figures in establishing important chapels open to the public that have been the impetus for the expansion of Santa Muerte devotion. The most famous person to make Santa Muerte devotion go public is Doña Queta, who is also known as Enriqueta Romero.[34]

Doña Queta set up a simple altar in the corner of her home kitchen where she sold quesadillas to locals. Her patrons could see the altar covered with Santa Muerte objects of worship and often asked permission to leave offerings. Doña Queta was most concerned about her son's incarceration because Mexican jails are perilous places where the threat of a violent death is ever present.[35] There was no one better to appeal to than death herself to free her son and lessen the risk of his demise than death herself, she thought. Queta believes her prayers were heard, as her son was released. To thank the saint, Doña Queta moved her altar onto the street. It burgeoned into a large shrine and became a renowned pilgrimage site, making it the first public shrine to Santa Muerte. Doña Queta must be credited with the devotion to death going public. Prior to this, Santa Muerte had been confined to homes.

National Geographic described Doña Queta as "an alternately fierce and motherly woman."[36] What the profile failed to note is that a woman can be simultaneously fierce and a mother and that this description summarizes Santa Muerte and reflects the many women who worship her. Santa Muerte mirrors their qualities. If, as Ludwig Feuerbach claimed, "Man . . . made God in his own image," then women also make Goddess in theirs.[37] Doña Queta, a loving mother, was determined to see her son freed. In placing her shrine out on the street and later fighting the authorities to prevent it from being closed down, she has ferociously defended her beliefs as well as her son's life by proving her faith to Santa Muerte with a grand gesture that up until then no one had dared to do.[38]

Doña Queta has acquired significant spiritual prestige. Regulars to the shrine ask her for advice not only on devotional matters but also on life. Her communal prominence, due to her foundational role in Santa Muerte devotion, has also protected her from the violence that characterizes her neighborhood, Tepito, which is one of the most violent in Mexico City. She recalled an incident when she and a group of friends were on their way to visit her critically injured son in the hospital. On the way, they crossed paths with a group of muggers but Santa Muerte "covered them with her holy shroud" and they went unnoticed.[39] In her eyes, the death saint has protected her. Nevertheless, her husband, Raymundo, was murdered in 2016. Her brother, Rafael, was also injured in the shooting but survived. Her husband's death took a toll emotionally on Doña Queta, though she says devotion to death has helped her to cope with it. Speaking to death daily and imagining her as a motherly figure taking care of loved ones beyond the grave has brought her reassurance.

Doña Queta no longer sells quesadillas. Instead, she runs a shop abutting the shrine, which supplies visitors with all the Santa Muerte accoutrements imaginable. Between this income as well as the constant *limosnas*, donations from devotees, she has gained financial independence. She has been attacked by both the church and the state, with authorities threatening to raze her shrine, but thus far she has resisted. Doña Queta can be seen day in and day out diligently dusting, and clearing away old candles in the chapel; she is fiercely faithful to her saint, who, in her feisty but caring nature, embodies the traits of the shrine's owner, whose strength of character allows her to survive in this hostile environment.

Enriqueta Vargas was a fierce mother, much like Doña Queta. She was heartbroken and furious when her only son, Jonathan, was shot and killed close to the shrine to Santa Muerte that he had built. Although Enriqueta venerated the Virgin of Guadalupe, at the time of her son's death, she made a pact with Santa Muerte.[40] She pledged she would devote herself to extending Santa Muerte's reputation if the saint brought justice to the murderers that took her son's life. In the months that followed, Vargas believed the saint of death answered her prayers.

Vargas went on to establish her own ministry, Santa Muerte Internacional. The first of its kind, it consisted of a transnational network of shrines spanning the Americas. Working around the clock, she rapidly became a public spokesperson who accrued such status and spiritual prestige that she was even asked to conduct weddings and baptisms. Vargas died of natural causes in 2018, and her daughter has taken up her mantle.

Doña Elena, an Indigenous Zapotec woman in her seventies, initially set up a small fane in 2003 in rural Oaxaca. Health-care services in rural Oaxaca are "very basic, lacking adequately equipped health clinics" and properly trained doctors.[41] Doña Elena credited Santa Muerte with the healing of an ailment that had consumed her for twelve years and for which she had received no proper medical care. She told me, "One night as I lay in my bed, death came," but not as she expected. Death flew in from the darkness in a long gown as black as midnight. Santa Muerte whispered to Doña Elena that she would be cured, and Doña Elena woke up to a miraculous recovery.

To thank the saint, Doña Elena, with her son's help, established a small public shrine in 2003. That shrine, along with the road it was on, was destroyed by the authorities in order to construct a major highway. Doña Elena saw the destruction as an opportunity to replace the shrine with a more impressive chapel, which caught the attention of the local populace. Many people who were not familiar with la Santa or reticent to worship death began to show interest and pray to the saint.

Numerous devotees who suffered from lack of access to adequate medical care told me that Santa Muerte allowed them to cope with the ramifications of the structural violence they encountered. The death of Josefina's father was not only devastating, it left her entire family further impoverished. She and her sisters were unable to feed their children or pay the bills. "We risked losing the small home we grew up in and finding ourselves on the street," Josefina related. She described how the children began wasting away from hunger. Josefina's meager pay only covered the costs incurred by the death of her father, with nothing left to spare. She began visiting Doña Elena's chapel on her way to work, leaving candles and whispering prayers, which were answered when the family had an unexpected windfall of cash that resolved everything. But she also found Santa Muerte's protection extending to other areas of her family's life. "My son later got very ill," she said. "And despite many visits to the doctor, they did nothing for him, could find nothing wrong and I thought he might die. I began to pray to la Santa." Josefina told me that Santa Muerte healed her son: "La Santa has never let me down, she takes care of us."

Spiritual Spaces

Doña Elena has become a central figure to local devotees of death, who revere her as spiritually powerful. As the owner of a known shrine, they turn to her for advice and consolation in the face of family tragedies, and she makes a modest living from the *limosnas* (alms) they give her. The domain of popular religiosity provides opportunities for women who are generally marginalized in the public sphere to emerge as leaders, allowing them to forge spiritual spaces within which they and others may find means to cope with danger, disease, distress, and death. Inadvertent leaders such as Elena, Enriqueta Romero and Enriqueta Vargas have established new social centers central to community relations and impelled the creation of a new folk form of World Christianity, which may even challenge the boundaries of Christianity itself.

Like Doña Queta, Doña Elena struggles to maintain her shrine. A local Catholic priest has threatened her many times and attempted to have the shrine razed. One night, the state police (*Estatales*) raided the shrine and her house. In her account, they menaced her, locked her granddaughter in a room, and mercilessly beat her son and grandsons. They also stole the *limosnas*, took machinery and tools, and desecrated the shrine, even lighting the hands of Doña Elena's favorite and oldest Santa Muerte statue on fire.

Despite such attacks, which once again speak to the violence of life in the Mexican postcolony, Doña Elena's faith has only grown. She tells me that Santa Muerte exacted her revenge on the police. Her son heard on the radio that the same state police force had raided a ranch that happened to have closed-circuit television. The owner of the ranch reported it and they were punished. Like Doña

Queta, Enriqueta Vargas, and many of the female devotees I have met, Doña Elena is caring yet ferociously devoted to looking after her shrine and her family. Santa Muerte's persona, as a saint who is both caring but also feisty, is the spiritual expression and personification of the women who are devoted to death. They have forged an icon in their own image that represents the many difficulties women have and the force and determination yet nurturing nature they must have to survive and attempt to keep their families safe in a state where violence and death are ever present.

Conclusion: Devotion to Death as Distaff

Santa Muerte has emerged as a unique form of World Christianity that women have forged as a means to cope with death, danger, distress, and disease. Within the Mexican state, levels of death and violence have been spiraling out of control and have been met with impunity. Femicide figures have also boomed. Women are also faced with the dangers caused by unjust economic and social systems. Santa Muerte has emerged as a spiritual response to this environment. Female leaders of death have impelled the faith to flourish by providing safe public spiritual spaces, thereby acquiring prestige. They are not strict spiritual clerics but rather laissez-faire leaders who focus on helping devotees overcome threats of death, danger, and disease rather than seeking capital or prestige. Santa Muerte highlights women's agency in innovating new forms of devotion and piety.

Devotees supplicate the fierce, maternal folk saint for protection from death and violence, both for themselves and for their loved ones. They turn to Santa Muerte to deal with structural violence and its consequences: sickness, poverty, and precarity. She is sought out for her spiritual aegis and she allows women to voice their fears and find healing when violence has been committed against them, as in the case of Maria.

In the face of state impunity, Santa Muerte is imagined as enacting revenge for devotees, such as in the case of Enriqueta Vargas, avenging those who killed her son, and in the case of Doña Elena, punishing the policemen who pillaged her chapel. The folk saint's character traits are the personification of female devotees who, in petitioning her for favors both vengeful and benevolent, fashion her in their own image, as mothers but also as women who long for justice and who do not turn the other cheek, unlike the pious Virgin.

Ironically, rather than being malevolent, as the Catholic Church and the press portray her, Santa Muerte arms the many women who worship her with spiritual weapons to face evils that lurk in the patriarchal postcolony of Mexico—whether death, disease, or untold danger. If some women are turning away from Guadalupe and other, more conventional forms of Christianity, it is because, as Zaniyah stated, "*lo unico seguro que hay es la muerte*" (the only thing that is certain is death).

NOTES

1. Elizabeth Ellen Brusco, *The Reformation of Machismo: Evangelical Conversion and Gender in Colombia* (Austin: University of Texas Press, 1995); Dana L. Robert, *American Women in Mission: A Social History of Their Thought and Practice* (Macon, GA: Mercer University Press, 1996); Cynthia Hoehler-Fatton, *Women of Fire and Spirit: History, Faith, and Gender in Roho Religion in Western Kenya* (Oxford: Oxford University Press, 1996).

2. Joel Cabrita and David Maxwell, "Introduction: Relocating World Christianity," in *Relocating World Christianity: Interdisciplinary Studies in Universal and Local Expressions of the Faith*, ed. Joel Cabrita, David Maxwell, and Emma Wild-Wood (Leiden: Brill, 2017), 14.

3. Cabrita and Maxwell, "Introduction," 6.

4. Frank Graziano, *Cultures of Devotion: Folk Saints of Spanish America* (New York: Oxford University Press, 2006), 6.

5. R. Andrew Chesnut, *Devoted to Death: Santa Muerte, the Skeleton Saint* (New York: Oxford University Press, 2011), 3.

6. Chesnut, *Devoted to Death*, 4.

7. Kristin Norget, *Days of Death, Days of Life: Ritual in the Popular Culture of Oaxaca* (New York: Columbia University Press, 2006), 163.

8. J. A. F. Martos, "Iconografías Emergentes y Muertes Patrimonializadas en América Latina: Santa Muerte, Muertos Milagrosos y Muertos Adoptados," *Revista de Antropología Iberoamericana* 9, no. 2 (2014): 115–140; Kate Kingsbury and R. Andrew Chesnut, "Syncretic Santa Muerte: Holy Death and Religious Bricolage," *Religions* 12, no. 3 (2021): 220.

9. Wil G. Pansters, ed., *La Santa Muerte in Mexico: History, Devotion, and Society* (Albuquerque: University of New Mexico Press, 2019), 26.

10. Although several churches have been opened by people such as David Romo and Enriqueta Vargas who have attempted to create national and even transnational networks of believers, these are exceptions to the rule.

11. Pansters, *La Santa Muerte in Mexico*, 27.

12. Chesnut, *Devoted to Death*, 3.

13. Jeanette Favrot Peterson, "The Virgin of Guadalupe: Symbol of Conquest or Liberation?," *Art Journal* 51, no. 4 (1992): 40.

14. Laura Roush, "Santa Muerte, Protection, and 'Desamparo': A View from a Mexico City Altar," in "Lived Religion and Lived Citizenship in Latin America's Zones of Crisis," special issue, *Latin American Research Review* 49 (2014): 129–148.

15. Chesnut, *Devoted to Death*, 54.

16. Michael Deibert, *In the Shadow of Saint Death: The Gulf Cartel and the Price of America's Drug War in Mexico* (Guilford: Rowman & Littlefield, 2014).

17. D. F. Eickelman, "The Study of Islam in Local Contexts," *Contributions to Asian Studies* 17 (1982): 1–2.

18. See the information center at https://www.gesmujer.org/, accessed August 5, 2020.

19. See INEGI, "Estadísticas a propósito del día internacional de la eliminación de la violencia contra la mujer (25 de noviembre)," datos nacionales, 2019, https://www.inegi.org.mx/contenidos/saladeprensa/aproposito/2020/Violencia2020_Nal.pdf.

20. Executive Secretariat of the National Public Security System, "Informacion sobre Violence contra las Mujeres," Report, April 30, 2019.

21. See their website and reports at Observatorio Ciudadano Nacional del Feminicidio, accessed June 5, 2022, http://observatoriofeminicidio.blogspot.com/p/publicaciones .html.

22. Cited in Deborah Du Nann Winter and Dana C. Leighton, "Structural Violence: Introduction," in *Peace, Conflict, and Violence: Peace Psychology for the 21st Century*, ed. Daniel J. Christie, Richard V. Wagner, and Deborah Du Nann Winter (Upper Saddle River, NJ: Prentice Hall, 2001), 99.

23. Arthur Kleinman, Veena Das, and Margaret Lock, eds., *Social Suffering* (Berkeley: University of California Press, 1997).

24. Kleinman, Das, and Lock, *Social Suffering*.

25. Kate Kingsbury, "Doctor Death and Coronavirus: Supplicating Santa Muerte for Holy Healing," *Anthropologica* 63, no. 1 (2021): 1–23.

26. See *Panorama sociodemográfico de Oaxaca 2020*, INEGI, https://www.inegi.org.mx /contenidos/productos/prod_serv/contenidos/espanol/bvinegi/productos/nueva _estruc/702825197933.pdf.

27. Kate Kingsbury, "Death Is Women's Work: Santa Muerte, a Folk Saint and Her Female Followers," *International Journal of Latin American Religion* 5 (2021): 43–63.

28. As Carlsen points out, in her work for the Americas Program, 70 percent of search parties for the disappeared are led by women. See Laura Carlsen, "Mexico's Search Brigades for the Disappeared: Rebuilding Society from the Ground Up," Americas Program, March 2019, https://www.americas.org/mexicos-search-brigades-for-the-disappeared -rebuilding-society-from-the-ground-up/.

29. Norget, *Days of Death*.

30. Norget, *Days of Death*, 147.

31. Norget, *Days of Death*.

32. Norget, *Days of Death*, 143.

33. Kate Kingsbury, "At Death's Door in Cancun: Sun, Sea, and Santa Muerte," *Anthropology and Humanism*, June 18, 2021, 1–22.

34. Chesnut, *Devoted to Death*, 13.

35. Chesnut, *Devoted to Death*, 38.

36. Alma Guillmermoprieto, "The Vatican and Santa Muerte," *National Geographic*, May 14, 2013, https://www.nationalgeographic.com/news/2013/5/130512-vatican-santa-muerte -mexico-cult-catholic-church-cultures-world/.

37. Ludwig Feuerbach and Elliot George, *The Essence of Christianity*, trans. Marian Evans (London: Trubne & Co., Ludgate Hill, 1881; repr. 1957).

38. Her son was later gunned down in 2017.

39. *La Santa Muerte*, directed by Eva Aridjis (Dark Night Pictures, 2007).

40. R. Andrew Chesnut, "Top Santa Muerte Leader Enriqueta Vargas Is in the Bony Lady's Embrace," *Skeleton Saint*, December 19, 2018, https://skeletonsaint.com/2018/12/19/top -santa-muerte-leader-enriqueta-vargas-is-in-the-bony-ladys-embrace/.

41. Jennifer J. Salinas, Soham Al Snih, Kyriakos Markides, Laura A. Ray, and Ronald J. Angel, "The Rural-Urban Divide: Health Services Utilization among Older Mexicans in Mexico," *Journal of Rural Health* 26, no. 4 (2010): 334.

6

Modern-Day Martyrs

Coptic Blood and American Christian Kinship

CANDACE LUKASIK

On a winter afternoon in 2018, Romany Melek Hetta, a Coptic Christian asylum seeker, visited the Museum of the Bible in Washington, D.C.[1] Waiting for a friend from the local Coptic Orthodox church to arrive, he sat on a bench on the museum premises. A woman and man from the managerial staff of the museum approached and began questioning him. Romany grew uncomfortable, ended the conversation, and entered the museum without his friend. A while later, security officers approached Romany and directed him into a private room. The managerial staff and security officers began interrogating him about his friend, why he had not come, and who he was. The museum eventually advised the U.S. Federal Bureau of Investigation (FBI) that Romany was a possible terrorist and security threat and opened a counterterrorism investigation into him. To preserve his asylum claim, he agreed to an interview with the FBI to clear his name. During the interview, Romany was informed that the museum believed him to be a possible security threat because he used both legal surnames (Hetta and Melek), claiming that this usage was particularly common among Muslim terrorists.[2] Romany filed a lawsuit against the Museum of the Bible in early 2019, citing that the museum spuriously caused his personal information to be entered into FBI counterterrorism files. In a subsequent interview on the case, Romany lamented that people like the museum staff would "never be able to comprehend there is a Christian person who doesn't look like them."[3]

In recent years, American politicians, think tanks, and nongovernmental organizations (NGOs) have channeled their efforts into "saving" Middle Eastern Christians, especially in the wake of the so-called Arab Spring and the rise of the Islamic State. Over the past decade, Coptic Christians, the largest Christian community in the Middle East, have increasingly immigrated to the United States by means of the Diversity Immigrant Visa (or Green Card Lottery), asylum, and family reunification.[4] The growth of the Coptic community in the United

States, along with lobbying efforts and a rise in ISIS-affiliated attacks on their places of worship and pilgrimage in Egypt, have pushed them into the political spotlight. Since the 1990s, attacks on Egyptian Copts have been made legible to American (particularly evangelical) audiences through the global, moral imaginary of the "Persecuted Church."[5] Egyptian Copts are configured as Americans' Christian kin in their suffering for Christ, and American Copts, as well as Coptic clergy, have engaged this imaginary in their advocacy and social interactions. American persecution discourse has restructured Christian kinship along these imperial lines and has shaped how Eastern Christians have come to translate their specific histories and contemporary homeland contexts differently.

Images of bloodied Egyptian Coptic bodies and their hagiographic accounts of witness to Christ have circulated among Western Christian religiopolitical networks in what I term an "economy of blood": an economy of Christian kinship that performs the double movement of glory and racialization. In one movement, the suffering of Coptic Christians in Egypt is theologically engaged by American evangelicals and their kin as a triumphalist vision of Western Christendom, while also being the grounds of Coptic inclusion into American Christian kinship. Thus, the Persecuted Church has positioned the strengthening of Western Christianity on the death of Eastern Christians such as the Copts, who purify the faith and strengthen claims of besiegement.[6] The persecution of Copts in Egypt dually offers the grounds of claims-making practices among American Copts in their lobbying practices, and in their own identity formation, as immigrants, within a conservative American Christian landscape.

In another movement, American Copts, as immigrants of many different social classes, are also racialized as Middle Eastern, Arab, Muslim, and nonwhite others by the U.S. government in the context of War on Terror security. The racialization of American Copts is a dual process oscillating between Christian kinship with white America and the optics of nonwhite suspicion. Racialization is a multi-scalar process that proliferates through these different religio-racial divisions within the geopolitics of persecution. American Christians mobilize Eastern Christian suffering, yet those Christians ultimately remain "Eastern," nonwhite bodies in everyday interactions within American society. Many American Copts, including Coptic clergy and hierarchs, have reimagined indigenous Coptic collective memory of blood and persecution through the political, theological, and affective formations of this economy of blood. The power of this economy shapes the contours of American Coptic politics and the grounds of solidarity with the Christian Right.

By unpacking the ambiguity of American Christian kinship, this chapter analyzes how Coptic collective memory of persecution and martyrdom is remapped by this kinship. I argue that this geopoliticized, transnational economy of blood has reconfigured older economies of blood in Christian conceptions of kinship and the broader politics such conceptions have historically authorized.[7] Coptic Christians have historically engaged the blood of martyrs as a part of a figuration that connects the community to past forms of persecution and contemporary contexts of political subjugation and sectarian strife in Egypt.[8] I show what becomes of such Coptic conceptions and practices of kinship in the encounter with the evangelical and geopolitical economy of blood in post-9/11 America.

By studying Coptic experiences of racialization in post-9/11 America, we can better understand how the pervasive logics of whiteness alter everyday interactions, configure political orientation, and reinterpret histories of trauma through new contexts of empire expansion.[9] Whiteness is the process of variegation, whereby whiteness becomes the structure of parsing out who belongs as kin and who is marked by suspicion, which is not encompassed simply by phenotypical distinction but also by political affiliation. Racialization is the process of becoming a subject of this parsing. White supremacy and American imperial power discipline Coptic diasporic life by rewarding the suppression of emblems of Middle Easternness and emphasizing shared Christian values.[10]

My analysis is grounded in twenty months of ethnographic fieldwork among recent Coptic migrants; first-, second-, and third-generation American Copts; and clergy members moving transnationally between Egypt and the New York–New Jersey area of the United States, as well as Washington, D.C., lobbying networks. Based on this fieldwork, I examine the economy of blood as a kinship formation and investigate how this formation structures and obscures the everyday lived experiences of racialization. I focus on the tensions that are internal to the economy of blood, and show how this parses kin through the dialectic of community building ("kin") and suspicion ("not-kin"). Through this dissection, I analyze what kinship becomes in Coptic encounters with American Christianity.

Transvaluing Persecution

Beginning in the early 1970s and flourishing in the 1990s, American evangelicals developed a set of foreign policy objectives that focused on human rights advocacy and blended their spiritual and political beliefs, employed skillful lobbyists to promote their interests in Congress, and created a strong network linking them with their coreligionists throughout the world. In the 1990s, former Cold War think tanks like the Hudson Institute, Freedom House, and the Institute for Religion and Democracy partnered with evangelicals and also consulted a few Coptic diaspora activists in shifting from the fight against godless communism toward the fight against fundamentalist Islam. Today, in such think tanks and other advocacy organizations, Copts now hold positions of power, shaping policy through the lens of human rights language and Christian persecution discourse. As diasporic representatives, they engage and add authority to right-wing discourses, such as *dhimmitude*, which argues that if the global war on Christians is not won, the situation of American Christians will resemble that of Middle Eastern Christians—subjugated by Islam under conditions in which their religion is kept private and care is taken so public acts do not offend the state religion.[11] To this conservative coalition, Copts, as both symbols and actors in their own right, have offered a striking portfolio of bloody narratives and imagery, which reinforces persecution discourse.[12]

The Christian persecution movement has positioned Eastern Christians as martyrs for Western Christendom, in that their fate is not seen as negatively impacting Christianity as a whole, because Western Christianity—in particular white evangelicalism and its ecumenical proponents—benefit from this persecution. It is by the spilling of their blood that American Christian kinship is opened to Eastern Christians; Coptic blood becomes shared American Christian blood. The death of Copts in Egypt thus becomes a purifying function for white evangelicalism.[13]

Melani McAlister has argued that the suffering of Eastern Christian bodies is recounted and put on display in an evangelical public sphere. The examination and display of those persecuted bodies have offered Americans a new kind of Christian selfhood. This new "evangelical internationalism" is marked by fear and a sense of threat from Islam and defined by increased attention to the suffering and the needs of Christians outside the United States.[14] In this fight, American evangelicals have made significant alliances with Catholics, Jews, Mormons, and Eastern Orthodox Christians, as well as American Copts.[15] Evangelicals have found ways to work more ecumenically on issues they deem important to the overall project of "saving America," and part of that work has also been the work of "saving" Middle Eastern Christians from Islamic oppression. Events and subsequent images of Coptic bloodshed, ranging from the twenty Copts and one Ghanaian beheaded on the shores of Libya by Islamic State affiliates to the spate of bombings that have ravaged large churches and cathedrals throughout Egypt, have been transvalued and remapped onto this moral imaginary of global Christian persecution.[16]

In December 2017, I attended the Third International Archon Conference on Religious Freedom, which was held at the Trump International Hotel in Washington, D.C. The Archons of the Ecumenical Patriarchate are a society of laity chosen by the patriarch of Constantinople for their service to the Greek Orthodox Church and their respect within the community. The conference was titled "The Persecution of Christians in the Holy Lands and the Middle East: Consequences and Solutions," and the schedule was theologically eclectic, with speakers comprised of politicians of evangelical backgrounds, Greek Orthodox influencers, Syriac and Coptic bishops, and upper-middle-class Copts involved in advocacy work in Washington, D.C.

The second session, entitled "Persecution of Christians and Possible Solutions," took place at an auditorium on Capitol Hill. The auditorium was dark

except for bright lights focused on a large stage projection of the twenty-one martyrs of Libya, darkened to black and white, lined up on their knees in front of
masked members of ISIS standing ominously behind them. Following opening
remarks, clerical leaders from various Middle Eastern churches gave speeches
regarding their positions on persecution and Western intervention.

Bishop Angaelos of London spoke on behalf of the Coptic Orthodox Church.
Bishop Angaelos has explicitly addressed the persecution of Copts, appearing on
the BBC and numerous other outlets following attacks in Egypt. During the panel,
he commented:

> We come at a time when there are 200–500 million Christians persecuted
> around the world. In scores of countries . . . they are suffering at a time
> when we as humanity are in an era of our development that prides itself
> in international treaties, international conventions and a right to life. . . .
> The Christians of whom we speak are those that deny and reject minor-
> ity status, for they are indigenous people. If what is happening in the
> Middle East were to happen to the indigenous people of America or Can-
> ada or the aborigines of Australia, the world would be up in arms. They
> live the faith that was born in the region.

Against the backdrop of the Libya martyrs on their knees, the bishop described
how he was compelled by the image to mark his own body:

> The 21 martyrs of Libya have changed the world. Typically, the Copts have
> a cross tattoo on their inner right wrist. Just as a sign of who they are.
> I grew up in Australia. I didn't have one, I didn't see the need. But when
> I watch this video and the . . . man in the middle having to mask his face
> so we would not know who pointed that knife and said, "We are after the
> nation of the cross." I felt a need to get a cross for them. We hear the sto-
> ries of the saints and the martyrs in our church every day. Another bomb-
> ing, another martyr, another saint, it's still happening. It happened on
> our screens. We saw it before us.[17]

The persecuted body not only marks Christians as under global siege, but also
points to the argument that through the blood of persecuted (Eastern) Christian bodies, all of Western Christendom and its imperial formations are sanctified. The global efficacy of the evangelical public sphere and its remapping of
Coptic martyrology persuades even a Coptic bishop—who otherwise saw no need
for an identitarian tattoo—to mark the Coptic cross on his right wrist.[18]

In ballroom at the Trump Hotel, just down the street from the White House
itself, President Donald Trump's closest associates were the keynote speakers and
key figures of the conference dinner. The first remarks came from Jordan Sekulow, executive director for the American Center for Law and Justice (ACLJ). His
father, Jay Sekulow, is a frequent commentator on the Christian Broadcasting

Network (CBN) and on Fox News, a Messianic Jew, and one of Trump's personal lawyers. Jordan, Jay's son, remarked on the persecution of Christians around the world, but especially in the Middle East, as an *American* problem. By looking to the faith and tragic circumstances of the Copts, he argued, America should be inspired to carry the light of religious freedom to all corners of the globe. Sekulow proclaimed:

> We cannot forget that our brothers and sisters in Christ, whether they be of the Orthodox faith or just the Christian faith generally, are facing immense persecution around the world. For all of us, do not forget those Coptic Christians who are in the heart of Egypt, worshipping on Christmas Day, worshipping on Easter and hundreds are killed. And yet, next Easter, hundreds more show up. And that is a symbolism of their Christian faith, but it is also unacceptable in the world that we live in. . . . Here we are in the United States of America. . . . You have a government that accepts freedom. And we're unique. In the United States, we have to learn in a unique way how to take that understanding that we have been born into and ingrained into us, and take that to parts of the world where that is not ingrained. Where the free exercise of religion is not the first right. We have so much to do for the Persecuted Church.[19]

In this discourse, America is the leader, the savior, and the exemplar for the world. America can bring freedom to other parts of the world where persecution and devastation have prevailed. Coptic blood is shed and displayed as a spectacle on the world stage. Bombings, attacks, and shootings were brought to bear not only against Egyptian Copts, but against all Christendom. This economy of blood includes Copts in the role of martyr and maimed body, an imagery that the Coptic Church has also championed as a communal identity marker. This constellation of conservative discourses that include the Copts as persecuted figures at the hands of Muslim militants have bound American Copts into particular characteristics of racial-religious legibility that have mediated interfaith relations in the United States.

Suspicious Bodies

After 9/11, Islamophobia and anti-Muslim rhetoric affected not only American Muslims but also Sikhs, non-Muslim Arabs, and people of South Asian descent.[20] One of the early victims of this violence was the Egyptian-born Coptic Christian Adel Karas, who was shot dead by two white men inside his grocery store in San Gabriel, California, on September 15, 2001.[21] Scholars have argued that the racialization of Muslims in post-9/11 America has meant that certain bodies have been made "suspicious."[22] Copts have been included among these suspicious bodies even though many have tried to combat suspicion by emphasizing their Christian faith and claiming racial-religious misrecognition.[23]

On a cold winter evening in Staten Island, I sat across from Abouna (the Arabic term for father, or priest) Girgis in the kitchen of the administrative center of the local Coptic diocese. A man in his late thirties who had been recently elevated to the priesthood, Abouna grew up in Bayonne, New Jersey, and had strong ties to his clergy-filled family back in Luxor, Upper Egypt, visiting them regularly. We talked about the protests that had stalled zoning board approval of Bayonne's first mosque. (The same zoning board approved the expansion of a Coptic church in 2011.) After purchasing the property in 2015, the local Muslim community's proposal was denied by the zoning board in early 2017, citing traffic and parking issues. The property was protested and even vandalized, with crude phrases such as "F-ck Muslims" and "F-ck Arabs," in the name of Donald Trump, the then-Republican nominee for president.

Bayonne is a working-class neighborhood, where historically many Italian, Polish, and Irish immigrant communities took up residence. More recently, Bayonne has become home to many Middle Eastern communities, especially Egyptians, both Muslims and Coptic Christians. When he was growing up, however, Abouna's family was one of a few Middle Eastern families. "You could tell, even at that age, that people weren't used to your complexion. They weren't comfortable with having people of your complexion around," he said. Now, the community has two Coptic Orthodox churches, and is expanding with a new influx of Coptic immigrants from Egypt. Though the community also faces its own share of discrimination, Copts joined in the protests against the Bayonne mosque. Protestors held signs that said, "Stop the mosque!" "If the mosque comes, the mayor goes!" "No mosque—remember 9/11!" I asked Abouna Girgis what he thought about the protests in his hometown. "Look," he answered, "if you're Coptic you're going to protest Islam. When you've seen and gone through the harassment, the persecution in Egypt and everything, can you blame them?" Coptic protests against mosques and their engagement in Islamophobic rhetoric are practices that not only signify the collective memory of persecution manifesting itself in diaspora.[24] These actions also reflect the need to secure the recognition of Copts as *Christians* in America.

Abouna recounted how he and a group of friends had stopped at a local convenience store on the evening of September 11, 2001. While there, he began to be heckled by a group of men (whom he took to be "Hispanic") who hurled insults at him. "We had the wrong complexion," he recounted. "They said to us, 'You f'in terrorists. Look what you did. We're going to get you!' . . . [After 9/11], you felt like you were a target and it wasn't your fault." A local priest in the days following 9/11 even went under house arrest because of his supposed resemblance to Osama bin Laden, another Coptic interlocutor later recounted. After 9/11, Copts changed their attire to sartorially distance themselves from Arabs and Muslims. Coptic clergy in New Jersey noted that Pope Shenouda III, the late patriarch of the Coptic Orthodox Church, allowed priests to wear a wooden cross similar to that of Catholic clergy and to trim their beards in the hopes that this would prevent them from becoming the targets of backlash or hate crimes after 9/11. In Los Angeles since 9/11, Metropolitan Serapion has allowed clergy to forgo their traditional head covering ['amma]—an informal requirement throughout the Coptic Church—because, according to one priest, "they look like Islamic turbans." Coptic religious practices (such as priestly garb) have reformed in diaspora to reconcile with post-9/11 racial infrastructures that code such aesthetics as threatening.

The power of whiteness within American society is structured in and through such disciplinary measures and everyday relations, and the transformation of Coptic religious and social life in the United States gestures to the power of (white, Western) Christianity.[25] Copts are Eastern Christians, yet they must contend with, and are transformed by, an imperial and geopolitical form of Christianity, one that is intertwined with the power and privilege of whiteness. Such racial distinctions have never been tethered to a defined set of categories whereby avoiding detection in those categories (name, dress, language) would somehow help to avoid the white gaze. Thinking with Barbara Fields and Karen Fields's notion of "racecraft," the racialization of Coptic Christians in American society is pieced together in the ordinary and extraordinary course of everyday doing. Racecraft governs racial imagination—"what goes with what and whom"—and guides imagination and human action.[26] Thus, the "deference and dominance" of racial distinctions lies in the dense set of prior representations and practices on which they build—the Muslim, the undocumented, the immigrant, the Jew, the Black person—their histories interweaving with one another. The shifting gaze of racecraft in the United States can be traced in the ways the racialization of different groups circuits and overlaps.

Especially after 9/11, many Copts were identified by law enforcement as potential threats. Magdy Beshara was the Coptic owner of the St. George's Shell Gas Station in Bayville, New Jersey. Shortly after 9/11, the FBI came to the family's home in the middle of the night and questioned Beshara as to whether Marwan al-Shehhi, one of the 9/11 hijackers, had worked at the gas station. Beshara's stepson Michael described the aftermath of the initial FBI raid: "People would drive by and say, 'We're going to kill you terrorists,' and throw a big liquor bottle at me and my sister." Under the PATRIOT Act, the government confiscated anything it desired from the gas station and their home. Their mail was opened, their phones were tapped, and Michael was followed to school by federal agents. The family even faced death threats, and despite their pleas to the police to intervene, they were refused. Michael described how the incident forced him to differentiate. "It made me feel weird to say out aloud, but I always thought to myself, 'I'm not a Muslim, I'm a Christian.' I felt like I was putting them [Muslims] down to say, 'Hey, look, I'm the good guy.' I felt like we had to do anything to defend ourselves." At school, Michael was bullied and physically assaulted on dozens of occasions. At one point in the months following the raid, an unknown assailant set the family's house on fire while Michael and his little sister were sleeping upstairs. All this took place even after the FBI notified Magdy Beshara that he was no longer a subject of investigation.[27]

As Junaid Rana has argued, racial infrastructures interact with one another by means of cultural and institutional forms of discrimination in a complex social system of racialization.[28] Yet the process of racialization is never complete; identifying who is the "Muslim" is part of the apparatus of racialization. As Magdy Beshara noted during an interview after the FBI raid of his gas station, "Middle Eastern people, we all look alike, you know what I mean."

Beyond post-9/11 contexts in the New York–New Jersey area, Copts, along with other immigrant communities, experience everyday forms of racism that displace the logics of persecuted Christian personhood. Abanoub, an asylee from Alexandria, Egypt, had been in the United States for nearly five years, working his way up from a gas station attendant to an Uber driver and now to a building inspector. Throughout his twenties he was a mechanical engineer in the oil fields of southern Algeria. He explained to me that as a Copt growing up in Egypt and working in Algeria, he was discriminated against as a Christian and colleagues would question his name and his background. Yet when he came to the United States, he experienced a novel form of difference. Over dinner in Bay Ridge, Abanoub lamented: "Here, what matters is your accent [lahga] and your color [lown]. As soon as a white superior or client meets me, hears my accent, they ask where I'm from, and some even go so far as to question my qualifications. 'How did you get this position?' one person asked me. White people here think if you're a gas station attendant or work as a dish washer, that's your place—they are okay with that. But if you get into skilled labor, like myself, people ask you how you got there. They are suspicious of your success."

In close proximity to Egyptian Muslims, Copts occupy a liminal space of difference within difference. Their theological and racial difference from the West has placed them into similar matrices of subjugation as with other non-Christian peoples, yet their new enmeshments with Western geopolitical imaginations of Christian persecution have positioned them as kin in the fight against Islamic terrorism. In everyday life, however, they continue to contend with their racial difference from white America. During our conversation, Abanoub joked about his name and the politics of misrecognition at work. "They think my second name is 'Saddam.' I had white people ask me if I'm related to Saddam Hussein of Iraq. Saddam is not my second name, but for them they can't tell the difference."

In the contemporary racialization of Arabs and Muslims in the United States, religion, national origin, and color articulate into complex subject formations that determine and differentiate the citizen and the terrorist.[29] Caught in the web of this racial-religious form, the work of differentiation done by some Copts gestures toward the power of whiteness, as a structure of assimilation, to mold sensibilities, relationships, and practices and avoid the gaze of suspicion.[30] Strategies of separation evidence Coptic desire to disentangle from post 9/11 racial infrastructures—to not be identified as the enemy. Yet such strategies are also conditioned by Coptic inclusion in the economy of blood, where American Copts see themselves as kin with the Christian Right in their shared narratives of persecution and interest in preserving Christian values in conservative America.

Saving America, Saving Egyptian Christians

Following a liturgy one Sunday in August 2020, I sat with George and Verina, who had just dropped their youngest son off at college. The elections and Black Lives Matter protests had consumed news media and the conversation naturally directed itself there. George explained that he was concerned about where American society was going, even hinting that if protests continued (protests reminiscent of the 2011 Egyptian revolution and the downfall of former Egyptian president Hosni Mubarak), he would move back to Egypt. "Trump is a Christian, and he's trying to keep America a Christian nation," he said. "Obama supported the Muslim Brotherhood in Egypt. The Muslim Brotherhood was against the Copts, leading to more violence. With Trump, he supports the Christians back there." Verina chimed into the conversation, "Under Obama, it was Happy Holidays! Now, we can say Merry Christmas again. We came to the U.S. to escape discrimination in Egypt. We don't want to be stripped of our rights again as Christians here."

In the New York–New Jersey area, Egyptian immigration—of both Copts and Muslims—is a consistent fixture of communal life. Coptic support for the reelection of Donald Trump was structured through the economy of blood, whereby American Copts of various socioeconomic classes understood themselves as linked to the conservative values Trump espoused regarding immigration, the economy, and Islam. Ramy immigrated to the United States in the late 1990s on the Green Card Lottery from Nag Hammadi, Upper Egypt. He later married Marina in Egypt and brought her to Jersey City, where they had two sons. They recently purchased a home in Bayonne, leaving the Jersey City apartment where they had lived for more than a decade. Since the beginning of the COVID-19 pandemic, Ramy had been unemployed, relying on Marina's salary as a teacher's aide to support the family. Both Ramy and Marina were vocal supporters of Trump. "So many people don't want to work here. They take money from the system and don't want to give back," Marina lamented over lunch after Sunday liturgy. "I think they should do a merit-based immigration system. We don't know who they are letting in!" The conversation shifted to Egyptian Muslim migrants in particular. "Look at France! We don't want those extremists to come here. They need to be able to assimilate. They come here and demand that people conform to their perspective. They want America to be Islamic!"

Similar sentiments conditioned more public support for Trump's 2020 reelection among the Coptic community of New York and New Jersey. "God bless America and Egypt" was the motto highlighted on the Egyptian Christians for Trump website.[31] Board members appeared on the Coptic SAT TV show *Ask with Mira* on October 23, 2020, to garner support for the advocacy group and discuss why Egyptian Christian support for Trump was so crucial to the community in diaspora.[32] A viewer who was a second-generation American Copt called in to express his support for the organization:

> I don't think it's any coincidence that in the new capital city that [Egyptian] President Sisi has built, the biggest Coptic cathedral in the Middle East is built there, and President Sisi is very excited to highlight this to the world and to show this to President Trump—[implicitly saying] "Look at what I'm doing for the Coptics!" and that's what we want, we're happy with that. I'm glad President Sisi did that. We want him to continue . . . and the way we're going to get there is by supporting our great President Trump and letting him know "Hey! The Coptic community supports you and we expect you to support our brothers and sisters back home."

American Coptic support for Trump is woven into a political imaginary of diaspora advocacy, but it also aligns with the idea that Copts in the United States belong to a broader constellation of the Christian Right, which strives for the advancement of a Christian nationalism entailing the fusion of Christianity and American civic life.[33] Although Christian nationalism is understood to be a discourse related to white, Protestant, native-born, culturally Christian Americans, some of its tenets—on immigration, social welfare, cultural issues pertaining to abortion and LBGTQ rights, and especially fear of Muslims—are adopted by minority groups, such as the Copts, that are in many instances the target of Christian nationalist ire, as immigrants from the Middle East.

With a framed picture of Trump on the desk behind him, the vice president of the organization, a financial adviser, connected support for Trump to support for Egypt's el-Sisi but also encouraged Coptic immigrants to become model minorities.[34] "If you stay on welfare and Medicaid and wait for social services . . . this is what happened to the Blacks [as-sud] and Hispanics [espan] here. They vote for Democrats so they can get food stamps. To all of our family, who immigrate from Egypt, please don't get stuck with Medicare and food stamps. Go achieve your dream, work hard don't wait for people to give you money." Concern for the persecution of Egyptian Copts interweaves with the limits of that concern once they leave Egypt for the United States. They must achieve economic success in the United States so as to avoid association with failed minorities—Blacks and Hispanics. This brings to mind what Toni Morrison has argued—that "only when the lesson of racial estrangement [from the native-born Black population] is learned is assimilation complete."[35] American Copts imagine themselves in relation to the Christian Right as kin. The extension of kinship from American Christians to Eastern Christians such as the Copts is a relation of persecuted blood. Thus, American Copts see their ties with the Christian Right in terms of persecuted blood rather than as a racial formation. Although the diaspora offers opportunities to form new intersectional solidarities, the happy convergence of otherwise divergent persecution narratives has placed American Copts into vectors of religiopolitical belonging with the Christian Right, which seeks to preserve a white, conservative Christian America.

Secular Threat, Coptic Difference

Every Labor Day weekend for over a decade, Abouna Thomas, a popular priest from Cairo with a major following in the diaspora, holds seminars on family, social issues, and evangelism in Upstate New York. With one of the largest programs of missionary activity in Egypt and throughout the African continent, Abouna Thomas has made a reputation speaking on cross-cultural communication, ethics, and relationships. Before beginning the first seminar, Abouna answered questions from the audience, which were brought to him on white pieces of paper. One question asked how youth in America should approach issues such as same-sex marriage. Abouna began, "In my opinion, you have persecution here more [as Christians] than we do in Egypt. Here, you have a secular society that imposes demands on you as Christians that are against your faith. In Egypt, we may have a terrorist come and blow up a church, but it doesn't affect our faith. You all are more of a minority [here, than we are there]."

The bombs and attacks on Egyptian Copts, to Abouna Thomas, do not affect the faith—they only strengthen it. Yet in the United States, American Copts have been subjected to the liberal politics of pluralism, whereby ethical choices must be made in the everyday. In Egypt, minority politics of separation, repression, and resistance are reconfigured within the current American culture wars, in which Copts have, in common with evangelical and conservative others, feelings of threat to religious values. While Copts are a minority in both Egypt and the United States, in the latter nation Copts have to reckon their values in a public sphere that is dominated both by pluralism and also by pervasive evangelical politics.

During the nomination of Amy Coney Barrett to the Supreme Court, Copts took to social media to voice their support and expressed concern over the encroachment of their Christian values by secular political forces. In October 2020, a Coptic youth meeting was held in New Jersey to discuss the confirmation hearings and the questioning of Coney Barrett's Catholic faith. The meeting was entitled, "A Successful PATRIOT: Because of Faith, NOT In-Spite Of," and those in attendance grappled with their Coptic positionality within American Christianity.

"Sometimes you feel like you're the minority, and now we're less than the minority," a Coptic mother and doctor in attendance commented. While the priest and organizer of the event framed the discussion around culture war politics and the decline of Christianity in America, he noted that much of this decline stemmed from evangelical influence:

> By us staying silent, by us not living our faith and demanding our right to voice our love, to voice the right, balanced message of Christ, we are allowing the incorrect view of Christianity to prevail. . . . I think that we get so embarrassed and so intimidated because of the backlash because of what this misrepresentation of Christianity has caused that we ourselves get intimidated. And it has made the non-Christians or those who do have a strong opinion on the bigoted vision or version of Christianity to come out to the extent that at a Senate hearing, publicly on television, somebody's faith can be attacked or at the very least criticized.

Mina, a Coptic man from the audience chimed in: "We have to recognize that the definition of the word Christian in American society is far from what our Middle Eastern brown background understands this word to be." Gesturing toward the politics of translation and a clash of (Western/Eastern) Christian traditions, Mina conveyed to the priest that not everything described as "Christian" is reconcilable or even compatible with Coptic Orthodox histories, sensibilities, and pedagogies. Beyond this, Coptic, and more broadly, Oriental Orthodox racial difference from white, evangelical America lend themselves to divergent experiences of being Christian in American society. American Coptic politics are remapped by these U.S. culture wars, which chart religious public life onto a left-right spectrum. These culture wars are conditioned by racial difference and, ultimately, white supremacy, which incite Copts to adopt, to varying degrees, positions that diverge from their own theology and religious traditions. The priest grimaced at the comment, and sought a more pragmatic political angle: "We have power in numbers, though!" The Coptic man replied: "If you're with the wrong numbers, you have the wrong power."

The economy of blood extends kinship from American Christians to Eastern (Coptic) Christians. Despite racial difference from white America, American

Copts overwhelmingly see their ties to the Christian Right in terms of religious kinship and blood. Copts are a racial minority in the United States, but they are also part of the Christian majority. As a Middle Eastern Christian immigrant community, American Copts have contended with their lack of power in numbers and have sought allies among conservative forces on the right that have dually instrumentalized them. The economy of blood, as this chapter has suggested, incites American Copts who are engaged in advocacy and conservative politics into certain narratives and values, and binds them into particular strategies of differentiation from the Middle Eastern/Arab/Muslim other, ultimately effacing the conflicts within and struggles over their racial and religious difference from white, Protestant America in the process.[36]

Community in Blood and by Blood

Within the economy of blood discussed in this chapter, Coptic suffering circulates to advance religiopolitical policies that exceed the direct needs of the Coptic community in the United States or in Egypt. Caught between whiteness and its racialized others, American Copts connect Egyptian contexts to these new imperial formations. On the Upper East Side one August afternoon, I sat on a black crate next to the food cart owned by Wael, a Copt from Asyut, Upper Egypt, who came to the United States six years ago through the Green Card Lottery. "Everyone dreams of working abroad to make better money," he said with a tired smile. Wael explained that he felt marginalized back home and described what made him ultimately decide to apply for the Green Card Lottery: "Since I can remember, things are just not safe back home for us. . . . They kidnap Coptic girls and kill us. Recently, there's been even more violence against Christians . . . like the bombing [at al-Qudiseen church] in Alexandria and the bus attack on the way to the monastery in al-Minya. . . . Because of things like this I supported Trump's ban on Muslims to the United States." As Halal food carts drove by us, Wael waved to his Egyptian Muslim colleagues, but he was quick to tell me about his dislike for them and their discrimination against him as a Copt, even in New York City.

As more Copts immigrate to and build family in the United States, histories of persecution and sectarian violence in Egypt are remapped onto a transnational economy of blood, reconfiguring Christian kinship through American empire building. The blood of Coptic martyrs relates them as kin to American Christians, thus building community in blood and by blood. Yet American Copts are placed into racial partition. Persecution politics and American Christianity interpellate and incite Copts to a bloody kinship—one that includes and simultaneously excludes them in white America. The economy of blood requires a multiscalar approach to analyzing how American Christianity religiously includes them and how U.S. empire racially excludes them. The ways in which

American Copts inhabit such a formation is important for understanding the difficulties they face as Middle Eastern, immigrants, and also Christians in the contemporary United States.

NOTES

1. The Museum of the Bible was founded and is funded by Hobby Lobby CEO Steve Green. The members of the Green family are prominent American evangelicals.

2. This narrative is based on *Hetta v. Museum of the Bible, Inc.*, complaint, Superior Court for the District of Columbia, Civil Division, January 17, 2019, https://d3n8a8pro7vhmx .cloudfront.net/justiceonline/mailings/234/attachments/original/Museum_of_the_Bible _Complaint_public_%280081747xB3827%29.pdf?1547753191. This particular description on the part of the plaintiff's attorneys is noted on pages 2, 3, and 5.

3. Dominic Holden, "A Middle Eastern Man Is Suing the Bible Museum for Racial Profiling and Reporting Him to the FBI," *Buzzfeed News*, January 18, 2019, https://www .buzzfeednews.com/article/dominicholden/bible-museum-lawsuit-racial-profiling-fbi.

4. As part of the Immigration Act of 1990, the United States instituted the lottery, which encouraged nationals of countries that historically sent few migrants to the United States to apply for one of 50,000 legal immigrant visas. As of the 2018 results (the latest statistics available), Egypt ranked third in Green Card Lottery winners from Africa. Over the past ten years, the number of Coptic immigrants, particularly those winning the lottery, increased exponentially, with Copts applying for it from cities as well as the most remote villages of Egypt. See U.S. Department of State—Bureau of Consular Affairs, "DV 2018—Selected Entrants," accessed May 26, 2022, https://travel.state.gov/content/travel/en /us-visas/immigrate/diversity-visa-program-entry/dv-2018-selected-entrants.html.

5. I use *evangelical* as a political construction and one connected to institutional power. Conservative, white Protestants, led by Christian Right organizations, have been key players in cultivating the Persecuted Church moral imaginary, especially as it pertains to Muslims and Middle Eastern Christians. Within the broader framework of American evangelicalism, Catholics, Jews, Eastern Orthodox Christians, Episcopalians, and other Protestants have also participated in such a coalition of the faithful that is guided by evangelical aesthetics, sensibilities, passions, and politics.

6. Elizabeth Castelli, "Praying for the Persecuted Church: US Christian Activism in the Global Arena," *Journal of Human Rights* 4, no. 3 (2005): 321–351.

7. Sarah Bakker Kellogg, "Syriac Christianity, Ethnicity, and Secular Legibility," *Current Anthropology* 60, no. 4 (2019): 475–498.

8. Anthony Shenoda, "Cultivating Mystery: Miracles and the Coptic Moral Imaginary" (PhD diss., Harvard University, 2010).

9. Junaid Rana, "Anthropology and the Riddle of White Supremacy," *American Anthropologist* 122, no. 1 (2019): 99–111; Aisha Beliso-De Jesús and Jemima Pierre, "Introduction: Special Section: Anthropology of White Supremacy," *American Anthropologist* 122, no. 1 (2020): 65–75.

10. Andrew Whitehead and Samuel Perry, *Taking America Back for God: Christian Nationalism in the United States* (Oxford: Oxford University Press, 2020).

11. For more on this specific language, see Mary Ann Glendon, "The Naked Public: A Symposium," *First Things*, November 2004, https://www.firstthings.com/article/2004/11 /001-the-naked-public.

12. Paul Sedra, "Writing the History of the Modern Copts: From Victims and Symbols to Actors," *History Compass* 7, no. 3 (2009): 1049–1063; Paul Sedra, "Class Cleavages and Ethnic Conflict: Coptic Christian Communities in Modern Egyptian Politics," *Islam and Christian-Muslim Relations* 10, no. 2 (1999): 219–235.

13. Andrea Smith, *Unreconciled: From Racial Reconciliation to Racial Justice in Christian Evangelicalism* (Durham, NC: Duke University Press, 2019), 118.

14. Melani McAlister, *The Kingdom of God Has No Borders: A Global History of American Evangelicals* (New York: Oxford University Press, 2018).

15. Neil J. Young, *We Gather Together: The Religious Right and the Problem of Interfaith Politics* (Oxford: Oxford University Press, 2015).

16. John Dulin, "Transvaluing ISIS in Orthodox Christian-Majority Ethiopia: On the Inhibition of Group Violence," *Current Anthropology* 58, no. 6 (2017): 785–804.

17. "Persecution of Christians and Possible Solutions," Session 2, accessed May 26, 2022, https://www.youtube.com/watch?v=10iToAH4Z-k.

18. Melani McAlister, "What Is Your Heart For?: Affect and Internationalism in the Evangelical Public Sphere," *American Literary History* 20, no. 4 (2008): 870–895.

19. "Grand Banquet, 3rd International Conference on Religious Freedom," accessed May 26, 2022, https://www.youtube.com/watch?v=JMQqGkbiV4Q&t=1737s.

20. Jaspir Puar, *Terrorist Assemblages: Homonationalism in Queer Times* (Durham, NC: Duke University Press, 2007).

21. Joe Mozingo, "Slain Egyptian Was a Fixture in San Gabriel," *LA Times*, September 19, 2001, http://articles.latimes.com/2001/sep/19/local/me-47275.

22. Saher Selod, *Forever Suspect: Racialized Surveillance of Muslim Americans in the War on Terror* (New Brunswick: Rutgers University Press, 2018).

23. Yasmeen Hanoosh, *The Chaldeans: Politics and Identity in Iraq and the American Diaspora* (London: Bloomsbury Publishing, 2019).

24. Ghassan Hage, *White Nation: Fantasy of White Supremacy in a Multicultural Society* (London: Routledge, 2000), 60–61.

25. W.E.B. Du Bois, "The Souls of White Folks," in *Darkwater: Voices from Within the Veil* (New York: Harcourt, Brace, and Howe, 1920).

26. Karen Fields and Barbara Fields, *Racecraft: The Soul of Inequality in American Life* (New York: Verso Books, 2012), 25.

27. Michael Winerip, "Our Towns; A Terrorist at the Shell Station? No, but That Goatee Looks Suspicious," *New York Times*, September 30, 2001, https://www.nytimes.com/2001/09/30/nyregion/our-towns-a-terrorist-at-the-shell-station-no-but-that-goatee-looks-suspicious.html.

28. Junaid Rana, "The Racial Infrastructure of the Terror-Industrial Complex," *Social Text* 129 34, no. 4 (2016): 119.

29. Sally Howell and Andrew Shryock, "Cracking Down on Diaspora: Arab Detroit and America's 'War on Terror,'" *Anthropological Quarterly* 76, no. 3 (2003): 443–462.

30. Sylvia Chan-Malik, *Being Muslim: A Cultural History of Women of Color in American Islam* (New York: NYU Press, 2018); Sonja Thomas, "Cowboys and Indians: Indian Priests in Rural Montana," *Women's Studies Quarterly* 47, nos. 1–2 (2019): 110–131.

31. https://egyptianchristiansfortrump.com/en/.

32. "Asa'l ma'a Mira" (Ask with Mira), *Coptic SAT TV*, October 23, 2020.

33. Perry and Whitehead, *Taking America Back*.

34. Stanley Thangaraj, "Playing through Differences: Black-White Racial Logic and Interrogating South Asian American Identity," *Ethnic and Racial Studies* 35, no. 6 (2012): 988–1006.

35. Toni Morrison, "On the Backs of Blacks," *Time Magazine*, December 2, 1993.

36. Nadine Naber, "Imperial Whiteness and the Diasporas of Empire," *American Quarterly* 66, no. 4 (2014): 1107–1115.

PART THREE

Communities

Community is an essential component of religion. The field of World Christianity has typically focused on the ways in which Christian churches and communities have been formed by generative processes of conversion, translation, and agentive cultural adaptation. The following chapters, however, explore how violence has helped to constitute new Christian communities and networks. These chapters draw new attention to the ways in which a World Christian narrative of expansion has been predicated on forms of social constraints, persecution, and violence that have often been historiographically marginalized. In varying ways, they ask how Christians utilized the theological, spiritual, and ritual resources of their traditions in order to form new communities amid violence and persecution. Together, these chapters show new intersections of religion, violence, power, and agency in regions that have been central to the field of World Christianity.

Perhaps no other region has been as celebrated within the field of World Christianity as sub-Saharan Africa, which has seen dramatic demographic growth in Christianity since the end of the nineteenth century. While scholars have argued that Christian conversion in the colonial era as a means to escape from colonialism's destructiveness, Harvey Kwiyani argues that colonial violence did not stop after Africans were converted to Christianity. Kwiyani uses his home context of Malawi to show the ways in which Christianity has both used and served colonial violence against peoples of the world. He also insightfully explores how localized expressions of Christianity resisted Western Christianity, while arguing for the need to contend with Western Christianity's ambivalence toward the violence of slavery, colonialism, racism, and white supremacy.

Such dynamics of racism, cultural violence, and marginalization in a different context can also account for why, as in the case of Dalits and tribals in India, they converted to Christianity in the first place. In doing so, these communities moved out of the abject places to which they were assigned by dominant caste religious logic. Sunder John Boopalan builds on psychologies of perception, exploring how social status and power produce affect in caste-based societies. He highlights the agency of marginalized Christians, who resist the ways in which violence and discrimination are realized in interpersonal relations and daily ethics, both in India and in the networks of its diaspora.

The constitutive power of diasporic networks, violence, and communities is likewise explored by Christie Chui-Shan Chow, who follows the remarkable development of the Church of Almighty God in China and around the world. Tracing its emergence from an independent house church network in Henan province, to a global church with a robust online presence, Chow describes how the group typifies China's vigorous underground Christian sects, which resist the pressure to be absorbed into the state-controlled system of patriotic religious associations. These sects offer a distinctly new analytical lens by highlighting the ways in which these experiences of state persecution and intra-Christian suspicion have been integrated into its global spread in the twenty-first century. As China's Christian communities continue their rapid pace of growth and transformation, Chow's case study explores the crucial role of violence and disruption in challenging the concept of World Christianity.

7

Bishop Colenso Is Dead

White Missionaries and Black Suspicion in Colonial Africa

HARVEY KWIYANI

As the people gathered for their usual Sunday worship on January 24, 1915, at the Providence Industrial Mission at Mbombwe in the Shire Highlands of southern Malawi, many were aware that the service would not be business as usual.[1] There was both a great sense of excitement and a heavy cloud of fear in people's hearts. William Jervis Livingstone (here referred to as W. J. Livingstone), the estate manager at the nearby Alexander Low Bruce Estates at Magomero, had been killed just the day before. Many people were paralyzed with fear because they knew that the colonial British government that sat in Zomba, less than an hour away, would retaliate with full force. They fully expected that many people would die and that many more would be jailed because of the angry yet joyful transgressions of their pastor and leader, John Chilembwe, and his militia. Chilembwe was an independent Baptist preacher who had led his industrial mission at Nguludi since his return from ministerial training in the United States in 1900. During the three years he had spent in America, Chilembwe had come into contact with some of the leading African American minds of the time who influenced his thinking on the emerging colonialism in Africa (which was actually only starting at the time). He had seen with his own eyes the enduring plight of Black people in America. He came back to Malawi wishing for an Africa that was free from white rule. Then he set up his church at Mbombwe and led it rather quietly until January 1915, when he led an uprising.

Chilembwe's 1915 uprising was made necessary by several factors. First among them was that Chilembwe's church was located just outside the Alexander Low Bruce Estates (known in literature as the A. L. Bruce Estates, or by locals, including my grandmother, Bruce Estates), where W. J. Livingstone caused a great deal of trouble to the local community. Many of Chilembwe's followers were tenants on Bruce Estates and often on the receiving end of Livingstone's cruelty. Livingstone not only displaced and moved people around the estate at will, he constantly terrorized them. He is said to have been a very short-tempered man who loved to beat up any locals who did not meet his job requirements.[2] Second, after World War I broke out in 1914, the colonial British government rounded up and drafted many young men in Malawi to serve as porters to the British army, which was fighting against the Germans in northern Malawi.[3] Many young women and children were left vulnerable and without care. Chilembwe found this disturbing and wanted to convince the colonial British government that the Great European War should not cost the lives of young Africans who had nothing to do with its causes. Third, the introduction of a European-style taxation system caused misunderstanding and frustration to Malawians as it forced them to work at the very colonial farms that they generally despised. In Malawi, just like in many other colonies, the taxation system, which levied taxes on wives, huts, livestock, and land, essentially forced Africans to work on colonial farms, and the revenues generated by these taxes helped the colonies pay for their own colonization and save European governments money.[4] The British colonial government also required Malawians to work *for free* at the colonial estates to reduce costs for European farmers. This was called *thangata* (which literally means "to help" voluntarily, not under coercion). Under the *thangata* system, every year Malawians would be forced to work for one to two months on a colonial estate without pay. Needless to say, Malawians resented the colonial government and the British farmers a great deal for this.

In this chapter, I reflect historically, as a Malawian from Magomero, on the general theme of colonial violence in relation to Christian mission. I propose that because Christian mission has been closely based on white supremacy and the Europeans' desire to dominate the worlds they came into contact with, it has both used and served colonial violence against peoples of the world. This connection between mission and colonialism has been very well explored by such scholars as Andrew Walls, Lamin Sanneh, and Stephen Neill (whose conclusion in *Christian Mission and Colonialism*, that there is little to no collaboration between the mission and colonialism, gave birth to the critique being made here).[5] This chapter offers a history from below that suggests that colonial violence did not stop after the local people were converted to Christianity. Interracial violence continues today within the Christian communities of the world because racism and colonialism, in various forms, still exist. This chapter ultimately asks Christian leaders to confess these sins and change their ways instead of pretending that Christianity does not have this horrendous past.

Magomero Uprising

The central location of the events of January 1915 was Magomero (which happens to be my home). It was then—and remains today—a small village situated between Blantyre (forty miles to the south) and Zomba (twenty miles to the north), in southern Malawi. Blantyre back then was an emerging commercial town in the Shire Highlands, which was named after David Livingstone's birthplace in Scotland. It was also home to the Blantyre Mission of the Church of Scotland. Zomba was the colonial capital, where the government sat with its newly built barracks of the King's African Rifles. Magomero was the first European mission station in Malawi (and possibly within all of Central Africa). The Universities Mission to Central Africa (UMCA), under the leadership of Bishop Charles McKenzie, came to Magomero in 1861. David Livingstone, the famous Scottish missionary, himself chose Magomero to be their mission station. To Livingstone's dismay, they left Magomero in 1863, largely because of malaria and the unfortunate fact that a slave trade route ran through the village. Bishop McKenzie, the leader of the mission, died of malaria less than six months after arrival. During those six months and for the remaining time at Magomero, the missionaries spent a great deal of energy rescuing kidnapped Africans, an effort that felt rather counterproductive to them.[6] As a result, the UMCA relocated to Zanzibar in 1863, only to come back to Likoma Island on Lake Malawi in 1875.

Over thirty years after the UMCA arrived at Magomero, in 1892, David Livingstone's son-in-law, Alexander Low Bruce (who was married to David's eldest daughter, Agnes), bought up 170,000 acres of land in Malawi, a larger portion at Magomero, and the old mission station and a smaller portion at Likulezi, not too far away in Phalombe/Mulanje. The former UMCA mission station became a colonial property of the Livingstone family, who used the estate for growing coffee and cotton, among many other crops. In 1893, Bruce sent a relative of the Livingstone family, William Jervis Livingstone, to manage the estate at Magomero. Bruce's own two sons, David L. Bruce and Alexander L. Bruce, would have to wait until they were of age to manage the business. Alexander L. Bruce joined W. J. Livingstone at Magomero in 1908 before proceeding to settle down as manager at the Likulezi Estate. W. J. Livingstone managed the A. L. Bruce Estate at Magomero for twenty-two years, a period marked by extreme violence against local Malawians. He was, in fact, a good example of a violent colonial farmer who exploited locals at every opportunity. The estate took time to return a profit after making losses in the late 1890s, when he relied on the free labor of *thangata* to keep it financially afloat. Like many other colonial farmers, he believed he had to *break* the Indigenous Africans in order to assert his white colonial superiority and make them work for him for little to nothing. He followed the lead of Alexander L. Bruce, who was deeply suspicious of African Christians, especially those who had some education. W. J. Livingstone burned down schools and church buildings on and around the estate, some of which belonged to John Chilembwe's Providence Industrial Mission.[7]

In the weeks leading to January 1915, Chilembwe collaborated with a circle of other influential Malawians to organize a militia to try to return the country to local rule. On January 23, he sent part of his militia to Blantyre to steal ammunition while another part went to Magomero with strict instructions to bring Livingstone's head but to do no harm to the women and children. Thus, on that fateful Saturday night, Livingstone was killed, while his wife and children were saved and escorted to another colonial farm nearby. When Chilembwe's congregation gathered for service on Sunday, January 24, Chilembwe preached his sermon with W. J. Livingstone's severed head perched on a stick right next to the pulpit. The people celebrated—Chilembwe was their Moses, their Messiah, the liberator who broke the yoke of the Livingstones at Magomero. Having been successful, perhaps he could break the yoke of British colonialism in Malawi and possibly throughout southern Africa as well. By the end of that Sunday, however, the British government, whose colonial capital was only a short distance away, in Zomba, had learned of Livingstone's killing and prepared to quell the uprising.

Chilembwe's people understood the risk. They knew Chilembwe's actions against Livingstone were tantamount to declaring war on the colonial government and that there was virtually no way they could win. They understood that their mission was simply to "strike a blow and die" or "to be buried alive alternatively," and they believed that their "blood [would] surely mean something at last."[8] The British government did as Chilembwe and his followers expected. The one hundred soldiers who remained at the K.A.R. Barracks in Zomba and the groups of volunteer reserve troops (most of the soldiers had gone to the northern part of Lake Malawi to fight against the Germans in Tanzania) combed through southern Malawi, rounding up anyone connected to Chilembwe. Many men—calculating an actual figure is impossible—were summarily shot by firing squads and many more were imprisoned (for life with hard labor) at the Zomba Prison.[9] Chilembwe himself was killed on February 3, 1915, by a Malawian reserve soldier as he tried to escape to Mozambique.

The wider country of Malawi was relatively peaceful prior to World War I. The British colonial government had, for almost twenty-five years, tried to rule it with an iron fist—and it was this violently enforced peace that made the uprising possible. Harry Hamilton Johnston, the first governor of the British Protectorate of Central Africa beginning in 1891, had quashed any form of anticolonial resistance. By 1898, when he was sent off to establish peace in Uganda, he had killed every local chief who seemed to resist British rule. There was even talk of the Pax Britannica, the British violent pacification of Malawians to ensure submission to the Crown. By 1915, it seemed the British had everything under control. When World War I broke out, many of the colonial leaders, including Alexander L. Bruce, mobilized to the north of Malawi to fight against the Germans in neighboring Tanzania. Thus, it was a perfect time for Chilembwe to strike—most of the country was quiet and soldiers of the King's African Rifles were occupied in the north. However, it was also the most dangerous time for Chilembwe to act as the colonial government was mobilized for war and had no interest in negotiating. It was expected to act swiftly and decisively to make an example of Chilembwe and scare anyone else who had thoughts of uprising against it.[10]

While his uprising failed to change anything for the people of Malawi—and in a sense, it made colonial rule in Malawi even harsher—Chilembwe continues to be celebrated today for his courage to stand up against the violence of colonial rule. His uprising, which was based deeply in his Christian faith, initiated an anticolonial movement that sought to free Nyasaland from British colonialism. Similar Christian insurrections against colonialism would eventually help bring the entire colonial project to an end some fifty years later. Most of Chilembwe's coconspirators were Christians and many of them were leaders in African independent churches. For instance, Elliot Kamwana was a leader of the Watchtower movement, Philippo Chinyama led the African Baptist Church, Charles Domingo worked with the Seventh-Day Adventists as well as the Churches of Christ, and John Gray Kufa was an elder in the Blantyre Mission. All these men were educated to some extent, and that education had been provided by the missionaries. The education was necessary—local Christians needed to be able to read the Scriptures, but education also made them more useful to the colonial government. However, in providing education, the missionaries also planted seeds that would enable local Africans to fight for their independence. Later, in the 1950s and 1960s, the fight for independence in many African countries was led by mission-educated freedom fighters such as Kamuzu Banda of Malawi, Kenneth Kaunda of Zambia, and Robert Mugabe of Zimbabwe.

Christianity, Commerce, and Civilization

In 1859, long before Chilembwe's uprising, David Livingstone traversed the land that is now southern Malawi, dreaming of a possible British colony in that part of Africa. Livingstone's time in southern Malawi followed a successful visit to England between 1856 and 1857 during which he completed his popular 1858 monograph, *Missionary Travels,* and gave lectures in several cities and universities: Dublin, Manchester, Glasgow, Oxford, Leeds, Liverpool, Dundee, Halifax, Birmingham, and, of course, his home, Blantyre (near Glasgow).[11] The climax of the speaking tours was at Cambridge University on December 4, 1857, where he concluded his speech with a shout: "I beg to direct your attention to Africa. I know that in a few years I shall be cut off in that country, which is now open. Do not let it be shut again! I go back to Africa to try to make an open path for commerce and Christianity. Do you carry on the work which I have begun. I leave it with you!"[12]

In immediate response, some students at Oxford and Cambridge Universities formed a mission association that they called Oxford and Cambridge Mission. Later, Durham and Dublin Universities joined and the association changed

its name to the Universities' Mission to Central Africa (UMCA). Livingstone
returned to Central Africa straight away, finding his way up the Shire River and
seeing Lake Malawi for the first time in September 1859. His understanding of
mission in Africa was built on what he called the "Three Cs": Christianity, commerce, and civilization. He believed that Europe would Christianize, civilize, and
bring a new form of commerce (to replace the slave trade) to Africa. In one letter to a friend, a Professor Sedgwick, he stated, "All this [expedition's] ostensible
machinery has for its ostensible object the development of African trade and
the promotion of civilisation, [but] I hope may result in an English colony in the
healthy highlands of Central Africa."[13] The outworking of Livingstone's Three Cs
led to a fourth "C"—colonialism—that would eventually overshadow the first
three. Livingstone himself was convinced that it was "the mission of England to
colonize and to plant her Christianity with her sons [sic] on the broad earth
which the Lord has given to the children of men [sic]."[14] Indeed, it was Livingstone's desire for Britain to have a colony in Central Africa, and the Shire Highlands would be his ground zero. Between 1859 and 1860, he wrote extensively to
his dear friends Sir Thomas Maclear and Sir Roderick Murchison: " The interior
of this country ought to be colonised by our countrymen. . . . I see more in that
for the benefit of England and Africa than in any other plan. . . . I am becoming
everyday more convinced that we must have an English colony in the cotton-
producing districts of Africa. . . . Colonization from a country such as ours ought
to be one of hope, and not despair[;] . . . the performance of an imperative duty to
our blood, our country, our religion, and to humankind."[15]

In Livingstone's defense, Tim Jeal suggests that his ideas of colonialism were
quite different from what we understand to be colonialism today. He said that
to Livingstone, colony meant "British men and women had settled in distant and
previously thinly populated parts of the world, and were there reproducing all
that was best in the British way of life—a free press, trial by jury and government by representative institutions."[16] I am not convinced that Tim Jeal is correct. We know that the British Raj in India was established in 1858, long after
British colonialism had started in India through the British East India Company
and long before the so-called Scramble for Africa started. I doubt that the Raj
was about "reproducing all that was best in the British way of life." Thirty
years after Livingstone brought the UMCA to Magomero, in 1891, Malawi became
a British protectorate and in the following year, Livingstone's daughter, Agnes,
and her husband, Alexander Low Bruce, acquired the UMCA land. My great-great-
grandfather, Mtimawanzako Nacho, settled close to Magomero in the early days
of the Bruce Estates.[17] In 1885, he studied at Stewart's College in Edinburgh, Scotland, as one of the first Africans from the Blantyre Mission to train for church
leadership and, of course, to improve his English so he could help his missionary-
sponsor, David Clements Scott, in the making of his Nyanja dictionary. He spent
almost the entire first half of the twentieth century trying to serve his church,

the Church of Central Africa Presbyterian (which was born largely out of Scottish missionary work in Central Africa), while contending with his neighbors, the Livingstone family at the Bruce Estates. This continued up to 1945 when he, as an older man, took his life because, just like Chilembwe thirty years before him, he could not take colonialism anymore. Alexander L. Bruce, on the other hand, became a very influential member of the colonial legislative council as he was one of the major British landowners in Malawi. He ultimately lived in Malawi for forty years before returning to the United Kingdom in 1948 (he died there in 1954).

Africa for the African

Chilembwe's mentor, a Derbyshire man by the name Joseph Booth (1851–1932), had already spent some years as a missionary in New Zealand and Australia when he arrived in Malawi in 1892 and started the Zambezi Industrial Mission.[18] His operational principle was to "train and cultivate native converts' spiritual gifts and lead to *self-reliant action* in preaching and planting industrial missions in the 'regions beyond.'"[19] Because of his anticolonial ideas, he was almost always in bad books with other missionaries in southern Malawi. He also inevitably found himself out of favor with the colonial government of Harry Hamilton Johnstone, probably because he was an independent and lone missionary of a small network of churches and tended to identify more with Africans than with his fellow Europeans.

In 1896, Booth visited South Africa to promote his vision of the African Christian Union, especially among the Zulu Christians, who had some connections with the other missionaries in Malawi. As a white man, however, he was met with extreme suspicion. In the 1890s, the Zulus had a reminder for anyone wanting to deal with white people: "Bishop Colenso is dead."[20] That was to say that since the only white man they could trust, Bishop Colenso, was dead, it was of no use trusting any other white man because white men—both missionaries and colonial farmers—were all violent "men of guns." The Zulus challenged Mataka, Booth's Malawian companion on the trip that, saying that "there was no white man living who was a safe guide for native African people. . . . Bishop Colenso of Natal, *Sobantu*, adviser of Cetewayo, was the last of the race of true white man friends, and . . . no matter what Mataka thought, no living white man, whether carrying guns or not, would in the end, when war came, be friends of black men."[21]

While in South Africa, Booth learned more about Colenso, which helped him galvanize his thoughts into a fiery anticolonialist manifesto, entitled *Africa for the African,* that he published in the United States in 1897. Of course, it was immediately banned in Malawi, but Booth was unfazed. Back in Malawi in 1899, Booth led a group of Malawians to petition Queen Victoria for education, political participation, and justice on behalf of all Africans. The petition, which was delivered to Alfred Sharpe, second governor of the protectorate, demanded that hut-tax (a form of land tax introduced by British Government in their African colonies levied on a "per hut" basis) revenue be spent solely on education to the point of equality with an average British education, that the government pledge not to surrender the protectorate to any control other than a native government, and that the protectorate be restored to native ownership and government within twenty-one years. Booth concluded the petition with the hope that the queen would wish to "put into practice the Christian precept, 'Therefore whatsoever ye would that man should do unto you, do ye so unto them.'"[22] Naturally, the colonial administration was not happy with this petition. An attempt was made to arrest and deport Booth but he escaped to Mozambique before he could be arrested. He remained there until 1900, when he was allowed to return on condition that he stay away from politics. Of course, he could not keep the promise, and he was finally deported from Malawi in 1902, and in 1907, officially barred from ever returning. Of course, by the time he returned to settle back in Britain in 1915, he had been deported by the British government (from Malawi, Cape Colony, Basutoland, and other places) altogether seven times.

Booth must be commended for speaking against colonialism while the Scramble for Africa was still in progress. He paid heavily for it—those seven deportations were for a reason. His theological persuasions were inconsistent (he was a Seventh-Day Adventist for a while and later became a Watch Tower missionary), which worsened the situation. However, his anticolonial stance was the trademark of his ministry. He stated, "The ingenious heartlessness to which the modern spirit of greed can descend in the exploitation of African ignorance and helplessness. Whether we look at the government, mining capitalists or the planter class the spirit is the same. . . . Even missionaries, many of them need teaching that the African is inferior in opportunity only."[23] Charles Domingo, another Malawian disciple of Booth's brought this critique home in a letter sent to Booth in 1911:

> There is too much failure among all Europeans in Nyassaland. The Three Combined Bodies: Missionaries, Government and Companies or Gainers of money do form the same rule to look upon a Native with mockery eyes. It sometimes startle us to see that the Three Combined Bodies are from Europe, and along with them there is a title "CHRISTNDOM." And to compare or make a comparison between the MASTER of the title and His Servants, it pushes any African away from believing the Master of the title. If we had power enough to communicate ourselves to Europe, we would advise them not to call themselves "CHRISTNDOM" but "Europeandom." . . . Therefore the life of The Three Combined Bodies is altogether too cheaty, too thefty, too mockery. Instead of "Give," they say "Take away from."[24]

The Flag and the Bible

For the colonized, it is usually impossible to separate mission from colonialism. Indeed, for most Africans, mission and colonialism were two sides of the same coin of *imperialism*. If there is something we can learn from Magomero, it is why missionaries have been called the "religious arm of the colonial empires . . . the ideological shock troops for the colonial invasion whose zealotry had blinded them,"[25] "the spiritual wing of secular imperialism,"[26] or even "imperialism at prayer."[27] Just as the missionary enterprise was closely associated with the imperial expansion of the West, the word *missionary* was also attached to this expansion effort and often taken to imply as "the earliest foot-soldiers of colonial empires"[28] or "colonial administrators."[29] Yet historian and missiologist Andrew Walls is rather kind in his assessment, stating, "The missionary movement from the West was a semi-detached part of the European migration—semi-detached because its essential motor derived not from the economic, political, and strategic interests that produced the migration, but from the nature of the Christian message."[30] However, in the eyes of most of the colonized, the missionary made way for the colonizers; the Christian message was used to pave way for the colonizer and reduce resistance from the Indigenous people. Reading between the lines of mission history in most of sub-Saharan Africa, it becomes evident that European missionaries changed their disposition toward Africans after the formal partitioning of Africa at the Berlin Conference (1884–1885). Prior to the "scramble" that the conference produced, missionaries depended on African goodwill to survive in Africa. They had to be humble, to submit to African kings, and to ask for permission from local chiefs to enter a village and settle among their people. They had to pay taxes to African chiefs to access their roads, buy their foods, and evangelize their peoples. But once the Scramble for Africa started, many European missionaries employed their superiority with abandon. They no longer had to submit to African leaders (for those leaders were now under European rule) and could therefore refuse to pay taxes with impunity. It was the famous Church Mission Society (CMS) missionary to East Africa, Bishop Alfred Tucker, who, in 1890, wrote, "We are going forth on our long journey [to Buganda] neither depending upon not trusting in the arm of flesh, nor courting the patronage of the world, *much less that of an African potentate*."[31]

A result of this changed context is that the missionaries' efforts suddenly became more successful. The Scramble for Africa made it clear that Christianity was the religion of the colonizing powers and, as such, it brought many benefits, including education, security, and health care. Where the missionaries had labored for years with little success, colonialism brought in the converts. For example, Kenneth Scott Latourette, writing about Malawi, says that the Livingstonia Mission, founded by the Free Church of Scotland in 1874 and led by Robert Laws, could only point to fifteen converts in 1890.[32] The next year, British rule was extended over the area. By 1914, there were 49 new missionaries and 9,500 communicants had been added in addition to 900 schools, 1,600 teachers, and 57,000 students.[33] Of CMS in the Mamboya, Berega, and Nyangala areas of Tanzania, Thomas Beidelman writes that in 1904, after nearly twenty-eight years of work and before the German pacification process started, there were 11 African teachers, 109 baptized members, 14 catechists, 32 schools, and 738 students. Ten years later, in 1914, following German pacification, they reported 74 African teachers, 355 baptized members, 1,057 catechists, 125 schools, and 3,077 students.[34]

Mission and colonialism have been strange bedfellows starting in the fifteenth century, when Europeans became aware of the wider world beyond North Africa and western Asia. Mission, as Christians speak of it today, is a European creation (of course, the same can be said of both its ecclesiology and theology). The word *mission* itself did not mean "the sending of Christians from Christian lands to non-Christian lands to convert the 'heathens' or 'pagans'" until after the Reformation. It was the Jesuits (the Society of Jesus was formed in 1540) who first used the term the way we do today. David Bosch points out that many of the modern connotations of the word can be dated only back to the sixteenth century. He adds that the new usage was introduced by Ignatius of Loyola and the Jesuits to designate ecclesiastical agents who were sent to regions being colonized by the kings of Spain and Portugal to propagate the reign of Christ.[35] An intimate connection between colonialism and this new conception of Christian mission was thereby established. "The new word, 'mission,' is historically linked indissolubly with the colonial era and with the idea of a magisterial commissioning. The term presupposes an established church in Europe with dispatched delegates to convert overseas people and was such an attendant phenomenon of European expansion."[36]

Contemporary mission is a European creation of a particular era when Europeans were becoming aware the wider world beyond the bounds of Western Europe. That world, in the minds of the Europeans, needed to be Christianized and civilized by Europeans who were lucky to have been chosen to be both Christians and civilized people of that time. Beginning in the West Indies, moving down to Latin America, then up to North America, and, simultaneously, into Asia and Africa, Europeans worked hard to Christianize and civilize the world. At the center of that effort was the belief that Europeans were destined to be superior to all the other peoples of the world. Mission, understood in this Eurocentric sense, could be easily used to serve European interests around the world. For these reasons, the very concept of mission as we understand it today is intrinsically built on racism and white supremacy.

The rebellion in Magomero is just one example of what happens when mission and colonialism become one. Unfortunately, the story Magomero is a synecdoche of the general history of the spread of Christianity throughout the past

500 years (I am intentionally leaving out the Crusades). This is a story of my countryman, John Chilembwe, a significant part of which takes place in my village, touching my family and including my great-great-grandfather. The story also includes David Livingstone and his offspring, with another British missionary, Joseph Booth, somewhere in the web of connections, revealing the problematic theology and praxis of European missionary work in Africa. That David Livingstone's mission station became his daughter's colonial estate where his grandson persecuted local Christians, burning down their churches and schools and forcing them to work on the estate without pay shows the intertwined legacies of the mission of God and the mission of empires—the problem *of defining Christian mission through the praxis of colonialism.* After the murder of W. J. Livingstone, the British government killed many Malawian Christians and jailed many more, including several British missionaries who sympathized with the Africans, especially those of the smaller denominations, such as the Churches of Christ. The government passed laws that required all the major churches to have white leaders.[37] Moreover, any new churches that required registration had to have Europeans as leaders. All Black-led churches were closely monitored to make sure there would be no repeat of Chilembwe's uprising.

To convince those who, like Stephen Neill, want to believe that European mission had little to do with colonialism, we can point to secular literary sources, especially those written by Africans during the colonial era. Fiction of mid-twentieth-century Africa is unified and clear about how Africans understood and spoke about the relationship between mission and colonialism. More often than not, missionaries and colonialists helped each other's causes. This is a point that Africans have long emphasized in the stories they have told about colonialism. Mongo Beti's *The Poor Christ of Bomba,* which was published in Cameroon in 1956, tells a story of Catholic missionaries and French colonialism in 1930s Cameroon.[38] Beti's story is, in essence, a critique of the French presence in Cameroon. The book tells of a French missionary, Father Drumont, who spends twenty unfruitful years working among the Tala people of Cameroon, during which time the evils of colonialism become increasingly apparent both to him and to the Tala. The crescendo of Beti's critique of colonialism comes when Father Drumont, having reached the end of his twenty years of Catholic missionary work in Cameroon and while preparing to return to France as a defeated missionary, tells Monsieur Vidal, a new colonial administrator, "I can stay in this country along with you, associated with you, and thus assist you to colonize it, with dreadful consequences; softening up the country ahead of you, and protecting your rear—for that is how you envisage (the role of the missionary). Or else, I can truly Christianize the country; in which case I'd better keep out of the way, as long as you are still here."[39] Many missionaries caved to the demands of the colonialists. Some fought against them and, generally speaking, lost. Many others, like Father Drumont, ended up willfully leaving the mission field, afraid that evangelization only helped colonization gain a foothold on the continent.

Beti's Father Drumont is correct. It is impossible to truly Christianize a people and colonize them at the same time. The gospel of Christ liberates and humanizes people. Colonialism does the opposite: it dominates and dehumanizes people. When the colonized are fellow Christians, it is an expression of Christian violence against other Christians. This is the ambiguity of Christian mission for most of the past five centuries—that it succeeded through the help of colonialism. However, in the development of World Christianity as we have witnessed in the decades after the 1960s, it was only after the collapse of European colonialism that Christianity expanded in Africa. This is perhaps because anticolonial seeds were planted in the conversion of people to Christianity. For many African countries, the Christian faith became the very tool that destroyed colonialism. The combination of the Christian message and education produced educated Christians who, like Chilembwe and Domingo (with the help of some missionaries such as Booth), believed that it was their Christian duty to fight against colonialism. Chilembwe's time among African Americans in Virginia had taught him the dangers of white rule, the importance of civil resistance, and the need for sacrifice to maintain independence.[40] This message resonated with many fellow Africans in Malawi to the point that Chilembwe's uprising was a form of Christian uprising against colonialism. Chilembwe, like many other converts who died resisting the Scramble for Africa, emboldened other African Christians, who would fight against colonialism in the 1950s and 1960s. This struggle for independence by local Christians against colonizers also represents Christian violence against other Christians, which is a recurring dynamic within World Christianity.

If my suggestion that converting people to Christianity also empowers them with the seeds of the ability to resist being colonized is correct, a great deal of the history of world Christianity must be rewritten for, while scholars of World Christianity might appreciate the many Western missionaries who braved the seas to evangelize the world, their work would not be complete without the help, or even the resistance, of the many who sacrificed their lives for the freedom of their people. People like Chilembwe were often labeled enemies of the colonial government and the missionaries—my great-great-grandfather's conflicts with the Bruce Estates made him an enemy of the colonial government. However, it is the resistance of these men, often passive as it was, that have us a type of Christianity that is uniquely African. Their keen interest in a de-Europeanized Christianity brought about a Christianity that is indeed, in many ways, foreign to Europeans. Unfortunately, even today, a great deal of mission history is written by Westerners and tends to focus on Western missionaries. Yet we know that, for example, Africa has been evangelized by Africans. It is my hope that new history books will emerge to shine the light on the African agents of Christianity.

Conclusion

Christianity, being the predominant religion of the empires of Western societies—Spanish, Portuguese, British, and American—has taken part in their imperial atrocities. One might say that it has only been used by those empires for their own purposes and interests, but one can also argue that Christianity was a knowing accomplice, often using the might of the empires to its advantage. Contemporary World Christianity continues to be an agent of globalization even as localized forms of Christianity can resist Western expressions of Christianity (such as evangelicalism). This resistance is largely because of Western Christianity's ambivalence concerning issues involving slavery, colonialism, racism, and white supremacy. Western denominations such as the Church of England seem reluctant to acknowledge the part they played in the slave trade and colonialism more broadly. As Azariah Francis-Williams shows us, even after they were forced to admit to this history, they cannot abandon the systemic racism that has been a constitutive part of their identity quickly enough.[41] In this fast-changing postimperial, neocolonial world, Christian leaders would do well to acknowledge Christianity's violent past as they seek new ways to share their faith peacefully. Those of us who are Christian cannot remain silent about European Christianity's slave trading and its violent colonial past. We need to boldly investigate these histories in the spirit of the Apostle Paul, who wrote that if one part of the body of Christ suffers, then the whole body suffers with it. Only then can we begin to heal.

NOTES

1. Malawi is a landlocked country in the southeastern part of Africa. Like many other African countries, it came into existence as a nation-state following the colonization of the tribal kingdoms in that area in 1891. The British called it *Nyasaland* after David Livingstone had wrongly named a local lake *Nyasa* in 1859. "Nyasa" is a Yao word for "lake," and Lake Nyasa is, for locals, "Lake." The country of Nyasaland changed its name to Malawi at independence in 1964. *Malawi* means "flames of fire," recognizing the Maravi iron smelters who settled the land around 1500 A.D. In this chapter, I use *Malawi* except for the few times where *Nyasaland* must be used.

2. John McCracken, *A History of Malawi, 1859–1966* (Suffolk: James Currey, 2012), 131.

3. The British government had recruited many Malawian young men to be involved in their wars across southern Africa since the 1890s. In World War I, 1 million Africans were conscripted to be porters of the British army across the colonies of Britain. Out of these, 95,000 Africans died.

4. See Leigh Gardner, *Taxing Colonial Africa: The Political Economy of British Imperialism* (Oxford: Oxford University Press, 2012).

5. Stephen Neill, *Colonialism and Christian Missions* (New York: McGraw Hill, 1966).

6. Bishop McKenzie died in January 1862 and was replaced by Bishop William Tozer, who initially assessed that the UMCA had wasted time and energy in Malawi and resolved to move the mission to Zanzibar. See Landeg White, *Magomero: Portrait of an African Village* (New York: Cambridge University Press, 1987), 67.

7. These industrial missions were organized to provide vocational training to Africans in addition to converting them to Christianity. In calling his mission the Providence Industrial Mission, Chilembwe followed the lead of Joseph Booth, his mentor, whose mission was called the Zambezi Industrial Mission and is remembered for the agricultural training it provided to Malawians in the 1890s. Such missions believed that vocational training would improve the lives of the Africans.

8. George Simeon Mwase and Robert I. Rotberg, *Strike a Blow and Die: The Classic Story of the Chilembwe Rising* (Cambridge, MA: Harvard University Press, 1975), 36.

9. Mwase's book, *Strike a Blow and Die*, was based on accounts of his interviews conducted in 1932 with people who had been jailed in Zomba in 1915.

10. Of course, the uprising caught international attention. Chilembwe, himself, is mentioned in Theodore Lothrop Stoddard's 1920 novel, *The Rising Tide of Color against White World Supremacy*, where he is described as an Ethiopian preacher who engaged in a bitterly antiwhite propaganda, asserting that Africa belonged to the Black man and the white man was an intruder. In discussing Chilembwe's uprising, Stoddard first celebrates that "the Whites acted with great vigor, the poorly armed insurgents were quickly scattered, and Chilembwe himself was soon hunted and killed." In conclusion, he says, "In itself, [Chilembwe's] incident was of slight importance, but, taken in connection with much else, it does not augur well for the [white supremacist imperial] future" (Theodore Lothrop Stoddard, *The Rising Tide of Color against White World-Supremacy* [New York: Charles Scribner's Sons, 1921], 99).

11. David Livingstone, *Missionary Travels and Researches in South Africa* (New York: Harper & Bros, 1858).

12. Meriel Buxton, *David Livingstone* (Basingstoke: Palgrave, 2001), 106.

13. Quoted in Oliver Ransford, *David Livingstone: The Dark Interior* (London: J. Murray, 1978), 159.

14. Ransford, *David Livingstone*, 159.

15. Ransford, *David Livingstone*, 160.

16. Jeal, *Livingstone*, 188.

17. Mtimawanzako Nacho begat Margaret Nacho, who begat my grandmother, Abiti Uledi, who begat Jonathan Kwiyani, my father.

18. For a short critical biography of Joseph Booth, see Harry W. Langworthy, "Joseph Booth, Prophet of Radical Change in Central and South Africa, 1891–1915," *Journal of Religion in Africa* 16, no. 1 (1986): 22–43.

19. George Shepperson and Thomas Price, *Independent African: John Chilembwe and the Origins, Setting and Significance of the Nyasaland Native Rising of 1915*, Kachere Monographs (Blantyre: Christian Literature Association in Malawi, 2000), 26.

20. Bishop John William Colenso was born in Cornwall in 1814 and died in Durban in 1883. He was the first bishop of Natal and, as his biographies say, he was a fervent defender of the Zulu against both the Boer and British aggressions, including during the Anglo-Zulu War of 1879. He also defended other African tribes, in the process gaining the title *Sobantu*—the father of the people. He was widely regarded as the last honest white man. Colenso's death at a time when the Scramble for Africa was brewing made it even more difficult for the Africans to trust Europeans. Several biographical accounts were written about Bishop Colenso. See, for instance, George William Cox, *The Life of John William Colenso, D.D., Bishop of Natal* (London: W. Ridgway, 1888).

21. Shepperson and Price, *Independent African*, 71.

22. Langworthy, "Joseph Booth," 31–32.

23. Shepperson and Price, *Independent African*, 110.

24. John McCracken, *Politics and Christianity in Malawi: The Impact of the Livingstonia Mission in the Northern Province*, Kachere Monographs (Zomba: Kachere Series, 2008), 216.

25. Edward E Andrews, "Christian Missions and Colonial Empires Reconsidered: A Black Evangelist in West Africa, 1766–1816," *Journal of Church and State* 51, no. 4 (2009): 663–664.

26. John D. Omer-Cooper, A. E. Afigbo, E. A. Ayandele, R. J. Gavin, and Robin Palmer, *The Making of Modern Africa: The Growth of African Civilisation*, vol. 2 (New York: Longman, 1968).

27. Lamin O. Sanneh, *Translating the Message: The Missionary Impact on Culture*, American Society of Missiology Series (Maryknoll, NY: Orbis Books, 1989), 88.

28. John H. Darch, *Missionary Imperialists?: Missionaries, Government and the growth of the British Empire in the Tropics, 1860–1885* (Colorado Springs: Paternoster, 2009), 1.

29. Mongo Beti, *The Poor Christ of Bomba* (Long Grove, IL: Waveland, 1971), 153.

30. Frieder Ludwig and J. Kwabena Asamoah-Gyadu, *African Christian Presence in the West: New Immigrant Congregations and Transnational Networks in North America and Europe* (Trenton, NJ: Africa World Press, 2011), 409.

31. Alfred Tucker to Lang, June 11, 1890, G3 A5/06 CMS Archives, Oxford (my emphasis).

32. Kenneth Scott Latourette, *The Great Century in the Americas, Australia and Africa A.D.1800–A.D.1914*, vol. 5 of *A History of the Expansion of Christianity* (New York: Harper & Brothers, 1943), 394.

33. Latourette, *Great Century*, 394.

34. T. O. Beidelman, *Colonial Evangelism: A Socio-Historical Study of an East African Mission at the Grassroots* (Bloomington: Indiana University Press, 1982), 77–79.

35. David J. Bosch, *Transforming Mission: Paradigm Shifts in Theology of Mission*, American Society of Missiology Series (Maryknoll, NY: Orbis Books, 1991), 228.

36. Bosch, *Transforming Mission*, 228.

37. See, for instance, Ulf Strohbehn, *Pentecostalism in Malawi: A History of the Apostolic Faith Mission in Malawi, 1931–1994*. Kachere Theses (Zomba, Malawi: Kachere Series, 2005), 63–64.

38. Beti, *Poor Christ of Bomba*. Other books that can shed a helpful light on this topic include Chinua Achebe, *Things Fall Apart* (New York: McDowell, 1959).

39. Beti, *Poor Christ of Bomba*, 153.

40. George Shepperson's biography of Chilembwe is titled *Independent African* for this reason.

41. Azariah D. A. France-Williams, *Ghost Ship: Institutional Racism and the Church of England* (London: SCM Press, 2020).

8

Religions and the Production of Affect in Caste-Based Societies

SUNDER JOHN BOOPALAN

"*Tch Tch*": An Introduction to Affect

In 2011, I attended a public lecture co-sponsored by the Hindu students' association at Princeton University. During the event, one of the presenters asserted that Dalits were peddling stories of false victimhood in order to break India's unity. A Dalit activist contested this Hindu nationalist claim during the Q & A by offering the example of the Khairlanji murders of 2006, when a family of Dalits was massacred by a casteist mob in broad daylight.[1] In response to the mention of "Khairlanji"—a "household word" today among those who understand how caste works[2]—members of the largely dominant caste audience started heckling the Dalit speaker, asking, "Where is the evidence?" That is a question that only dominant-caste persons, who are unaffected by caste-based violence, have the luxury of asking.

As the heckling continued, a moderator of the discussion came and grabbed the microphone from the hands of the Dalit speaker. While this effort to silence him is certainly problematic, what struck me was the palpable affect that surrounded the activist as he spoke—the loud "*tch tch*" that echoed around the room. "*Tch tch*" is a primal affective sound that most Indians would be familiar with. It is quite remarkable that this sound, while not captured by a particular word, conveys a wide range of negative meanings, expressing a mix of displeasure, disgust, and dismissal. The "*tch tch*" began with the woman in front of me and soon caught on as several heads moved in disapproval and dismissal of the questioner. It was the movement of this negative affect through the room that prompted the moderator to come up and grab the microphone. It is the very same negative affect, which spread through the room like wildfire, that gave away the dominant caste composition of the audience.

The majority of Christians in India are converts from historically marginalized communities, namely Dalits and tribals. "Dalit" is the name chosen for themselves by communities that were historically discriminated against and cruelly treated as "untouchables." Tribals (also called *adivasis*, meaning "first peoples") are India's Indigenous communities. In the act of conversion to Christianity, these communities moved out of the abject places to which they were assigned by dominant-caste religious logic. This moving "out of place" produced, and continues to produce, the negative affect that forms the basis for much anti-Christian violence in India today. That negative affect—based on social status and power—is also transnational. Persons with (South Asian) Indian heritage often think and feel with caste-inflected emotional and intellectual registers even when they are as far away from India as Princeton.

This chapter argues that events of violence against Dalit and tribal Christians are better understood as events produced by caste-inflected affect. While obvious in some respects, readers would do well to focus on the affective terms that appear throughout the chapter. These affective terms—shame, pride, humiliation, honor, betrayal, disgrace, family values, happiness, contempt, enjoy, resentment, exotic, smell, foul—serve as guideposts for understanding the intersections between caste, tribe, affect, and violence. While the first part of the chapter is devoted to the negative affect produced by dominant-caste religious logic, the latter part also argues that converts' positive affect produced by another set of religious logics assists in encountering and transforming the negative affect. This chapter thus highlights the role of society's emotional life as a key factor in interpersonal relations.

Affect: Nowhere and Everywhere

Abraham, a South Indian friend of mine, boarded a train in Maryland along with his family. It was a busy morning and they were taking their seats. A white person looked at them and remarked, "You guys are smelling like your food." Abraham was quick to look back and say, "You have really a good nose, almost not human; by the way, we had pancakes for breakfast." The incident is both tragic and humorous. The incident is tragic because Abraham and his family had to endure what may have been racialized harassment but humorous because the stranger likely did not expect a comeback that destabilized the discriminatory logic. If it was racialized harassment, Abraham and his family would have found it extremely difficult to prove the intent had they reported the incident. "You guys are smelling like your food" might simply be interpreted as smelling like pancakes, and, perhaps, even a compliment from a person who loves pancakes. But to the person who experienced the harassment, the tone, the inflection, and the negative affect from the white person would have conveyed without a doubt the racialized nature of the encounter. Acts of discrimination are better understood as conditioned by affect. Affect is everywhere, and yet, when it comes to proving malevolent intent, it seems to be nowhere.

Despite the impact on persons' physical, emotional, and mental well-being, caste-based and race-based wrongs are difficult to prove. Unless we understand "how injustice comes to be lived affectively," violence will always slip away from being fully understood.[3] Violence is better understood when attention is paid to such affects and how they are differently felt and framed in emerging postcolonial nation states that get away with internal colonial violence under the guise of national unity or some other seemingly benign pretense.

In landscapes with histories of oppression, emotion plays a significant role in producing subjects.[4] Dominant religious (and ideological) frameworks in such landscapes condition subjectivity in such a way that feelings of shame, disgust, honor, and pride are dispersed differently based on people's caste and tribal identities. Dalit theorist Gopal Guru, for instance, uses the affective category of humiliation to analyze the violence against Dalits.[5] Joel Lee, an anthropologist who works on caste and religion, observes rightly that "caste functions, among other things, as a spatial-sensory order."[6] Caste, in other words, produces "particular configurations and concentrations of visual, aural, olfactory, gustatory, and tactile materiality."[7] Lee's commentary is also helpful because it indicates how caste informs global ideas of India's societal relations. Lee notes, for instance, how Annie Besant, a figure otherwise known for her anti-imperialism, nevertheless, in referring to Dalit children noted—based on the prevailing dominant-caste derogatory logic—that Dalit children "are ill-odorous and foul with the liquor and strong-smelling food, out of which for generations they have been built up."[8] Such tactile and material understandings of caste inform Indian realities both then and now.

Sarbeswar Sahoo offers an account of violence that emphasizes the extraphysical dimensions of violence. Indeed, the emotional and intersubjective aspects of violence are crucial to understand the sociopolitical consequences of affect.[9] While physical violence involves the "manipulation and destruction of the body," "intersubjective violence can consist of a word, a gesture or a look either between individuals or as supported by institutions. Such violence can inspire fear, strike at the core of one's identity, or make a way of living and being impossible even without physical intimidation or destruction."[10] Affect enables one to understand this range of violence.

Affect-Laden Encounters with Caste

The 2020 Netflix series *Never Have I Ever*, created by Mindy Kaling and Lang Fisher, centers on a first-generation Indian American girl, Devi. Kamala, Devi's cousin from India, lives with Devi's family as she pursues her Ph.D. Kamala dates Steve, an Asian American man. Their romance begins to get complicated when a groom for an "arranged marriage" lingers on the horizon. "Arranged marriage" is code for marrying into the same caste rank. While Kamala and Steve seem well suited for each other, Kamala feels uncontrollably pulled into the caste vortex. Episode 3 captures an interesting verbal exchange—laden with affect—between Steve and Kamala:

STEVE: Your parents can't force you to marry this guy.

KAMALA: They're not forcing me. I have a choice between my family and a life of shame that will disgrace me and my descendants for generations.

STEVE: That's bullshit.

KAMALA: Maybe it is, but I can't betray my family. I'm sorry.

STEVE: I can't believe that a woman who was brave enough to travel halfway around the world to pursue her dreams would allow anyone to dictate who she can be with.[11]

The exchange between Kamala and Steve captures the global reach of caste. Indeed, "a woman who was brave enough to travel halfway around the world to pursue her dreams" finds herself choosing an arrangement dictated by caste. It is important that the choice is, in her own words, one that is influenced by affective categories such as "shame" and "disgrace." The remark that she would live "a life of shame that will disgrace [her] and [her] descendants for generations" if she does not accept an arranged marriage certainly fits a comedy-drama plot line. But Kamala's words simultaneously reveal how affect conditions life choices and how caste drives such affect even outside India. "Disgrace" and "shame" are affective categories that have violent sociopolitical consequences.

While caste is assumed throughout the series, the noticeable absence in naming caste is worth highlighting. It is akin to what Shefali Chandra notes about many academic studies on caste that "have notoriously claimed to understand caste while actually finding ways to disappear it."[12] Indeed as Chandra further notes, "the fiction of Indian democracy plots 'caste' as a collection of atavistic religious rituals, hence obscuring the systematic yoking of upper- [dominant-] caste interests with Indian modernity."[13] In this sense, it might be said that the fictional television series inadvertently highlights the fiction of Indian democracy and the corresponding transnational transportation of such fiction overseas. It is hard to tell if television fiction becomes real-life horror or vice versa.

Documentary filmmaker and reporter, Kavita Pillay, in an essay for WGBH, Boston's National Public Radio platform, confesses, "I was born and brought up in America, and my Indian-American friends and I never discuss caste."[14] Referring to caste-based conventions in the United States, Pillay observes with a somber note, "It turns out that there are Indians who still embrace their caste status, even in America."[15] The particular caste convention Pillay is referring to is the Nair Service Society of North America (NSSONA), which is essentially a gathering of scores of Nair (a dominant caste in the south Indian state of Kerala) families. Pillay's commentary is insightful:

This was a gathering of people of the same caste, however, and beliefs about caste lay deep within what anthropologists call the "cultural iceberg." The caste system came up, explicitly and unexpectedly, at an event billed as a "Youth Seminar." It was a rambling, half-hour lecture intertwining religious history with what was meant to be career advice, led by a man closer to middle age than "youth." . . . The man continued, making no mention of Dalits, the lowly outcastes formerly known as "Untouchables" in the religious and social hierarchy of Hindus. "This casteism is not to be taken literally," he added. "This system is followed throughout the world, including U.S." He segued to comparing the caste system to the structure of a company—with manual labor at the bottom, management and sales in the middle and upper strata, and executives at the top. It was a muddled explanation, both a justification of caste and a dismissal of its realities. There was no time for questions at the end, and it was not clear whether anyone present disagreed with his stance.[16]

Pillay's commentary is insightful because it offers a window into the active world of caste-based associations in the United States. The NSSONA is not the only caste-based association in the United States—there are several. For instance, the American Telugu Association is dominated by the Reddy caste group.[17] Another Telugu group, the Telugu Association of North America (TANA), is a diaspora organization dominated by another dominant caste group, the Kammas.[18] The caste composition of the organization may not be apparent to an uncritical reader just as an uncritical reader will miss how *Never Have I Ever* is thoroughly inflected by caste. If one reads TANA's self-description under "About Us" on their webpage, the words *caste* and *Kamma* do not appear at all. The words *culture* and *community*, however, appear frequently. *Culture* is often code for caste. When one hovers from "About Us" to "Matrimonials Listing" under "Services," one will readily notice the explicit mention of particular caste identities. In addition, the phrases "Indian values" and "family values" make several appearances.[19] These values are not dissimilar from the ones that Kamala is afraid of "betraying"—recall her conversation with Steve—and Anderson Jeremiah rightly notes that "caste prejudices do not end in the Indian subcontinent, but travel wherever people go."[20]

According to caste logic, each caste community is necessarily either "higher" or "lower." Two persons are "equal" only if they belong to the same caste rank. Whether acknowledged or not, this is the logic that informs such caste-based conventions. As I note in my other work, "in marrying from the same caste, therefore, Indians inherit and perpetuate a discriminatory caste system that undergirds othering and exclusion."[21] This enables one to better understand how seemingly benign phrases—such as "family values," "culture," and "national unity"—can and do function as catalysts for caste-based violence.

The chapter now turns to the politics of marriages based on caste ranking, the affect that accompanies those politics, and the sociopolitical consequences of that affect.

Caste-Inflected Affect as Producer of Violence

In India, caste-based associations continue to order the murders of people who are perceived to violate caste-based norms and feelings in seeking marriage partnerships outside their caste. Such murders are popularly called "honor killings."[22] These acts of physical violence derive their sanctioning power from affective categories such as disgrace and shame if the affected part is casteist, on the one hand, and pride and honor, on the other, if the affected party is the one who transgresses the boundaries of caste.

Consider a few cases from the South Indian state of Tamil Nadu. In 2015, Gokulraj, a Dalit engineering student, was kidnapped by a dominant caste gang for dating a dominant-caste girl. His beheaded body was found near a railway track.[23] In 2016, a dominant-caste couple entered the home of a Kalpana, a Dalit woman, and hacked her to death because her younger brother had eloped with the couple's daughter.[24] In another honor killing, in 2016, Shankar, a Dalit man, and his wife, Kausalya, who was from a dominant caste, were hacked to death by a mob in broad daylight.[25] In all these cases, the aggressors acted ostensibly to protect their honor, which had been disgraced by transgressive Dalit agency.

In 2018, a twenty-four-year-old Dalit Christian man, Pranay Perumalla, was hacked to death in the South Indian state of Telangana. The father of Pranay's wife, Amrutha,—perceiving his dominant-caste honor to have been violated—hired hitmen to murder Pranay. The couple were expecting a child. Amrutha's father deemed the birth of a child through an intercaste union humiliating. Superintendent of police AV Ranganath, who was overseeing the case at that time, told reporters, "Rao [the father] came to know that Amrutha was pregnant and Rao thought if she delivered the baby, it would be all the more humiliating for him."[26] Apparently, the father's anger was further fueled by the fact that the couple had hosted a celebratory party. When viewed through the logic of caste, the happiness of a couple transgressing caste norms seems to be directly proportional to the negative affect felt by those who perceive their honor as being violated by others' freedom from caste.

Though it ended by murder, Pranay's freedom to transgress caste boundaries may be seen as a consequence of his Christian faith. Pranay's father, Balaswamy, in an interview with the *News Minute* at his home, noted, "Even [though] he was aware that they'll kill him, yet he was with the girl."[27] Balaswamy does not mention anything about faith or religion. Nevertheless, he describes Pranay's transgressive love while seated on the porch below a pictorial representation of Jesus. Dalit Christians have long been inspired by Jesus. From the time of their

encounter with Christian missionaries, Dalits embraced Christianity for its lib-
eratory impulse. In the words of Victor, a Dalit Christian interviewee in an ethnographic study of missions, "The confidence to challenge injustice whenever
we confronted it" is tied to Christian identity.[28] Victor recalls the Christian message as "you have blood, they have blood; it's the same blood."[29] In noting that
human persons have "the same blood," Dalit Christian logic sees through the
lie of caste, which pits people against one another based on false categories of
high-low and pure-impure.

It is significant that the state in which Pranay was murdered is prominent
for witnessing the historical Dalit mass-conversion movements in the nineteenth
century and the emergence of secular Dalit movements as well. Pranay's Dalit
Christian identity is best understood in this context. Pranay's example fits
Dalit commentary in this context: "In spite of the ongoing atrocities against
them, Dalit communities today are increasingly asserting themselves. This assertion manifests itself in naming themselves as Dalits, writing themselves into
history, converting to religions which they perceive to be egalitarian, celebrating their religion and culture, reclaiming Dalit rights as human rights and
engaging actively in the political processes of the country."[30] Pranay's father,
reflecting on his son's murder, seems to draw from the power inherent in Dalit
assertion when he highlights the need to promote intercaste marriages so that,
casteism (invoking B. R. Ambedkar) can be "weeded out."

Dalit youth are often accused of ensnaring women from dominant castes.
Dominant-caste contempt against Dalits is expressed in statements such as,
"They wear jeans, T-shirts and fancy sunglasses to lure girls from other communities."[31] Such contempt may be analyzed as the result of Dalit youth moving
out of the assigned place of abjectness. This is a double entendre with respect to
happiness, it seems. For Dalit Christians, there is happiness in breaking free
from caste-based humiliation. For dominant-caste persons, however, happiness
is tied to their own caste identity, and part of that necessarily means keeping or
"putting" Dalits in their place.

Pranay's father's observation in the interview that "even after 70 years of
independence, caste has not been annihilated" brings to the fore the famous
debate between B. R. Ambedkar and M. K. Gandhi.[32] Ambedkar rightly argued
against Gandhi that political independence from the British does not necessarily mean social independence for India. In other words, there is no independence
from caste in India today. While Dalits and tribals see caste as an oppressive lie
that needs to be "weeded out," dominant-caste persons—not unlike Kamala in
Never Have I Ever—align themselves with partners from similar castes in order
to maintain their "caste capital." "Caste capital," as Sanam Roohi observes,
"refers to the (largely invisible) symbolic, cultural or social capital that an actor
may possess by virtue of upper or dominant caste affiliation, capital that accords
advantages not enjoyed by people from other castes."[33] Roohi further notes that

"one of the ways in which caste and kinship operate on a transnational plane is through marriages."[34] Categories of affect such as "shame" and "disgrace" are employed in the service of maintaining such caste capital in both national and transnational settings. This analysis simply makes the connection between such caste-inflected affect and violence.

How Does This All Come Together (or Does It)?
An Interdisciplinary Excursus

In the next section, the chapter will utilize, among other things, the lens of affect to analyze violence against India's tribal Christians. This is a contested terrain. The terms *adivasi* and *Indigenous*, which the chapter uses in the introduction to describe India's tribals, are not officially accepted by the Indian government. The government uses the term *Scheduled Tribes* (STs) for tribals and *Scheduled Castes* (SCs) for Dalits, mostly to indicate that these communities are scheduled for affirmative action. The term *adivasi* (meaning original or first inhabitants) was "a term used by tribal rights activists in the early twentieth century to express their political identity as indigenous inhabitants in central and other parts of India."[35] There is an interesting Christian connection in the emergence of the term *adivasi* as Christian missionaries played a role in its production.[36]

Using the term *adivasi* to refer to India's Indigenous communities is mostly done in reference to tribal communities in central, northern, and southern parts of India. Tribals from India's northeastern states generally do not use the term *adivasi* and prefer to simply say "Indigenous" or "tribal" to refer to themselves. (I will elaborate on that, including how "race" plays a role, later in the chapter.)

It is interesting to note that states that witness violence against Christians also have a notable tribal presence.[37] This is a significant data point. While the presence of Dalits in most states aligns with the national average of about 16 percent, the percentage of tribal communities can drastically vary across states. Tribals make up a little over 8 percent of India's population. In states such as Rajasthan, however, tribal communities make up almost double that percentage.[38] Because these states witness disproportionate levels of anti-Christian violence, one better understands such violence as both anti-Christian and antitribal—in other words, violence against people who have been historically marginalized by caste discrimination but are now moving out those abject places by exercising their agency for freedom.

After India's political independence from British colonial rule in 1947, there were several movements for separate states. One prominent case—which later came to be known as the Jharkhand movement—occurred when the tribals of Central India organized to demand a separate state based on tribal identity. Sarbeswar Sahoo's observation that "a majority of these tribals who demanded a separate state were Christian" is worth noting.[39] In other words, tribal *Christians*

were, and are, moving out of their assigned places and making demands for freedom. Here, religious identities (that is, Christian) and ethnic identities (that is,
particular tribal locations) come together in the exercising of agency for freedom. Bara's phrase, "bending Christianity for self-defense," captures how many
tribal communities used Christianity for resisting oppressive feudal practices
and strengthening their positive self-identity.[40]

On the dominant-caste side of things, on the other hand, one perceives negative affect in relation to such agency. In Rajasthan, resentment is expressed
regarding religious conversion and, interestingly, also regarding intercaste marriages.[41] Whether one consciously expresses it as such or not, marrying within
the same or similar caste ranks creates the conditions for these affects—affects
that have violent sociopolitical manifestations. This is a major reason why the
chapter had analyzed the politics of affect with intercaste marriages.

When one moves to the northeastern region of India to consider tribals, several interesting features are worth mentioning. Some northeastern states, such
as Nagaland and Mizoram, are majority Christian, far exceeding the national
average of 8 percent. This majority-Christian composition threatens the self-
identity of the Indian nation-state, which increasingly—with a Hindu nationalist
government in power at the time of this writing—portrays itself as "Hindu" in
essence. Nagas, for instance, have long asserted their ethnic and geographical
independence contrary to the Hindu hegemony. Commentators note how, at a
very basic level, Nagas use their conversion to and subsequent Christian identity as political resistance in "opposition to their immediate non-Christian
colonizer, that is, India."[42] Christianity, in other words, for the Naga tribals, "has
become coterminous with Naga political identity."[43]

As we consider tribal Christians from the northeastern region of India, there
is another element that must be named. Theoretical and national understandings of violence against tribals from the northeastern region often emphasize
"cultural difference," but this framing "elides the problem of racism faced by
people from the Northeast, and at the same time, culture becomes a substitute
for race."[44] Violence against tribals from the northeastern states of India is usually not analyzed as racism. This is a major gap in research and the violence
against them has become what Papori Bora called a "problem without a name."[45]
Violence against tribals from India's northeastern region is often "invisibilized"
because of this "gap" in dominant approaches to theorizing that is often done
with the lens of caste.[46]

I am not arguing that caste is not a necessary lens through which to analyze violence in India, but when it comes to tribals from northeastern states,
caste may be a lens that is necessary but insufficient. This is more than a theoretical imbroglio, and it has to do with dominant imaginations of nation and
the nation-state's coercive desire for unity. An understanding of anti-Christian
violence needs to take these intricacies into account as well.

The next two sections describe violence against Dalit and tribal Christians, focusing on dietary practices. Both tribals and Dalits eat meat, including beef, and enjoy it. Violence against Dalits and tribals is often enacted in the name of protecting the sacred cow, and anti-Christian violence is often enacted in the context of politics surrounding meat. To highlight, however, that violence is produced from affect in more complex ways, I intentionally choose to analyze the violence against tribals in the first of the two sections by entering the scene with a vegetarian tribal food.

"Is This Curry Made of Shit?": *Akhuni*-Eating Tribals

"What kind of food do Northeast people eat? Is this curry made of shit?" The question arises from an affect of felt disgust. The questioner is Anita's neighbor in India's capital. Anita is a tribal Christian from the state of Nagaland. In an interview with anthropologist Dolly Kikon, Anita counters the derogatory question with pride, "This is how God created us and we should be proud of the way we live and what we eat."[47] Anita uses positive theological categories to counter the negative affect accompanying the question. Affect-based actions and reactions help in understanding caste, tribe, religion, and violence. Analyzing the question of Anita's neighbor may be helpful in understanding these connections.

Nagaland—one of eight states in northeastern India and home to Anita—consists of several distinct tribal communities, each of which is rich with their own language and culture. Over 80 percent of Nagas, the people of Nagaland, are Christians. Experiences of discrimination are common when they leave home. One reason behind such experiences of discrimination lies in the fact that these people look different from the stereotypical Indian. People from the Northeast are often mistaken as foreigners. In referring to Anita as "Northeast people," a first problematic lies in the erasure of Anita's particular religious and ethnic identity. Anita's identity is collapsed into a nondescript "Northeast." Furthermore, in addition to the derogatory nature of the question—"Is this curry made of shit?"—the questioner is using language that is foreign to Anita. "Curry" is not a Naga term.

The particular food, the smell of which evokes the questioner's affect, is a fermented dish called *akhuni*.[48] Kikon is right to note that "fermented food like *akhuni* shapes everyday practices and imaginations about citizenship, spaces of transgressions, and social meanings in contemporary India."[49] In 2007, the New Delhi police department issued a directive titled, "Security Tips for Northeast Students/Visitors in Delhi." Kikon notes that food items, including *akhuni*, were mentioned as likely to cause conflict, leading the police to offer the following advice: "bamboo shoot, akhuni, and other smelly dishes should be prepared without creating ruckus in neighbourhood."[50]

What does one do when a smell that evokes strong affective "feelings of repulsion" for one person is "the same smell [that] invokes feelings of comfort or memories of home" in another?[51] Such affective encounters make and break societal relations. As Angami Zapu Phizo asked famously in the context of the Shillong Accord of 1975 between Naga separatists and the Indian government, "How can there be peace when one side does not share the food of the other side?"[52] Feelings evoked in dominant persons by inferiorized others are best understood as affective reactions. Such affective reactions enable latent violence. Affective reactions certainly include jeering questions such as "Is this curry made of shit?" in reference to food. In addition to jeering, affective reactions also include leering.

Tribal women—often Christian—from states like Nagaland and others in the northeastern part of India often travel to India's metropolitan cities to study or work. Northeast India shares much of its borders with surrounding countries, such as Bangladesh, Bhutan, Burma, China, and Nepal. When Indigenous women from these parts come to India's metropolitan cities for work, they suffer racialized discrimination. Sociologist Duncan McDuie-Ra contextualizes the occupation of Indigenous women in the beauty industry. The facial features of Indigenous women are perceived as "exotic," observes McDuie-Ra, and "evoke a sense of other-worldliness fitting the cosmopolitan aspirations of many of the upper-middle class clientele."[53] Men in cities often have racialized perceptions of Indigenous women as "promiscuous" and "available." They further know that harming them has "limited repercussions" because they are deemed "other" within India's caste-based moral and mainstream national order, making wrongs suffered by such women often dismissible in the dominant imagination.

In her autobiography, Mary Kom, one of India's most successful athletes and a tribal Christian from the northeastern state of Manipur, notes how such stereotypical perceptions play out in everyday encounters: "Because of our oriental looks, people from the Northeast are often mocked in other parts of India. We're called Nepalis or Chinkies, and people call us names like ching-ching chong-chong. . . . When I used to say I am from Manipur people didn't even know where it was."[54]

People with facial features such as Anita (student), Mary Kom (world-famous athlete), and Reingamphi Awungshi (a beauty therapist whose murder was described by McDuie-Ra) are different from each another in more ways than one.[55] Yet, they are collapsed into the same category of "exotic other" and jeered at and harassed when they are in public in India's metropolitan cities. Such widespread affectual encounters form the basis for violence against them. While the sight of tribals itself is a kind of affective element that evokes latent violence in dominant subjects, it is not disconnected from other affective perceptions, such as the smell of their food. It seems that violence against Christians, in this sense, is best understood as the culmination of cumulative affects.

Beef-Eating Dalits and Tribals

The Mid-Day Meal Scheme is a program instituted by the government of India to ensure that school-age children nationwide get nutritional meals. One of the positive features of the scheme was that the Supreme Court took the recommendations of the National Advisory Council and issued a directive that privileged the employment of Dalit and tribal cooks for the program. Not surprisingly, there was dominant-caste backlash. Dominant-caste parents tried to block Dalit and tribal hires. Where that failed, they refused to have their children eat food cooked by Dalit hands. In other places, Dalit cooks were physically assaulted.[56] It seems that not much has changed from the 1910s, when Arya Samaj leader Swami Shraddhanand encouraged Indians to avoid eating food prepared by Dalits and choose to eat food prepared by dominant castes instead. Shraddhanand offered his advice by quoting Swami Dayanand, who said a Dalit's body "is filled with foul smell at the atomic level" and that such "is not the case" with dominant castes.[57]

Such notions—which are inflected with affect and othering logic—are part of the dominant Hindu sacred literature as well. The *Mahabharata* infamously notes, "If there were no meat-eaters, there would be no killers. A meat-eating man is a killer indeed."[58] It is not unlike the affect evoked when Gandhi, writing in his autobiography, observed, "My co-workers and I have seen by experience that there is much truth in the Indian proverb that as a man eats, so shall he become."[59] In the context of introducing nationwide bans on cow slaughter, the former prime minister of the Hindu nationalist government Bharatiya Janata Party (BJP), Atal Behari Vajpayee, stated, "I would rather die rather than eat beef."[60] The implication of such religious nationalism is that Dalit and tribal Christians—a majority of whom eat beef and other meats—are *not* Indian.[61] Identities are thus asserted and contested over dietary habits.

Such statements not only evoke negative affect against those with different dietary habits but also lead to the construction of violent identities that pit people against each other. Ethnonationalist political movements constantly try to peddle a version of India and Indian-ness based on such dominant interpretations. Religion and caste associations with respect to food culture are ambiguous in the Indian context, and food becomes an instrument of othering "and can often cross that already ambiguous relationship to become violent."[62]

If "a meat-eating man is a killer indeed," then a killer's killing, as it were, is problematically rationalized. Such a rationale, unfortunately, is not mere conjecture. In 2010, the state of Karnataka amended an already existing bill to propose the Karnataka Prevention of Slaughter and Preservation of Cattle Bill 2010. As Smitha Rao notes, "An intriguing addition is the provision for protection of persons acting in good faith."[63] Such provisions in the law make it convenient for self-appointed Hindu nationalist vigilante groups to perpetrate violence on those whom they deem "other." Violence, then, becomes not only possible, but even legitimated.

Most Indians are not strictly vegetarian. Meat eating, in this sense, simply points to the nonrepresentative absurdity of the "reductionist interpretation" that eating meat is a "marker of ritual impurity."[64] As James Staples argues based on his study of Dalit Christians, while meat eating is certainly employed as an "act of defiance," the sensibilities that inform meat eating are deeply affectual. Statements such as "meat is special," consuming beef "gives us a sense of satisfaction," "we honor people with it," and "it's for special days, for Sundays, weddings and festivals" reveal a nuanced aesthetics behind dietary habits.[65] For a great number of Christians, therefore, eating beef—not dissimilar from Anita's observation about *akhuni*—is part of their positive human identity.

Notwithstanding the positive affect that informs Dalit and tribal agency, Hindu nationalists are increasingly turning their attention to what may be called religiously inflected affective categories for producing "Hindu nation" subjects. For instance, Hindu businessman and yoga guru Baba Ramdev, who has active connections with the BJP, has now turned his attention to Christian-majority states such as Nagaland. Naga scholar Arkotong Longkumer observes that, under the guise of yoga, health, and dietary products, Baba Ramdev and his Pantanjali product brand operate in ways that may be seen "as a form of 'neo-Hindutva' that is increasingly diffuse and moves away from a more militant pathway of established Hindutva designs."[66]

Privileging vegetarianism, then, is certainly to "talk of caste by other means" or a way "to smuggle casteism through the backdoor."[67] Whether it is through physical violence, as when Hindu nationalist vigilantes attack those who process meat, or through the privileging of particular dietary habits through yoga-based and religiously inflected industries such as Ramdev's Patanjali, the so-called "nonviolence" that is often lifted up in dominant-caste Indian imagination is simply "empty rhetoric" conditioned by problematic religious affect.[68]

Conclusion: Feeling Religion and Violence

Religions are, then, understood not simply as a rational set of beliefs but also as entities producing and facilitating both negative and positive affect, which that reinforce or destabilize caste logic and domination. On the one hand, those who experience caste-based discrimination, "increasingly describe caste as an affect."[69] Caste-based violence is often simply felt by the discriminatory weight of expressions such as "*tch* " or "is that curry made of shit?" On the other hand, Anita's theologically inflected retort—"This is how God created us and we should be proud of the way we live and what we eat"—may partly be seen as arising from her Christian identity. The neighbor's negative affect informed by caste logic is destabilized by the positive affect informed by the theological conviction that "God made me this way."

Emotions, as Robin Markwica points out, are "deeply embedded in the processes and structures of world politics."[70] A global vision of violence, then, ought to include the task of "building an affective inventory."[71] This entails commentators from different parts of the world with different social locations deliberating about affect and its consequences.

NOTES

1. Anand Teltumbde, *The Persistence of Caste: The Khairlanji Murders and India's Hidden Apartheid* (New York: Zed Books, 2010); Anand Teltumbde, *Khairlanji* (New Delhi: Navayana Publishers, 2008).

2. Nicolas Jaoul, "The 'Righteous Anger' of the Powerless: Investigating Dalit Outrage over Caste Violence," *South Asia Multidisciplinary Academic Journal* 2 (2008): 26.

3. Kalpana Ram, *Fertile Disorder: Spirit Possession and Its Provocation of the Modern* (Honolulu: University of Hawai'i Press, 2013), 87.

4. Kamari Clarke, cited in Wahneema Lubiano, "Affect and Rearticulating the Racial 'Un-Sayables,'" *Cultural Anthropology* 28, no. 3 (2013): 541.

5. Gopal Guru, ed., *Humiliation: Claims and Context* (New Delhi: Oxford University Press, 2009).

6. Joel Lee, "Odor and Order: How Caste Is Inscribed in Space and Sensoria," *Comparative Studies of South Asia, Africa and the Middle East* 37, no. 3 (2017): 470.

7. Lee, "Odor and Order," 473.

8. Lee, "Odor and Order," 478.

9. Sarbeswar Sahoo, *Pentecostalism and Religious Conflict in Contemporary India* (New Delhi: Cambridge University Press, 2018), 1.

10. Dustin Howes, cited in Sahoo, *Pentecostalism*, 2. In other work, I make similar observations in my categorizations of wrongs as brutal and ordinary. While "brutal wrongs" may be compared to Howes's description on "physical violence," "ordinary wrongs" are similar to Howes's definition of "intersubjective violence." "Ordinary wrongs" are "those wrongs that have an everyday banal character but are nevertheless deeply violent, conditioned by discriminatory logics of exclusionary practices of the past and the present." See Sunder John Boopalan, *Memory, Grief, and Agency: A Political Theological Account of Wrongs and Rites*, New Approaches to Religion and Power (New York: Palgrave Macmillan, 2017), 122.

11. For a brief description, including the link to the TV series, see Priya Arora, "Mindy Kaling's Netflix Show Tells a New Kind of Story: One Like Hers," *New York Times*, April 27, 2020, updated April 29, 2020, https://www.nytimes.com/2020/04/27/arts/television/mindy-kaling-never-have-I-ever-netflix.html.

12. Shefali Chandra, "The: Caste, Sexuality and the Manufacture of Indian 'Democracy,'" *Dialectical Anthropology* 38, no. 2 (June 2014): 237–238.

13. Chandra, "World's Largest Dynasty," 237–238.

14. WGBH News and Public Radio International (PRI)'s *The World* worked in collaboration with the Pulitzer Center to produce a multipart examination of "Caste in America," accessed May 1, 2020, https://www.pri.org/categories/caste-america.

15. Kavita Pillay, "Love and Marriage: Rebels against an Indian Tradition That Endures in the U.S.," February 27, 2019, https://www.wgbh.org/news/national-news/2019/02/27/love-and-marriage-rebels-against-an-indian-tradition-that-endures-in-the-us?00000161-8b7f-d670-ad6f-abff33b10000-page=2.

16. Pillay, "Love and Marriage."

17. Jillet Sarah Sam, "Caste Diasporas beyond National Boundaries: Digital Caste Networks," *Perspectives on Global Development and Technology* 16, nos. 1–3 (2017): 146.

18. Dalel Benbabaali, "Caste Dominance and Territory in South India: Understanding Kammas' Socio-Spatial Mobility," *Modern Asian Studies* 52, no. 6 (2018): 31.

19. Telugu Association of North America, accessed May 1, 2020, https://www.tana.org/services/matrimonials-listing.

20. Anderson H. M. Jeremiah, "Race, Caste, and Christianity," *International Review of Mission* 109, no. 1 (2020): 96.

21. Boopalan, *Memory, Grief, and Agency*, 5.

22. For an analysis of and commentary on such "honor killings," see Rajpal Bhullar and Bala Rani Bhullar, eds., *Honour Killings & Human Rights in India* (New Delhi: Academic Excellence, 2013); Satnam Singh Deol, "Honour Killings in Haryana State, India: A Content Analysis," *International Journal of Criminal Justice Sciences* 9, no. 2 (2014): 192–208; Manpreet Kaur, *Honour Killings in India: A Crime against Humanity* (New Delhi: Anamika Publishers, 2015).

23. "Trial in Gokulraj Murder Begins," *Times of India*, August 31, 2018, http://timesofindia.indiatimes.com/articleshow/65615115.cms?utm_source=contentofinterest&utm_medium=text&utm_campaign=cppst.

24. "Dalit Activists, Women's Groups Thrilled; Political Parties Remain Silent [Times Region]," *The Times of India*, December 13, 2017, https://search-proquest-com.ezproxy.princeton.edu/docview/1975805195?accountid=13314.

25. R. Vimal Kumar, "'Honour' Killing of Dalit Youth Shankar in Tamil Nadu: Death for Six, Including Father-in-law," *Hindu*, December 12, 2017. https://www.thehindu.com/news/national/tamil-nadu/shankar-murder-case-father-in-law-gets-death-sentence/article21478790.ece.

26. Srinivasa Rao Apparasu, "Telangana Dalit Christian Killing," September 19, 2018, https://www.hindustantimes.com/india-news/for-honour-killing-of-dalit-christian-in-telangana-contract-killer-arrested-from-bihar/story-1KZYMqbG3lQoZXVL1JOFAK.html.

27. "Violence against Inter-Caste Couples: The Need for A New Law," October 18, 2018, https://www.youtube.com/watch?v=2RRRiIyJIsA&feature=emb_logo.

28. Joseph Prabhakar Dayam and Peniel Rajkumar, "Mission at and from the Margins: Patterns, Protagonists and Perspectives: A Critical and Constructive Contribution to the Edinburgh 2010 Conference," in *Mission at and from the Margins: Patterns, Protagonists and Perspectives*, ed. Peniel Rajkumar, Joseph Prabhakar Dayam, and I. P Asheervadham (Oxford: Regnum, 2014), 5.

29. Dayam and Rajkumar, "Mission at and from the Margins," 5.

30. Editors' introduction to Peniel Rajkumar, Joseph Prabhakar Dayam, and I. P Asheervadham, eds., *Mission At and From the Margins: Patterns, Protagonists and Perspectives* (Oxford: Regnum, 2014), xiii.

31. Dickens Leonard, "Spectacle Spaces: Production of Caste in Recent Tamil Films," *South Asian Popular Culture* 13, no. 2 (2015): 165.

32. "Violence against Inter-Caste Couples."

33. Sanam Roohi, "Caste, Kinship and the Realisation of 'American Dream': High-Skilled Telugu Migrants in the U.S.A.," *Journal of Ethnic and Migration Studies* 43, no. 16 (2017): 2763.

34. Roohim, "Caste, Kinship and the Realisation of the 'American Dream,'" 2759.

35. Papori Bora, "The Problem without a Name: Comments on Cultural Difference (Racism) in India," *South Asia: Journal of South Asian Studies* 42, no. 5 (2019): 854; also see Alf Gunvald Nilsen, "Adivasis in and against the State: Subaltern Politics and State Power in Contemporary India," *Critical Asian Studies* 44, no. 2 (2012): 251–282.

36. For more context, see Alpa Shah, "The Dark Side of Indigeneity?: Indigenous People, Rights and Development in India," *History Compass* 5, no. 6 (November 2007): 1806–1832.

37. Sahoo, *Pentecostalism*, 122.

38. Sahoo, *Pentecostalism*, 125.

39. Sahoo, *Pentecostalism*, 138.

40. Joseph Bara, "Colonialism, Christianity and the Tribes of Chhotanagpur in East India, 1845–1890," *South Asia: Journal of South Asian Studies* 30, no. 2 (2007): 219–220.

41. Sahoo, *Pentecostalism*, 147.

42. Tezenlo Thong, cited in Sashila Jamir, "Christianity in Nagaland," *Word & World* 37, no. 4 (2017): 392.

43. Jamir, "Christianity in Nagaland," 394.

44. Bora, "Problem without a Name," 849.

45. Bora, "Problem without a Name," 846.

46. Bora, "Problem without a Name," 845.

47. Dolly Kikon, "Eating Akhuni in India," in *Farm to Fingers: The Culture and Politics of Food in Contemporary India*, ed. Kiranmayi Bhushi (New Delhi: Cambridge University Press, 2018), 100.

48. *Akhuni*, although consumed by many Nagas, is a distinctive food of the Sumi tribe of Nagaland.

49. Kikon, "Eating Akhuni in India," 82.

50. Kikon, "Eating Akhuni in India," 96.

51. Kikon, "Eating Akhuni in India," 83–84.

52. Prasenjit Biswas and Suraj Gogoi, "Racism in India," *Statesman*, February 26, 2017, https://www.thestatesman.com/northeast/racism-in-india-1488142250.html.

53. Duncan McDuie-Ra, *Debating Race in Contemporary India* (New York: Palgrave Macmillan, 2015), 63–64.

54. Cited in McDuie-Ra, *Debating Race*, 7.

55. In 2013, Reingamphi Awungshi, a Christian Tangkul Naga woman from Manipur, working as a beauty therapist, was found dead in her apartment in Delhi, India's capital. Although she had brutal injuries, including a prominent wound on her face, and had been sexually assaulted, the police initially declared her death as a suicide without registering a criminal case and dismissed the evidence of her mutilated face as having been caused by rodents. The criminal case involving her murder is still pending (see McDuie-Ra, *Debating Race*, 57–59, 63–64).

56. For more context and details, see Aloysius Irudayam, Jayshree P. Mangubhai, and Joel G. Lee, *Dalit Women Speak Out: Caste, Class and Gender Violence in India* (New Delhi: Zubaan, 2012).

57. Lee, "Odor and Order," 478.

58. From the Mahabharata; cited in Lisa Kemmerer, *Animals and World Religions* (Oxford: Oxford University Press, 2012), 56.

59. Mohandas K. Gandhi, *An Autobiography: The Story of My Experiments with Truth* (Boston: Beacon Press, 1993), 272.

60. James Staples, "Beef and Beyond: Exploring the Meat Consumption Practices of Christians in India," *Ethnos* 82, no. 2 (2017): 240.

61. Staples, "Beef and Beyond," 240.

62. Biswas and Suraj Gogoi, "Racism in India."

63. Smitha Rao, "Saffronisation of the Holy Cow: Unearthing Silent Communalism," *Economic and Political Weekly* 46, no. 15 (2011): 85.

64. Staples, "Beef and Beyond," 232.

65. Staples, "Beef and Beyond," 235.

66. Arkotong Longkumer, "'Nagas Can't Sit Lotus Style': Baba Ramdev, Patanjali, and Neo-Hindutva," *Contemporary South Asia* 26, no. 4 (2018): 401.

67. Pandian, cited in C. Sathyamala, "Meat-Eating in India: Whose Food, Whose Politics, and Whose Rights?," *Policy Futures in Education* 17, no. 7 (2019): 86.

68. Pandian, cited in C. Sathyamala, "Meat-Eating in India, 87.

69. Sushrut Jadhav, David Mosse, and Ned Dostaler, "Minds of Caste—Discrimination and Its Affects," *Anthropology Today* 32, no. 1 (2016): 1–2.

70. Anand Teltumbde, *Khairlanji* (New Delhi: Navayana Publishers, 2008).

71. Duncan McDuie-Ra, Elaine Lynn-Ee Ho, Tanya Jakimow, and Bittiandra Chand Somaiah, "Collaborative Ethnographies: Reading Space to Build an Affective Inventory," *Emotion, Space and Society* 35 (2020): 7.

9

From Persecution to Exile

The Church of Almighty God from China

CHRISTIE CHUI-SHAN CHOW

Emerging in Henan province in central China in the early 1990s, the Church of Almighty God (CAG) successfully utilized social networking, itinerant evangelists, and literature evangelism to gain popularity among rural house church members.[1] In many ways, the CAG typifies China's vigorous underground Christian groups, which resist the pressure to be absorbed into the state-controlled system of patriotic religious associations.[2] But the CAG has become a headache to both the Communist authorities and the larger Chinese Protestant churches. The former's suspicions seemed to be confirmed when the movement made international headlines in 2014 after the Chinese authorities associated it with a murder in Zhaoyuang City, Shandong province. Six evangelists with former CAG backgrounds allegedly beat a woman to death at a McDonald's restaurant because she refused to give them her phone number.[3] This tragedy was a significant turning point in the global and Chinese domestic media coverage of the CAG. As part of clamping down on syncretic sectarian groups, around the same time the Chinese state mobilized its vast army of experts from the prestigious Chinese Academy of Social Science and national universities to conduct an ambitious full-scale propaganda crusade against these homegrown religious movements.[4] An official Chinese website portrays the group as dangerously destabilizing to the political order, seeks to undermine the intellectual credibility of the CAG's teachings, and publicizes accounts of deconversion from the group.[5]

Protestants blame the group for spreading twisted doctrines, the most controversial of which being that Jesus Christ has been reincarnated as a Chinese woman, while the Chinese government accuses it of employing coercive proselytizing methods to win converts. Stories concerning CAG evangelists' use of violence, seduction, and deception have made the movement a Christian pariah and an enemy of an authoritarian government that is fearful of social unrest.[6]

By the mid-1990s, the CAG was officially listed as an "evil cult," a label given to those religious actors that the Communists deemed as threatening the party-state.

While the debate concerning the CAG often focuses on its heterodox beliefs and practices,[7] little discussion is given to the effects of the brutal crackdown on the group inside China, where they share the same fate as groups such as Falun Gong, an indigenous Buddhist group that was also labeled an "evil cult" and criminalized for its political activism during the late 1990s.[8] CAG's core leaders fled to the United States in 2000 and gained political asylum in response to religious persecution the following year.[9] Since taking refuge in the United States, CAG leaders have set up headquarters in New York City, where they continue to spread the Almighty God's teachings. The group retains its apocalyptic outlook, warning about the coming of the end of the world and calling sinners to follow the teachings of the Almighty God while condemning the Chinese Communist Party as the anti-Christ and the red dragon metaphorically depicted in the New Testament book of Revelation.[10]

As more members go to live in exile abroad, they have not only built local CAG communities in their adopted countries but have also reached out globally through various social media platforms. A recent study suggests that their internet evangelism is most successful in the United States.[11] Their outreach to both Chinese and non-Chinese speakers worldwide should not come as a surprise. In fact, the CAG follows in the footsteps of some pro-democracy dissidents, as well as other officially banned religious movements, to adopt "decidedly high-tech, extremely mobile and multifaceted" organizational strategies.[12] Rebuilding themselves abroad and shifting much of their operations online, the CAG has waged an impressive multifront campaign against Chinese human rights abuses, lobbying national governments and global organizations for help. This chapter examines how the CAG has combined persecution narratives with human rights activism to reposition itself as a mainstream Christian movement. In this way, it challenges the boundaries of World Christianity and the inclusion of new religious movements within its contours.

Recent scholarship on CAG has focused on the movement's theology, liturgy, and organizational practices or is intended to dispel the Chinese government's demonizing accounts.[13] This chapter instead explores the CAG's virtual realm of activism as an open space for outsiders to witness its transformative trajectory from a persecuted Christian-inspired sectarian movement into a global, multiethnolinguistic Christian community. The CAG's movies about religious persecution are the dominant focus of my investigation. The choice of this methodology emerges from my early interest with the group and my own encounters with some CAG followers in New York City in 2017. In attempting to establish a rapport with members of the CAG, I found that their years of repression at the hands of the Chinese state made them suspicious of me. The chapter thus uses

CAG as a case study to reflect on the difficulty of conducting ethnography among clandestine Christian groups. It shows that fragments of ethnographic reality about the CAG can be "glimpsed at" through the methodology of *virtual ethnography*. By contextualizing the CAG's website as a site of knowledge production and a mode of identity invention, I ask what particular knowledge the CAG produces and projects online in order to win public sympathy. This research combines the methodologies of *physical ethnography* and *virtual ethnography* to explore the lives of these marginalized, secretive Chinese Christians in exile, with a focus on their effective use of universal human rights discourse and social media technologies and their persecution stories to reinvent themselves as an ordinary Christian community.

Experiences with CAG Members

The resilience of Christianity in contemporary China has become a major subject of scholarly inquiry. For years, archival research, theological discourse and textual analysis, and oral history have been common methodologies in the study of Chinese theology, church-state interactions, urban Christian life, and denominationalism.[14] The rapidity of China's liberalization during the 1990s and 2000s has enabled scholars to trace the development of both officially registered and unofficially recognized churches from the bottom up, delving deeper into the religious values and lived Christian practices of urban China, the enduring Confucian roots of Chinese Pentecostal revivals, and the interrelationship of Christian faith and ethnicity on China's western frontiers.[15] Underlying these case studies is the prioritization of fieldwork, through which scholars immerse themselves in faith communities, observing people closely, documenting their activities, and listening to their interlocutors in interviews. Scholars of contemporary Chinese Christianity have come to supplement this ethnographic information with data collected from church and local government archives, reconciling the temporal gap between past and present. The array of the sources offers a multifaceted understanding of the life and culture of Chinese believers.

In times of political uncertainty, however, gaining access to and trust from Chinese Christian informants can be immensely difficult. China is a single party-state in which the real authority lies with the Chinese Communist Party. The country is under a dual system of tight control, with two imposing bureaucracies coexisting side by side. The interests of the Chinese state and the Communist Party overlap. The state institutions control the ideological, political, social, economic, and religious spheres and the Communist Party runs the state. The question of state domination shapes the production of knowledge about Chinese Christianity. The decades of relative sociopolitical openness ended when the current president, Xi Jinping, came to power in 2012. Since then, many religious communities have been subjected to various degrees of suppression and the officials of the provincial and municipal archives have blocked foreign and local researchers' access to post-1949 materials on religious affairs.[16] Political sensitivity makes fieldwork precarious and uncertain, particularly with respect to the so-called forbidden Christian practitioners, labeled by the Chinese government as "evil cults." Equally challenging is the investigation of these Christians outside China. Religious suppression in their hometowns has made exiled CAG members cautious toward outsiders. Many CAG members also remain suspicious that intelligence agents from local Chinese embassies are infiltrating their gatherings. These social dynamics make ethnographic access to the group nearly impossible.

My interest in the CAG traces back to the late 2000s, while I was researching the development of Chinese Seventh-day Adventism. Adventists in China whom I interviewed often complained about losing their congregants to the CAG. For instance, an Adventist elder was surprised that their pastor, who was adept in the Adventist doctrines after receiving years of private doctrinal tutorship from an experienced senior pastor, left the church to join the CAG.[17] A younger church elder stated that the CAG's aggressive proselytization efforts had completely won over a local Adventist congregation in Yiwu, in northern Zhejiang province, and that it took an Adventist couple to rebuild the local ministry from scratch.[18] To prevent his flock from "drifting astray," a young church elder in Gongzhuling, Jilin province, reported a visiting CAG evangelist to the authorities and having that evangelist arrested. The elder later regretted his actions.[19] These oral accounts are one-sided and difficult to verify due to lack of access to the CAG in China. Yet they suggest the intense competition for converts within China's restricted religious market.[20] To me as well as to other outsiders, the scale of the CAG's activities and evangelistic outreach remains of interest.

In April 2017, I unexpectedly ran into two female evangelists of the CAG at an academic conference.[21] They came to a panel presentation given by two representatives of Freedom House, a human rights organization from Washington, D.C.[22] Their presence represented a new strategy adopted by the CAG to work with Western human rights organizations for religious freedom. These two members invited me to attend CAG services on September 16, 2017.

The services took place at 10 A.M. in a church basement. There was no indication about the CAG meeting outside the church, suggesting that their gathering was not open to the public. Inside the basement hung an eye-catching banner showing the three Almighty God's books hovering above a world map. A bilingual (Chinese and English) statement declared, "God's name will be magnified among the gentile nations." By the time I arrived, dozens of young adults were already gathered, with men and women segregated by gender. Two of them told me they had been recruited online, drawn in by the group's digital evangelism. In fact, the services demonstrated the CAG's dependence on their digital repository, with the praise songs and the Almighty God's words all download-able from their website. The trauma of suppression lingered as the worshippers sobbed and wept over prayers remembering fellow members who were suffer-ing for their faith.[23] After the service, CAG leaders invited me to a congre-gant's house for lunch. There, CAG members shared their thankfulness to "God's words," the Almighty God's utterances turned sacred writings. These testimonies sought to convince me about the power of the Almighty God's liter-ature. I also was told that the movement has a thousand followers in New York City, a figure that is difficult to verify. The synthesis of proactive digital prose-lytism and secretive gatherings created a vexing combination.

On June 9, 2018, I met two female CAG followers in Lower Manhattan's Chi-natown and we talked over dinner about the suppression of their church in China. Both had just gained permission to stay in the United States as asylum seekers but were worried about their parents, who were also followers of the Almighty God back home. One told of being followed by a government agent, an experience that prompted her mother to arrange for her to leave China. The other follower fled the country while her mother, an active CAG evangelist, lived in hiding. Both also mentioned that the church had lost contact with a male mem-ber since he returned to China. That was my last direct encounter with CAG members. Afterward they stopped responding to any emails, text messages, or phone calls, and I lost all personal access to the CAG. This data source evapo-rated. Nevertheless, new lines of inquiry moved into its place—involving perse-cution, virtual ethnography, and World Christianity.

The CAG and Virtual Ethnography

The success of fieldwork depends primarily on relationships. Lack of trust may be one reason for explaining the CAG's abrupt ending of our relationship. Being slow to reciprocate on my part may be another, as one female adherent had asked me for advice on applying for political asylum, a process I was ignorant of. Los-ing ethnographic access to the New York City chapter of the CAG did not com-pletely close the door for further research on the group, however. Modern anthropology has contested that the notion of "being there" only refers to being physically on the ground to investigate a group narrowly defined as a spatially bounded entity.[24] Deborah D'Amico-Samuels asserts that in this social media age, "the field is everywhere."[25] When studying the pervasive influence of Amer-ican fundamentalist preacher Jerry Falwell, Susan F. Harding insists that Falwell's sermons, TV shows, and writings are also her fields of inquiry.[26] Similar argu-ments apply to the CAG. The CAG's multilingual website is a virtual space that reveals the group's self-understanding and evangelistic strategies. The data extracted from its virtual platforms demonstrates its capability to reinvent and transform itself from a "made-in-China" Christian-inspired movement to a globalized Christian community.

The identity of the CAG is still hotly contested by Chinese Communist officials, Chinese and overseas Chinese evangelicals, and the international media. The demonizing label "evil cult" attached to the group has publicly politicized the CAG's identity as a socially transgressing entity. Until recently, very few international media outlets have challenged the Chinese government's aggressive propaganda against the CAG. In an effort to counter Chinese hostile allegations and Western negative media representation, the CAG has constructed for itself an identity of persecuted victim. For example, an earlier CAG website that I had consulted in 2009 drew on the history of Chinese Christian martyrdom to win sympathy, but it relied heavily on religious texts and audio, which were visually cumbersome. Since then their media campaign has been upgraded, with the older materials incorporated into a professionalized multimedia and multilingual website. The website includes thousands of cases of perceived religious persecution by province, documented in Chinese and English, of the arrests, incarcerations, torture, and death of CAG adherents.[27] Earlier reports concentrate on the description of harassment and physical violence that the Chinese state inflicted on the CAG. Later reports have gruesome narratives but also include investigative touches by drawing on Chinese religious policy documents, local court verdicts against the CAG, and comments by foreign human rights experts. This extensive documentation presents the scale and patterns of persecution against the CAG since 1990 and forms the basis of the persecution movies that I discuss later in the chapter.[28]

The CAG's visual representation of victimhood is enhanced with videos of interviews with human rights specialists critical of China, hearings on international human rights, and instances of human rights violations in China. For example, the group's web-based news channel Trumpet of Truth interviewed European human rights scholars such as Massimo Introvigne, founder of the CESNUR (Center for Studies on New Religions), and Raffaella Di Marzio, director of the Center for Studies on Freedom of Religion, Belief and Conscience (Libertá di Religione Credo Coscienza, or LIREC). Videotaped hearings of China's human rights violation include scenes of young Chinese, in neat and tidy uniforms, performing traditional dances and singing gospel hymns for European audiences. In another video, the South Korean chapter of the CAG is shown interviewing Do Heeyoun, head of the Citizens' Coalition for the Human Rights of Abductees and North Korean Refugees, at a time when many of the CAG asylum seekers, including Chinese of Korean descent, had their applications denied by the South Korean government because of strong diplomatic pressure from Beijing. Notably, the videos employ universal human rights discourse to defend their right to religion as a right that they possess by virtue of being human. Under the human rights legal framework, they position themselves as pro-democracy dissidents, a

TABLE 9.1

Number of CAG subscribers / followers via social media platforms in 2022

Social media	Number of subscribers / followers
YouTube	85.5K (Chinese); 569K (English)
Twitter	6,463
Facebook	17K

Sources: God Footsteps, YouTube, https://www.youtube.com/user/godfootsteps (Chinese); "The Church of Almighty God," YouTube, https://www.youtube.com/user/godfootstepsen; Almighty God Church, Twitter, https://twitter.com/churchAlmighty; The Church of Almighty God, Facebook, https://www.facebook.com/godfootstepsen. All sources accessed May 20, 2022.

persecuted community including Falun Gong adherents, Tibetan Buddhists, and Uyghur Muslims, and they join with these groups in peaceful demonstrations and parliamentary lobbying.

When reaching out to international human rights experts and advocates, the CAG is keen to describe its adherents as the victims of China's human rights violations. This normalization is more explicit in the CAG's portrayal of their Christian life. There is an online gallery of photos depicting the diversity of CAG followers: Chinese, Koreans, Caucasians, people of all colors and ages, men and women. Aesthetically staged in these photos, the global CAG followers appear to exchange fellowship with each other cheerfully and confidently, reading their most sacred text, *Word Appearing in the Flesh.* Religious piety appears to be compatible with global modernity, as these believers, shown in professional business suits and with beautiful makeup on the women, carry their iPads and iPhones. The photos show them publicly celebrating their faith in dancing and singing. Despite its indigenous origins in the hinterlands of China, the global CAG portrays the church as a cosmopolitan, inclusive, and urban religion, attracting people worldwide.

One can follow the CAG on YouTube, Facebook, and Twitter. Table 9.1 shows the number of followers on each of the social media platforms, keeping in mind that followers can access more than one platform at once. Hot lines are available in multiple languages in over thirty countries. Religious conversion makes up a significant portion of the virtual materials. An online video shares the conversion story of a couple in Arizona, who go by the names Tina and Charlie.[29]

Tina stumbled on the CAG's Facebook page accidentally, and got in touch with a CAG online evangelist, who recommended to her the Almighty God's writings and the CAG's online videos. An evangelical Christian since childhood, Tina was moved by the Almighty God's messages that "God is among us" and "the Lord Jesus has already returned to the world." Another video shows a group of Korean women around a big table, reading *The Word Appears in the Flesh* and clapping harmoniously. The uniformity of their bodily movements typifies the Korean public expression of collective solidarity. No longer a Christian sect of, by, and for Chinese, the CAG has presented itself proudly as an inclusive and enlightening global Christian body. This did not preclude, however, the embodiment of persecution narratives.

CAG's Religious Persecution Movies

Besides written documentation, interviews with experts, and church life snaps, the CAG has produced hundreds of movies that are freely available online. Made in their studios in South Korea, these films exhibit multiple genres, such as musicals, theater, stand-up comedies, and documentaries, aimed at promoting their faith practices against the hostility of the Chinese state. Unlike the well-developed industry of Nollywood, which has a global commercial infrastructure to distribute its Christian films worldwide, the CAG films are low-budget productions relying on free social media platforms to circulate. The phenomenon of the CAG's visual content typifies cultural transformation in China's current digital and social media age. Media scholar Yiman Wang points out that the availability of portable digital cameras in China since the late 1990s has given rise to "an expanding group of amateur practitioners, ranging from the 1960s generation to college students." Armed with a new medium, at first independent producers made low budget films, using the unofficial networks of distribution and exhibition to show films critical of the social ills and problems plaguing China.[30] The CAG production is part of this cultural legacy that combines amateurism, aesthetic, and social critique. When they took refuge in South Korea, they founded the Church of Almighty God Film Center. Some actors in the CAG films hold degrees in music and performing arts from Chinese universities, and many young exiled members are pursuing an arts education in South Korea and other places. The production of the church's films, therefore, was a result of being outside of China.[31]

The CAG persecution movies blend hagiography, sensationalism, emotional authenticity, and reenactment with visual and audio cinematic effects. Aimed at mobilizing affective responses from viewers, the cinematic interpretations of CAG's religious persecution movies should be understood as "rhetorical texts," "using visual, audio, and cinematic means" to convey a particular point of view rather than offering a verifiable truth.[32] In a way, the CAG movies do not have raw footage nor interviews with survivors, which are necessary ingredients in conventional documentary. However, all the persecution movies are allegedly performed by exiled CAG members, a casting decision intended to lend credibility to the films and keep the production within the church. The filmic aesthetics and subtexts of these movies make them more like "docudramas," historical reenactments of specific persecution incidents. On the other hand, one can make the critique that the CAG's persecution movies are arguably insufficient for presenting a "witness" mode of authenticity that speaks accurately to historical events. But these movies undeniably give audiences some degree of "experiential authenticity."[33] The actors follow the pre-scripted repertoire of performances, encouraging the viewers to sympathize with the victims and take their persecution stories as they are.

The context in which the religious persecution depicted in the movies is framed primarily through the prism of spiritual categories, but these movies' narratives are also indebted to Christian martyrologies and hagiographies. Juxtaposed with the "unjustly" persecuted CAG believers are the "devilish" Communist captors and torturers. This binary framework offers an easy mode of reimagining the violence and pain that its leaders and members allegedly suffer at the hands of Chinese officials. A literary ancestor of these genres may be *Biographies of China's Catholic Martyr Saints,* which documents the martyrdom of the Chinese Catholics during the Boxer Uprising (1899–1901) or John Foxe's *Book of Martyrs*, which tells the stories of the life, suffering, and triumph of the early Protestant church in sixteenth-century England.[34] The CAG movies fulfill what Pamela Grace calls a "hagiopic" function to make their saintly figures instantly recognizable.[35] Each movie opens by referring to the story as the "real experience of the Christians of the Church of Almighty God" and by showing a copy of *The Word Appears in the Flesh*, the key revelatory text from the Almighty God. It then reconstructs the temporal and spatial setting of religious persecution incidents. A didactic narration explains the causes and pattern of the religious violence. The wording indicates the group's resolve to authenticate the persecution tales as historically reliable and accurate. The fundamental message remains that the state persecutes them because of their faith in the Almighty God. The saintly characteristics of the protagonists are highlighted through their refusal to give information to the police, their moral courage to suffer in order to protect the church, and their steadfast trust in the protection of the Almighty God for them and their family even in the time of their anguish. By grounding the centrality of "faith," the CAG highlights the commonalities of their suffering in Chinese Christian circles and downplays its theological differences from other mainline Chinese churches—an ecumenicity of suffering.

On many occasions, the narrators of the CAG persecution movies describe the frequent outbreaks of suppression as the result of a top-down decision by the senior Communist rulers in Beijing. This depiction offers a response to the debate of whether religious suppression in China is not an isolated local phenomenon but rather a larger state effort to eliminate independent churches. The central theme that links the seemingly disparate CAG tales is a trajectory of linear faith development gradually strengthened through the ordeal of suppression. The Chinese authorities criminalize committed CAG adherents for, in the words of CAG, "doing the duty of God." Unyielding to intimidation and inducement, the protagonists refuse to renounce the faith and betray church fellows, and are punished with incarceration, hard labor, and torture. Some protagonists flee the country and live in exile, and many suffer incurable physical and mental illnesses. Some die of torture.

The movie *Chronicles of Religious Persecution in China*, the winner for Best Documentary at 2017 Christian Online Film Festival, memorializes Zhou, allegedly an active evangelist in Anhui province in east China. His captors tortured him to death in April 1997. Officials attempted to bribe the Zhou family with Chinese yuan 50,000 (U.S.$7,180), to purchase their silence. The Zhou family rejected the bribe and filed a lawsuit. They eventually won the lawsuit, but the local court only handed a light sentence on the captors.[36] The film addresses police violence and abuse, the cruelty of physical and psychological torture, and the severity of pain and suffering inflicted on CAG Christians and their families. The movie has been so successful that CAG uses its title as an archetypical theme for all the CAG persecution movies.

To dramatize the intensity of their persecutors' viciousness, CAG's movies use bloody and violent scenes to sensationalize the horrendous torture methods that the Chinese officials are said to have applied to its members. The movie *Who Forced Her to the End of the Road* recalls the death of Gao, a female evangelist, who perished in a detention center after being locked up for three months.[37] In particular, it details graphically the countless sessions of prison interrogation and the severity of physical assaults. The captors often held Gao, the main character, and two female believers, in stress positions for days; deprived them of food, sleep, and toilet access; forced them to perform hard labor; and made them stand outdoors under the blistering heat of the summer sun. Sadly, Gao died as a result of the torture; her family was subsequently denied an autopsy.

Capturing the voices of other female victims of religious persecution, *The Dark Hour before the Dawn* tells the tale of three female followers.[38] The women underwent a slow and painful process of torture, exploitation, and dehumanization after being held in a torture chamber disguised as a government-run hotel. They refused to denounce one another and expose fellow church members. The producer uses close-up and medium shots to show a variety of torture instruments, highlights the dark space trapping these women, and captures the sound of physical assaults. Mixing with the women's wailing are the torturers' laughs and jeers. "Even a pair of chopsticks became a torturing tool in the hands of the captors," says the narrator. The unimaginable cruelty becomes sensation-alized through the suffering.

In *The Long Road of Exile*, a middle-aged evangelist is captured after being on the run from public security for fourteen years.[39] The captors deprive him of food and sleep, waterboard him, and smash his head against the wall. Their cru-elest torture is to hang him upside down and swing him toward the wall. Inca-pable of breaking him and forcing him to expose the church networks, a public security officer tells him, "Donate your kidney, and we'll let you go right away." The incident reminds viewers of the forced organ harvesting from Falun Gong practitioners, executed prisoners, and Uyghur Muslims in China.[40]

The state's deliberate cover-up of the cause of deaths of many CAG victims is widely criticized in the movies. In *The Cover-up*, twenty-eight-year-old female leader, Song, is found dead inside her rental apartment complex.[41] The film offers a flashback before her tragedy, when the local public security agents secretly monitored Song. Under the cloak of night, security forces break into her apart-ment, beat her to death, and throw her body from the building rooftop. To hide the truth, the agents fabricate evidence, insisting that Song jumped to her death after drinking pesticide. This film appears more like a crime thriller, as the pro-ducer shows the determination of the Song family to investigate their daughter's mysterious death and claim justice for her.

The movies depict the state's expansive violence toward, not just the indi-vidual, but also the whole family. The damage is insidious, long-lasting, and cross-generational. This is a major theme in *To the Brink and Back*, winner for Best Documentary at the 2019 Oniros Film Awards. The movie narrates the disinte-gration of the Chen family. A young entrepreneur at a state enterprise in Dalian, Chen hides for ten years to escape from the municipal public security forces. Back home, the local authorities harass and threaten his family to uncover his whereabouts. While this movie does not contain gruesome scenes of torture, the mental agony of unceasing bullying and intimation takes a heavy psychological toll on the Chen family. Chen's elderly mother used to live comfortably. Now, she cannot endure the public security's harassment, escaping to live in poverty in a remote township. Chen's wife moves from place to place, but the government forces always track her down, summoning her for interrogation whenever they want. The biggest tragedy happens to Chen's son. The police officer psychologi-cally torture the boy by threatening him with a stun gun and twist his toy dog's head off. Feeling traumatized and hopeless, the boy hangs himself; the movie blames the police's mental torture for causing his death.[42]

The significance of these cinematic portrayals of religious persecution lies in the fact that the CAG victims are depicted as ordinary citizens who suffer from state violence that does not discriminate by age, gender, or class. In the movies, the suffering CAG adherents embed a moral critique of the violent regime with a testimony to the lordship of the Almighty God. Brutal treatment would not frighten the Almighty God's followers, the movies assert, and the CAG situation speaks to China's global threat to human rights.

Conclusion

The scholarly study of World Christianity holds China as an epicenter of the Christian transmission in the Global East, characterizing Christianity as a faith crisscrossing cultural, confessional, and religious boundaries.[43] The field of "Chinese Christianities," the plural term for denoting the multiple forms of practices and expressions, centers on the resurgence of Christian activities in China and among the Chinese diaspora. While many scholars have examined the indigeneity and agency of Chinese believers in creating new articulations of faith in various settings,[44] much work needs to be done on the shifting movements of indigenous faith in non-Chinese avenues. Following the recent call for attention to the development of connections and ruptures in World Christianity,[45] this chapter identifies the CAG's response to perceived suffering as an indigenous movement struggling for global human rights and freedom. The CAG straddles a line between evangelical Christianity and new religious movements because of its unique claim about a Chinese female Christ. This indigenous theology, which is recognized as a special revelation to the Chinese, cannot escape contestation from confessional Christianity. While theology is nonnegotiable, exiled CAG members appeal to the broader Christian aspirations of freedom, democracy, and social justice to forge a universal identity. Still maintaining its indigenous theological claims, the CAG identifies with the global discourse of human rights, social justice and civil society embraced by Christians worldwide. When operating in diaspora, many displaced CAG adherents make their faith intelligible to non-Chinese.[46] The group's members can be said to be "Christian transnationals" who come out of an indigenous locale while upholding an objective, moral agreement with the larger Christian world.[47] In this way, they are more than "Sinicized" Christians with kinship only to Chinese culture and society.[48] Such new trends readily constitute part of World Christianity with an indigenous flourish.

This investigation treats the CAG's website as a site of knowledge production that articulates faith practices in an array of factual and aesthetic representations. Like a digital archive, the website is an examinable ethnographic object for understanding the presumed identity that the CAG displays visually.[49] With a strategy of evangelistic expansion, the group reclaims control over its own narratives through the website, rejecting the Chinese official "evil cult" discourse, and constructing a peace-loving and cosmopolitan identity. The movement's claims won followers in rural China during the 1990s. But for its religious teachings to take roots in the free urban societies outside China, the movement has sought to modernize its image, ameliorate the exclusivity of its doctrines, diversify its evangelistic strategies, and above all, ingratiate itself as a socially acceptable Christian religion. Embracing universal human rights and fundamental freedoms of other faith communities and pro-democracy dissidents, they find much common ground with victims of Chinese human rights abuses and cross the religious boundary to engage in lobbying and activism.

In the online realm, the CAG has positioned itself as an open, peaceful, and independent house church movement. Such a positive image fits well into its usage of the human rights discourse to enhance the group's legitimacy. It has coordinated international evangelistic efforts among the Chinese diaspora, circulating their sacred texts in multiple languages and adopting online news formats to provide information about their activities and comment on Chinese politics. Frequent references to the "Almighty God's" revelatory writings continue to define the central tenets of the group's doctrines, and the cyber presence reveals its capability to build a virtual community that bonds zealous members from around the world. The ease with which their members communicate with one another, reach out to foreign experts for advice, and collaborate with international human rights organizations, provide materials for rebuilding an image of a typical Christian movement. They also empower the CAG's ability to elude the Chinese authorities.

In a social media era, denial of access does not foreclose ongoing research into secretive religious groups. Having established a strong social media presence, the CAG has taken its message to every corner of the globe, and the group is eager to gain sympathy and support through this newly constructed online identity. In Emily Dunn's words, the CAG's website is "a windfall for researching a movement that is illegal in China."[50] The brief ethnographic encounters with the group related in this chapter suggest that freedom in the United States does not presume the group's approachability. Virtual ethnography, then, remains a publicly accessible field for researching activities with communities whose histories are fraught with enduring experiences of persecution.

NOTES

1. Emily Dunn, *Lightning from the East: Heterodoxy and Christianity in Contemporary China* (Leiden: Brill, 2015), 138–154.

2. The Chinese Communist Party uses the official regulatory mechanism known as the Three-Self Patriotic Movement (TSPM) to control the Protestant population. This is a Protestant activist movement established during the 1950s to eliminate the missionary element of the church. In the Maoist era, TSPM served actively to promulgate Mao's radical political campaigns against the church. In the late 1970s, another Protestant association, known as the Chinese Christian Council (CCC), was established for dealing with church management and ecclesiastical affairs. The TSPM/CCC combinedly remains a bridge between the party-state and the church; see Philip L. Wickeri, *Reconstructing Christianity in China: K. H. Ting and the Chinese Church* (Maryknoll,

NY: Orbis Books, 2007), 224–225. For a discussion of Chinese underground Christians, see Lian Xi, *Redeemed by Fire: The Rise of Popular Christianity in Modern China* (New Haven: Yale University Press, 2010), 204–232.

3. "China Executes Two Cult Members for McDonald's Murder," *BBC News*, February 2, 2015, https://www.bbc.com/news/world-asia-china-31087839.

4. For a discussion of two of these anticult international conferences in 2017, see Massimo Introvigne, *Inside The Church of Almighty God: The Most Persecuted Religious Movement in China* (New York: Oxford University Press, 2020), 103.

5. China Anti-Cult Network, accessed December 31, 2019, http://www.chinafxj.cn/sp/qns/.

6. The Chinese official Protestant magazine *Tianfeng* published numerous complaints about the CAG doctrines and practices; see, for instance, Wang Bingsheng, "Resist the Heretics Eastern Lightning," *Tianfeng* 5 (1997): 23; Jing Huanxin, "Tricks Played by the False Christ, Beware of Eastern Lightning the Evil Cult," *Tianfeng* 7 (1999): 20–21.

7. Susanna Chen, "Eastern Lightning Who Worships Female Christ," in *Discerning Truth from Heresies: A Critical Analysis of the Alleged and Real Heresies in Mainland China*, ed. Susanna Chen and Daisy Ho (Taipei: Christianity and China Research Center, 2000), 94–99; Kristin Kupper, "Images of Jesus Christ in Christian Inspired Spiritual and Religious Movements in China since 1978," in *The Chinese Face of Jesus Christ*, vol. 3b, ed. Roman Malek (Sankt Augustin, Germany: Institut Monumenta Serica and China-Zentrum, 2007), 1365–1375; Paul Hattaway, "When China's Christians Wish They Were in Prison: An Examination of the Eastern Lightning Cult in China," Asia Harvest website, June 25, 2002. https://asiaharvest.org/when-chinas-christians-wish-they-were-in-prison/.

8. David Palmer, *Qigong Fever—Body, Science, and Utopia in China* (New York: Columbia University Press, 2007); David Ownby, *Falun Gong and the Future of China* (New York: Oxford University Press, 2008).

9. Dunn, *Lightning from the East*, 201; Introvigne, *Inside The Church of Almighty God*, 39–40.

10. For the group's theological claims, see Introvigne, *Inside The Church of Almighty God*, 27–48; Dunn, *Lightning from the East*, 62–98.

11. Introvigne, *Inside The Church of Almighty God*, 69.

12. Patricia M. Thornton, "The New Cybersects: Resistance and Repression in the Reform Era," in *Chinese Society, Chang, Conflict, and Resistance*, ed. Elizabeth J. Perry and Mark Selden (New York: RoutledgeCurzon, 2003), 249.

13. Dunn, *Lightning from the East*; Introvigne, *Inside The Church of Almighty God*; Massimo Introvigne, "Xie Jiao as 'Criminal Religious Movements:' A New Look at Cult Controversies in China and around the World," *Journal of CESNUR* 2, no. 1 (January–February 2018): 13–32; Massimo Introvigne, "Captivity Narratives: Did The Church of Almighty God Kidnap 34 Evangelical Pastors in 2002?," *Journal of CESNUR* 2, no. 1 (January–February 2018): 100–110.

14. Brent Fulton, *China's Urban Christians: A Light That Cannot Be Hidden* (Eugene: Pickwick Publications, 2015); Chloë Starr, *Chinese Theology: Text and Context* (New Haven: Yale University Press, 2017); Alexander Chow, *Chinese Public Theology: Generational Shifts and Confucian Imagination in Chinese Christianity* (Oxford: Oxford University Press, 2018); Carsten T. Vala, *The Politics of Protestant Churches and the Party-State in China: God above Party?* (New York: Routledge, 2018); Li Ma and Jin Li, *Surviving the State, Remaking the Church: A Sociological Portrait of Christians in Mainland China* (Eugene, OR: Pickwick Publications, 2018); Melissa Wei-Tsing Inouye, *China and the True Jesus: Charisma and*

Organization in a Chinese Christian Church (New York: Oxford University Press, 2018); Christie Chui-Shan Chow, *Schism: Seventh-day Adventism in Post-Denominational China* (Notre Dame, IN: University of Notre Dame Press, 2021).

15. Nanlai Cao, *Constructing China's Jerusalem: Christians, Power, and Place in Contemporary Wenzhou* (Stanford: Stanford University Press, 2011); Huang Ke-hsien, "Taming the Spirit by Appropriating Indigenous Culture: An Ethnographic Study of the True Jesus Church as Confucian-Style Pentecostalism," in *Global Chinese Pentecostal and Charismatic Christianity*, ed. Fenggang Yang, Joy K. C. Tong, and Allan H. Anderson (Leiden: Brill, 2017), 118–136; Aminta Arrington, *Songs of the Lisu Hills: Practicing Christianity in Southwest China* (University Park: Pennsylvania State University Press, 2020).

16. Joseph Tse-Hei Lee and Christie Chui-Shan Chow, "Methodological Reflections on the Study of Chinese Christianities," in *World Christianity: Methodological Considerations*, ed. Martha Frederiks and Dorottya Nagy (Leiden: Brill, 2020), 113–134.

17. Church elder, interview with author, August 6, 2012, Wenzhou.

18. Church elder, interview with author, October 20, 2012, Wenzhou.

19. Church elder, interview with author, April 22, 2019, Yanji.

20. Fenggang Yang, "The Red, Black, and Gray Markets of Religion in China," *Sociological Quarterly* 47, no. 1 (2006): 93–122.

21. 27th U.S. Catholic China Bureau Conference, August 11–13, 2017, St. John's University, Queens, New York.

22. Freedom House has long worked on behalf of Christian victims of persecution and for international religious freedom. See the organization's website, accessed March 15, 2020, https://freedomhouse.org.

23. The gender-based seating, spirited sharing, lay-led services, and the worship format resembles the Christian Assembly's rituals, widely practiced in China and Hong Kong, revealing the CAG's early connection with the Christian Assembly founded by the famous Chinese church leader Watchman Nee (Ni Tuoshen, 1903–1972) in the 1920s and managed by his successor Witness Lee (Li Changshou, 1905–1997) in Taiwan and the United States after 1949.

24. Tom Boellstorff, Bonnie Nardi, Celia Pearce, and T. L. Taylor, *Ethnography and Virtual Words: A Handbook of Method* (Princeton: Princeton University Press, 2012), 57.

25. Jeffrey A. Sluka and Antonius C. G. Robben, "Fieldwork in Cultural Anthropology: An Introduction," in *Ethnographic Fieldwork*, ed. Antonius C. G. Robben and Sluka A. Jeffrey (Malden, MA: Blackwell, 2007), 25.

26. Susan F. Harding, *The Book of Jerry Falwell: Fundamentalist Language and Politics* (Princeton: Princeton University Press, 2001).

27. The Church of Almighty God, "Reports on the Chinese Communist Government's Arrest of and Persecution to the Believers of Church of Almighty God," accessed January 9, 2020, https://www.godfootsteps.org/persecution.html.

28. Apart from the CAG website, these reports are available on many international human right organization websites, such as the Center for Studies on New Religions (CESNUR) or its affiliated electronic magazine *Bitter Winter* and the International Observatory of Religious Liberty of Refugees (ORLIR). See The Church of Almighty God, "2019 Annual Report on the Chinese Communist Government's Persecution of The Church of Almighty God," accessed March 22, 2020, https://www.holyspiritspeaks .org/news/annual-report-2019/; The Church of Almighty God, "2017 Annual Report on the Chinese Communist Government's Persecution of The Church of Almighty God,"

accessed December 20, 2019, https://www.cesnur.org/2017/almighty_china_report
.pdf; Marco Respinti, "The Bloody Tribute Paid by The Church of Almighty God," *Bitter Winter*, March 13, 2019, https://bitterwinter.org/the-bloody-tribute-paid-by-the-church
-of-almighty-god/; "The Church of Almighty God Releases Report on Persecution in China," ORLIR, November 20, 2017, https://www.orlir.org/church-of-almighty-god
-releases-report-on-persecution-in-china.html. Human Rights Without Frontiers (HRWF) published twenty CAG persecution stories in *Tortured to Death: The Persecution of The Church of Almighty God in China* (Brussels: HRWF, 2018).

29. See also Introvigne, *Inside The Church of Almighty God*, 53–54.

30. Yiman Wang, "The Amateur's Lightning Rod: DV Documentary in Postsocialist China," *Film Quarterly* 58, no. 4 (Summer 2005): 16.

31. Massimo Introvigne, "Church of Almighty God and the Visual Arts," *World Religion and Spirituality Project*, December 3, 2017, https://wrldrels.org/2017/12/04/church-of-almighty
-god-eastern-lightning-and-the-visual-arts/.

32. The discussion of "rhetorical texts" is drawn from Jouko Aaltonen, "Claims of Hope and Disasters: Rhetoric Expression in Three Climate Change Documentaries," *Studies in Documentary Film* 8, no. 1 (2014): 61–75.

33. The idea of "witness," and "experiential" modes of authenticity is drawn from Sara Jones, "Memory on Film: Testimony and Constructions of Authenticity in Documentaries about the German Democratic Republic," *European Journal of Cultural Studies* 16, no. 2 (2012): 194–210.

34. Taiwan Roman Catholic Bishops Committee, *Biographies of China's Catholic Martyr Saints* (in Chinese) (Taipei: Tianzhujiao Taiwan diqu zhujiaotuan, 2000); John Foxe, *Book of Martyrs* (Hartford: E. Hunt, 1851).

35. Pamela Grace, *The Religious Film: Christianity and the Hagiopic* (Malden, MA: Wiley-Blackwell, 2009), 1–3.

36. The film is also known as *The Way of the Cross*. YouTube video, 55:18, February 23, 2018, https://www.youtube.com/watch?v=6VwlZsXz3No.

37. *Who Forced Her to the End of the Road?* YouTube video, 34:12, March 3, 2018, https://www
.youtube.com/watch?v=covKrONHyuE.

38. *The Dark Hour before the Dawn*, YouTube video, 55:18, February 23, 2018, https://www
.youtube.com/watch?v=6VwlZsXz3No, begin at 32:24.

39. *The Long Road of Exile*, YouTube video, 39:42, June 6, 2018, https://www.youtube.com
/watch?v=OkIRk_GWVT8.

40. Saphora Smith, "China Forcefully Harvests Organs from Detainees, Tribunal Concludes," *NBC News*, June 18, 2019, https://www.nbcnews.com/news/world/china-forcefully
-harvests-organs-detainees-tribunal-concludes-n1018646 (accessed November 22, 2019).

41. *The Cover-Up*, YouTube video, 50:17, March 3, 2018, https://www.youtube.com/watch?v
=ytIIomPECHw.

42. *To the Brink and Back*, YouTube video, 47:35, March 5, 2018, https://www.youtube.com
/watch?v=TG2qmA6kaso.

43. Dale T. Irvin, "World Christianity: An Introduction," *Journal of World Christianity* 1, no. 1 (2008): 1–26.

44. Paul Woods, ed., *Shaping Christianity in Greater China: Indigenous Christians in Focus* (Oxford: Regnum Books International, 2017).

45. Joel Cabrita and David Maxwell, "Relocating Christianity," in *Relocating World Christianity: Interdisciplinary Studies in Universal and Local Expressions of the Christian Faith*, ed. Joel Cabrita, David Maxwell, and Emma Wild-Wood (Leiden: Brill, 2017), 1–44.

46. It is estimated that 30 percent of members in CAG's overseas communities are non-Chinese. See Introvigne, *Inside The Church of Almighty God*, 41.

47. The term "Christian transnationals" is drawn from David Maxwell, "Historical Perspectives on Christianity Worldwide: Connections, Comparisons and Consciousness," in *Relocating World Christianity*, ed. Cabrita, Maxwell and Wild-Wood, 51–52. Maxwell describes the missionaries in the eighteenth and nineteenth centuries as "Christian internationals" to stress the international connection between religious revivalist and social movements.

48. The Sinicization of Christianity has been a subject of debate in Chinese politics and in the field of Chinese Christianity. Scholars in the field of Chinese religions focus on the adaptation of Christianity to Chinese culture and society. See Zheng Yangwen, *Sinicizing Christianity* (Leiden: Brill, 2017). In China's political discourse, which uses the term as a political category, "Sinicization of Christianity" views Christianity as a foreign import that should be made compatible with socialism and Chinese authoritarianism.

49. This conceptualization follows Katherine Verdery, *Secret and Truths: Ethnography in the Archive of Romania's Secret Police* (Budapest: Central European University Press, 2014).

50. Dunn, *Lightning from the East*, 19.

Afterword

Global Visions of Violence–A Response

MELANI McALISTER

In the early 2000s, the contemporary Christian music group Jars of Clay collaborated on a book about the persecuted church titled *The Narrow Road*. The book was an expanded and redesigned version of the classic narrative of Bible smuggling behind communist lines, Brother Andrew's *God's Smuggler*, which was first published in 1967.[1] At the time, Jars of Clay was a Christian band with a mainstream following and a few Grammy awards behind them. Mostly their music was typical of much Christian music: apolitical, mildly countercultural, focused on loving Jesus. With "our narrow worldview," band leader Dan Haseltine wrote in the introduction to *The Narrow Road*, they had not realized that "there is a world beyond the safety of our insular church culture."

Then, as Haseltine described it, he read an article in the late 1990s about "Christian persecution" in the Sudan. The timing makes sense. The 1990s were the heyday of a political movement on behalf of the southern Sudanese, who were involved in a civil war against the leadership based in Khartoum. The movement was galvanizing U.S. Christian communities on behalf of people they saw as suffering fellow Christians who were facing a Muslim enemy. U.S. Christian news media, along with groups such as Voice of the Martyrs and Christian Solidarity International, were reporting widely on the conflict in Sudan as a religious war.

Haseltine described the moment of his own politicization this way: "I had seen the pictures of torture victims [before]. I had read the reports of Christian women and children sold into slavery. I had been confronted with the tales of murder, rape, and starvation. But all I knew were stories that seemed to fill that morbid curiosity that draws us to car wrecks and real-life TV shows. These people were not real to me. They were not brothers and sisters."[2]

Not long after, in spring 2000, several members of Jars of Clay went on a trip to Vietnam and China, under the auspices of a conservative Bible-distribution group.[3] There they met with underground Christian groups, and they came back deeply concerned about the "persecuted Church." They spoke out in interviews. They began working on *The Narrow Road*, augmenting Brother Andrew's story with a CD with a new Jars of Clay song and a photo gallery. The band held a benefit concert for Amnesty International and began taking up a collection for persecuted Christians at their concerts.[4]

In all these efforts, the members of Jars of Clay were acting very much in line with the priorities and activities of the modern U.S. antipersecution movement, which had a long history dating back to the Cold War but flowered in the 1990s, becoming a singularly powerful example of Christian political activism on foreign policy issues and a key player in the development of new forms of Christian narratives and cultural practice, both in the United States and globally.[5] Indeed, as the remarkable contributions to this volume demonstrate, the "global vision of violence" against Christians has become an animating concept—a reality in some cases and a distorted rendering of conflict in others, but overall a significant force in shaping Christian identity across borders and over many decades. In what follows, I focus on several key contributions of the volume—not as a summation of the many excellent essays here, but as a meditation on the cultural work that "visions of violence" do, as well as a reiteration of and reflection on the questions raised by many of the contributors, about what is seen and what is ignored in these constructs. I briefly explore four issues that emerge from the volume: (1) the cultural work of the discourse of anti-Christian violence in constructing community, (2) the power of media, (3) the significance of affect for "grassroots theology," and (4) the power of race and empire. In each case, I suggest directions for future scholarship. I also try to consider a question that is raised in the introduction to this volume and touched on in various ways in the chapters: how can scholars do justice to the realities of suffering, by Christians, among others, while also grappling with how the narrative of anti-Christian violence does its own kind of violence—to accurate understandings of global conflict, an honest reckoning with history, and the possibilities for nonsectarian community?

Visions of Violence Construct Community

The narrative of persecution does powerful work in forging identity and reshaping politics. This is true for many communities, not just Christians, but it is an animating force for Christians, in our own time and across much of the twentieth century. As the editors make clear in the introduction to the volume, there is often a potent form of misrepresentation that happens when complex conflicts are framed as being religious, given that the multifaceted realities of violence are, in fact, shaped by struggles over resources, ethnic conflict, government corruption, and the distorting influence of global capitalism. This is what happened in Sudan in the 1990s, and Nigeria and Iraq in the 2000s, as well as in many other places. The discourse of "persecuted Christians" posited complex conflicts as straightforward religious ones—thus as matters of morality, of defending the faith.

As the essays in the book show in numerous ways, a sense of struggle and suffering can create new forms of identity and community. From the heterodox teachings of the Church of Almighty God (Chow) to the new alliances created between Coptic and U.S. evangelical Christians (Lukasik), we see the ways that marginalization and even violence can create new networks. Indeed, the global movement on behalf of persecuted Christians has helped to constitute a kind of ecumenism among communities not always inclined toward it. Starting in the Cold War, and intensifying in the 1990s, a broad set of activists worked to create a sense of urgency about Christian suffering globally. In so doing, they made alliances among Protestants (ecumenical and evangelical), Catholics, and Orthodox.

In this embrace of the idea of a Christian community united by suffering, numbers mattered: it was important to show an urgent, growing problem. But some of the numbers could be misleading. There were a range of statistical methods to count Christians (Corrigan) and/or martyrs (Kirkpatrick and Bruner), and they were shaped for maximum effect. For example, in the 1990s it became common to claim that there were "more Christian martyrs in the twentieth century than in the previous nineteen centuries combined." That might be technically true (depending on how you defined martyr), but it ignored the massive increase in global population in the twentieth century; there were more Christians *overall* in the twentieth century than in the previous nineteen centuries as well.[6] Moreover, martyr numbers often included every Christian who died in a "religious" conflict, regardless of whether they were actually persecuted for their faith or simply died in a war.[7] But the point was not accuracy; it was about emotional and political power.

Indeed, the cultural work of such claims has been highly productive. By largely ignoring religious differences among Christians (even though conflict among Christian groups has arguably been the cause of most violence against Christians historically) and positing instead a pan-Christian community facing down unbelievers, the "persecuted Christians" narrative sutures a broadly ecumenical Christian identity. That ecumenical suturing has happened in the context of a larger rise in political tensions in which religion figures significantly. Most recently, as Bruner and Kirkpatrick argue in the introduction, the generalized claim about religious persecution against Christians that we see in the didactic literature is often translated (in the United States) into a story of Muslim attacks on Christians. This translation is so effective that "Muslim" has become a floating signifier of danger and stress, as in Kaell's description of the American woman who knows that someone she is supporting financially in

Ecuador is facing difficulty, and she vaguely gestures toward how this must have to do with the many Muslims there.

The fact that so much of the discussion of global violence today has come to be described or glossed in Muslim-Christian terms is due in part to the ways in which Christianity and U.S. empire have operated in tandem. This does not mean that every American Christian has advocated U.S. imperial reach or that the U.S. state was actually supporting missionary work (although it sometimes did). Rather, the Muslim-Christian framing resulted from the ways in which the United States operated on the global stage in recent decades—politically domi-nant, culturally Christian, and willing to impose its will through military force. The rhetoric of a "clash of civilizations" might be problematic for those in the United States and Europe who wanted to maintain the U.S. alliances with Muslim-identified governments in the Middle East (which is why President George W. Bush explicitly opposed the embrace of such language after 9/11 as he rushed to shore up the relationship with Saudi Arabia), but the idea of a fun-damental clash was embraced by people as different as the Islamist Osama bin Laden and the British evangelical activist Patrick Sookhdeo, both of whom found a usefulness in the ways that stories of conflict constructed community identities across internal lines of difference.[8]

At the same time, much of the suffering that persecution discourse tries to name is quite real. There is *religious* violence—in Nigeria and in New York, in Indonesia and Indiana. Ask any Muslim woman who wore a headscarf in the United States after 9/11, and she will tell you that, while there may not be any-thing like a "clash of civilizations," there are people bent on hurting others because of their religion. If those enactments of violence are not *only* about religion—what ever is?—they are not separate from it either. I make this rather obvious point because I think it is too often sidelined by scholars (myself included) who are anxious to show the distorting work that persecution dis-course does or that religion itself does as a category. When we see the U.S. Supreme Court rolling back rights for LGBTQ people in the name of religious free-dom or the Donald Trump administration declaring itself to be in the business of centering religious freedom abroad while discriminating against Muslim immigration at home, we are right to worry about the work being done to privi-lege certain religious groups as objects of state cultivation. But when Jews see their synagogues attacked, Christians see their churches burned down, or Mus-lims are attacked on the street—wherever it happens—then religious violence must be understood as being as viable (and as messy) a category as any other categorization of violence. This is the baseline reality on which the distortions of persecution discourse depends.

Indeed, thinking about religious communities in relationship—to each other and to other categories like race or ethnicity—requires adding religion, not subtracting it, from a layered picture. In collections such as this one, we gain a valuable addition to scholarship that accounts for transnational flows, working in multiple languages to unpack the many nuances and contexts of encounter. One further direction in this vein would be to engage in more work that deeply analyzes the relationships between religious groups—not only "how Christians view Muslims" or "how Hindus view Christians" (valuable as that is) but also the ways in which global and local contexts are reshaping relationships among communities. Ebenezer Obadare's work on Nigeria is one exemplary model.[9]

Visions of Violence Are Also Constructed through Media

Media has, for decades now, played a role in muddying the boundaries of Christian identities, working to create a broader, more loosely defined set of Christian values and performances. In the 1930s, radio brought Aimee Semple McPherson a national audience, while in the 1980s, TV put Pat Robertson's show into many non-Pentecostal homes, opening up the avenues for learning about both religion and politics. The boundary blurring became even more prevalent with the rise of the internet, where one might watch the Nigerian minister David Oyedepo give a sermon, listen to Brother Isaiah on Spotify, or follow Beth Moore's Twitter feed without knowing or caring about the theological differences that separate Pentecostals, Catholics, and Southern Baptists. In that sense, the cohabitation of diverse media products works like the discourse of persecution itself, capaciously crossing denominational and sectarian lines, creating sensibilities and orientations that help us construct connections.

However, media work to draw boundaries as well. In the nineteenth century, stories published by missionaries, who relied on such narratives to recount not only their success in gaining converts but also the suffering of those converts at the hands of an unbelieving world (Corrigan), we see the ideological work of media products, the us-them of the heathen and the believers. In the media products of Coptic Christians, we see a vision of Islam that shores up the anti-Muslim sentiments of white American evangelicals. Sometimes media does a different kind of work. Hillary Kaell's informants tell her that CNN tells the story of humanitarian crisis differently than Christian media do, and they long for a version that produces a possibility of connection, a sense of meaningful knowledge (even when that knowledge is, in fact, incorrect). Omri Elisha, in a similar vein, describes the power of "martyrological media" to produce an affective sense of witness and belonging. Crucially, he shows how the books and videos that circulate with stories of martyrdom are significant, not just for the stories they tell, but also in their status *as* media, as a kind of material manifestation of both the longing for connection and the reality of difference. We have a rich body of work that considers the impact of U.S. Christian media on both domestic and international audiences.[10] There is less that explores the full impact of global flows: how Christianity in India is being reshaped by YouTube videos from Nigeria, or how radio or TV from Mexico and Central America inform American Catholicism. As long as we operate from a model that implicitly or explicitly centers either U.S. imperialism (critically) or rising Global South Christianity (uncritically), we cannot fully account for the multiple connections that are reshaping religious-political formations across national and regional lines.[11]

Affective Practices and Ordinary Theology

A number of contributors to the volume explore how Christians encounter and engage with a complex series of affective stances that tie them to a larger community. Several of the essays describe the ways in which American evangelicals in particular struggle with a sense of connection and yet distance from Christians elsewhere in the world. Kaell, Elisha, Corrigan, and Lukasik explore the avenues through which Christians in the United States express an affective sense of *communitas* and longing for boundary dissolution, alongside a more or less developed ideological awareness of American privilege.

The working theologies of ordinary people are practiced in other contexts, too.[12] Kate Kingsbury describes how in Mexico, in a situation of drug cartel violence and danger, Catholic women construct a vernacular form of devotion to the saint of death. There is a theology here, albeit an unorthodox and even syncretic one, that calls on a folk saint for protection in the context of precarity—drug wars, economic insecurity, sickness, and gendered violence. But the theology or ideology of worshiping a fierce and sometimes vengeful figure also does affective work for its participants, creating a sense of power and resilience. Sunder John Boopalan describes affective relationships in a caste context in India as including visual, olfactory, emotional, and tactile components: disgust and contempt, complaints about smell or filth, and also fear, humiliation, and shame. In each case, feeling and belief are deeply connected, not as cause and effect but rather as intertwined and quotidian performances.

For decades now, scholars of religion have moved away from a "church history" orientation toward attention to lived religion. Indeed, an Asadian turn, built out of performance theory and Foucauldian analysis, has thoroughly reshaped the field. But what we see in this volume and in the work of a range of other scholars in recent years is a kind of return to theology, but via thinking through theology as part of lived, affective experience, built from what people feel and want to feel, which shapes what they know and believe. It is *not* that articulated belief does not matter, but rather that the work of thinking theologically happens in all sorts of ordinary spaces. Seminarians and theologians are perhaps no less saturated with emotion or affective reactivity than anybody else, but by taking the theorizing of ordinary believers seriously, we take account of a world of knowledge making that operates across the usual lines of authority.

Visions of Religious Violence and the Workings of Race and Empire

These structuring forms of power are singularly important for understanding what is unstated, or deliberately occluded, in many of the discussions of Christians as persecuted. The racial and gendered violence that structures global history in the modern era also fundamentally shapes Christian history, which is deeply divided along global fractures of national and racial power, however much theologies might (sometimes) aspire otherwise. As Harvey Kwiyani shows in the case of Malawi, white supremacy "both used and served colonial violence against peoples of the world." That violence was destructive and deadly, not only in the context of European colonialism but also in the realms of U.S. expansionist power and, of course, within U.S. borders. Racial and imperial violence could also take the form of appropriation and historical revisionism, as in Joel Cabrita's evocative discussion of a how a white "liberal" European scholar took credit for the work of a black woman in the context of the larger and systemic racial violence of apartheid. We can see how race works, historically and today, to divide Christians (within the United States and across the world). Yet the idea of "Christians," generically, as persecuted can work to ignore or suture those divisions.

It would be too easy, however, to assume that the perpetrators of this violence (whether literal or symbolic) are only and always white. As Candace Lukasik shows very well in the case of Coptic activists in the United States, there is a way in which incorporation into U.S. power politics does involve a kind of performance of, or affiliation with, whiteness; people who were parsed as brown-so-probably-Muslim in the context of U.S. Islamophobia manage to establish a separate space within persecution discourse. And yet, given the reality that American Christians are deeply and increasingly racially diverse, we must recognize that U.S. imperial power operates even in contexts where its representatives are not white.[13] There is a rich body of work that documents the ways in which African Americans and other marginalized groups have resisted U.S. empire.[14] But even before 9/11, and certainly since then, there also has been a vibrant scholarly conversation about U.S. global power that tries to account for racial diversity as a key component of the U.S. imperial brand.[15] When BIPOC American Christians go abroad, on short-term missions or as staffers for World Vision or InterVarsity, they cannot fully delink themselves from the power of the U.S. state. Race and empire are inseparable, and race and religion are often conflated, but it does not help our understandings of the contours of global power if we assume the whiteness of Global North Christianity.

In conclusion, I turn to a discussion of blood. In 2002, Jars of Clay founded a nonprofit called the Blood:Water Mission. This might seem to be a direct result of their immersion into the antipersecution activism in the 1990s, but actually it represented a self-conscious change of course. Not long after that first trip to

China and Vietnam to talk to persecuted Christians, band leader Haseltine was invited to tour parts of Africa (including Uganda and Malawi) to talk to African believers. Later, the band went to South Africa. From those trips, the band members became galvanized about the issue of HIV/AIDS, which they also understood to be connected to structural economic inequality, including the fact that many people in Africa lacked access to clean well water. The group founded their own charity, the Blood:Water Mission, whose work focused on the quotidian tasks of both building wells and promoting AIDS education. They also became involved with the ONE campaign, singer Bono's global antipoverty program, and later joined a larger group of evangelicals who prayed for aid for Africa at the G-8 summit in 2005. Soon Haseltine started speaking out politically as well. "Over the years, we really got tired of being lumped in with so many things we didn't believe," he told a reporter. "As the political process seems to be narrowing in on 'Republicans are all Christians, Christians are all Republicans,' we decided we don't really want to fall into those categories."[16] By working on HIV/AIDS and sanitation projects, the band said they wanted to highlight the importance of "clean water and clean blood" for developing countries in Africa. The band understood that both water (Jesus as living water) and blood (the blood of the lamb) are rich in Christian symbolism, and they used those images to invite an alternative kind of Christian activism from the persecution politics that first politicized them.

In this book, there is surprisingly little in the way of blood, and yet blood is both a reality and a metaphor that ties together a great deal of what we see in these marvelously rich and diverse chapters. Blood is central, of course, to the Christian narrative: the blood of Jesus as redemptive sacrifice. "Oh precious is the flow / That makes me white as snow," sings the globally popular worship band Hillsong. "The blood of the martyrs is the seed of the church," in the words of church father Tertullian—an aphorism that found renewed circulation with the rise of the antipersecution movement in the 1990s, quoted by everyone from Pope John Paul II to Voice of the Martyrs. This belief that violence is generative—that it actually creates a stronger community of believers—is deeply controversial among those who fight against such violence, but it runs through the sanctification that is everywhere in the global discourse about anti-Christian persecution. There is an "economy of blood," in Candace Lukasik's evocative phrase. That economy creates kinship from suffering—"my brothers and sisters," in the words of Jars of Clay's leader. It links Christians as family and victims, tying those "redeemed by the blood of the lamb" intricately to those who are steeped in the blood of violence, both as agents and victims. But blood is also a language of race, of difference—it works to differentiate across religious lines and within them. It shapes the power relationship that allows some Christians to appropriate others' work or enact colonial domination in a missionary context. It is the sign of violence that is both literal and symbolic, constructive and destructive, deeply spiritual and the most material of realities. It is at the heart of Christian global visions, including visions of violence.

NOTES

1. Brother Andrew, John L. Sherrill, Elizabeth Sherrill, and Jars of Clay, *The Narrow Road: Stories of Those Who Walk This Road Together* (Grand Rapids, MI: Revell, 2001); Brother Andrew, *God's Smuggler* (New York: New American Library, 1967).

2. Introduction to Andrew, Sherrill, Sherill, and Jars of Clay, *The Narrow Road*, 7.

3. The activist was Steve Hass, U.S. director of the International Day of Prayer for the Persecuted Church, but the members went to China and Vietnam with Open Doors and Voice of the Martyrs.

4. Jars of Clay Press release, April 20, 2001, http://www.jarchives.com/jartifacts18.htm ·

5. I discuss the antipersecution movement of the Cold War and post–Cold War eras in detail in several chapters of Melani McAlister, *The Kingdom of God Has No Borders: A Global History of American Evangelicalism* (New York: Oxford University Press, 2018 ; repr., 2022). See also Andrew Preston, *Sword of the Spirit, Shield of Faith: Religion in American War and Diplomacy* (New York: Knopf, 2012); Lauren Frances Turek, *To Bring the Good News to All Nations: Evangelical Influence on Human Rights and U.S. Foreign Relations* (Ithaca: Cornell University Press, 2020); Elizabeth Castelli, "Persecution Complexes: Identity Politics and the 'War on Christians,'" *Differences: A Journal of Feminist Cultural Studies* 18, no. 3 (Fall 2007): 152–180; Elizabeth Castelli, "Praying for the Persecuted Church: US Christian Activism in the Global Arena," *Journal of Human Rights* 4, no. 3 (September 2005): 321–351.

6. To give a quick sense of why this is so: in 200 A.D. there were probably 200,000 Christians in the world, so even if a high percentage of them were killed, the total numbers would still be small. Even in the last one hundred or so years, the global Christian population has more than tripled, from 600 million in 1910 to 2.2 billion today. So, again, if the same percentage of people were killed today as in 1910, the total numbers would be dramatically higher. See Pew Research Center, "Global Christianity—A Report on the Size and Distribution of the World's Christian Population," December 19, 2011, https://www.pewforum.org/2011/12/19/global-christianity-exec/. See also Christianity in View, "Statistics and Forecasts for World Religions: 1800–2025," February 22, 2016m. http://christianityinview.com/religion-statistics.html. On the early Christian era, see Philip Jenkins, "How Many Christians?," September 22, 2017, https://www.patheos.com/blogs/anxiousbench/2017/09/how-many-christians/.

7. Melani McAlister, "The Persecuted Body: Evangelical Internationalism, Islam, and the Politics of Fear," in *Facing Fear: The History of an Emotion in Global Perspective*, ed. M. Laffan and M. Weiss, 133–161 (Princeton: University of Princeton Press, 2012).

8. Patrick Sookhdeo, *A People Betrayed: The Impact of Islamisation on the Christian Community in Pakistan* (Pewsey, U.K.: Isaac Publishing, 2002); Lausanne Committee Issue Group, "LOP 32: The Persecuted Church," 2004 Forum Occasional Papers, Lausanne Committee for World Evangelization (Pattaya, Thailand), 2004, http://www.lausanne.org/documents/2004forum/LOP32_IG3.pdf.

9. Ebenezer Obadare, *Pentecostal Republic: Religion and the Struggle for State Power in Nigeria* (London: Zed Books, 2018).

10. Among the many good works in this field, see Marla Frederick, *Colored Television: American Religion Gone Global* (Stanford: Stanford University Press, 2016); Steve Brouwer, Paul Gifford, and Susan D. Rose, *Exporting the American Gospel: Global Christian*

Fundamentalism (London: Routledge, 2013); Jason C. Bivins, *Religion of Fear: The Politics of Horror in Conservative Evangelicalism* (Oxford: Oxford University Press, 2008); Jonathan L. Walton, *Watch This! The Ethics and Aesthetics of Black Televangelism* (New York: NYU Press, 2009).

11. Some examples of work that accounts for these flows includes Philomena Njeri Mwaura, "Nigerian Pentecostal Missionary Enterprise in Kenya," in *Religion, History, and Politics in Nigeria* (Lanham, MD: University Press of America, 2005), v–viii; Birgit Meyer and Annelies Moors, eds., *Religion, Media, And the Public Sphere* (Bloomington, Indiana University Press, 2005). There is also a vibrant scholarly conversation on this topic in Middle East studies; see Charles Hirschkind, *The Ethical Soundscape: Cassette Sermons and Islamic Counterpublics* (New York: Columbia University Press, 2006); Marwan M. Kraidy, "The Projectilic Image: Islamic State's Digital Visual Warfare and Global Networked Affect," *Media, Culture & Society* 39, no. 8 (2017): 1194–1209.

12. Jeff Astley, *Ordinary Theology: Looking, Listening and Learning in Theology* (Burlington: Routledge, 2002); Catherine Albanese, *America: Religions and Religion*, 5th ed. (Belmont, MA: Wadsworth, 2012).

13. Janelle S. Wong, *Immigrants, Evangelicals, and Politics in an Era of Demographic Change* (New York: Russell Sage Foundation, 2018).

14. Penny Von Eschen, *Race against Empire: Black Americans and Anticolonialism, 1937–1957* (Ithaca: Cornell University Press, 1997); Nikhil Pal Singh, *Black Is a Country: Race and the Unfinished Struggle for Democracy* (Cambridge, MA: Harvard University Press, 2004); Keisha Blain, *Set the World on Fire: Black Nationalist Women and the Global Struggle for Freedom* (Philadelphia: University of Pennsylvania Press, 2018).

15. Moustafa Bayoumi, "The Race Is On," *Middle East Report*, Middle East Research and Information Project, March 2010, http://www.merip.org/mero/interventions/race; Melani McAlister, *Epic Encounters: Culture, Media, and U.S. Interests in the Middle East since 1945*, 2nd ed. (Berkeley: University of California Press, 2005); Deepa Kumar, *Islamophobia and the Politics of Empire* (Chicago: Haymarket Books, 2012).

16. Kate Bowman Johnson, "So Much to Sing About," *Sojourners*, November 2005.

ACKNOWLEDGMENTS

This project was made possible by the time, energy, and support of many people. First among them are our colleagues who contributed their work to this volume. That work was produced, revised, and edited amid a host of intersecting challenges, including especially the COVID-19 pandemic. The fact that this volume came together at all is a testament to their diligence, commitment, and creativity. On our side, we would like to thank our spouses, Anna (David) and Keeley (Jason), for the flexibility, understanding, and care you provided to create the time we needed to complete it.

We also want to extend our sincere thanks to our editor at Rutgers University Press, Elisabeth Maselli, for her interest in and support of this project.

Support for research funding was generously provided in a project grant through the Louisville Institute to Jason Bruner for his project titled "An Ecumenism of Blood."

A special thanks to the College of Arts and Letters at James Madison University for funding that supported this book project, as well.

Three of the chapters in this volume are derived from earlier publications:

Omri Elisha, "Saved by a Martyr: Evangelical Mediation, Sanctification, and the 'Persecuted Church,'" *Journal of the American Academy of Religion* 84, no. 4 (2016): 1056–1080.

Harvey Kwiyani, "Mission after George Floyd: On White Supremacy, Colonialism, and World Christianity," *ANVIL* 36, no. 3 (2020): 7–13.

Candace Lukasik, "Economy of Blood: The Persecuted Church and the Racialization of American Copts," *American Anthropologist* (2021), https://doi.org/10.1111/aman.13602.

BIBLIOGRAPHY

ARCHIVES

Billy Graham Center Archives, Wheaton, IL

ChildFund Archives, Richmond, VA

Church Missionary Society Archives, Oxford, UK

Couzens, Tim. Papers. Greenside, Johannesburg

Institute for Social Research, Records, University of KwaZulu-Natal Archives, Pietermaritzburg

Kuper, Hilda. Papers. University of California at Los Angeles Archives

London School of Economics Archives

Sundkler, Bengt. Papers. University of Uppsala

University of Notre Dame Archives (UNDA), South Bend, IN

Wits Historical Papers, Johannesburg

Women's Board of Missions Records (WBMR), Burke Library Archives at Union Theological Seminary, New York, NY

World Vision International Archives (WVIA), Monrovia, CA

BOOKS, ARTICLES, AND REPORTS

Aaltonen, Jouko. "Claims of Hope and Disasters: Rhetoric Expression in Three Climate Change Documentaries." *Studies in Documentary Film* 8, no. 1 (2014): 61–75.

Achebe, Chinua. *Things Fall Apart.* New York: McDowell, 1959.

Adam, Barbara, and Chris Groves. *Future Matters: Action, Knowledge, Ethics.* Leiden: Brill, 2007.

Adorno, Theodor. *The Culture Industry: Selected Essays on Mass Culture.* Edited by J.M. Bernstein. London: Routledge, 2001.

Ahern, Laura. "Agency." *Journal of Linguistic Anthropology* 9, no. 1–2 (1999): 12–15.

Ahlstrom, Sydney E. "The Scottish Philosophy and American Theology." *Church History* 24 (1955): 257–272.

Ahmed, Sara. *The Cultural Politics of Emotion.* New York: Routledge, 2015.

Albanese, Catherine. *America: Religions and Religion,* 5th ed. Belmont, MA: Wadsworth, 2012.

Allen, John, Jr. *The Global War on Christians: Dispatches from the Front Lines of Anti-Christian Persecution.* New York: Image, 2013.

Almighty God Church. Twitter. Accessed May 20, 2022. https://twitter.com/churchAlmighty.

"American Board of Missions." *Missionary Herald,* February 1828, 60.

Anderson, Alan. *Spreading Fires: The Missionary Nature of Early Pentecostalism.* Maryknoll, NY: Orbis Books, 2007.

Andrew, Brother. *God's Smuggler.* New York: New American Library, 1967.

Andrew, Brother, John L. Sherrill, Elizabeth Sherrill, and Jars of Clay. *The Narrow Road: Stories of Those Who Walk This Road Together.* Grand Rapids, MI: Revell, 2001.

Andrews, Edward E. "Christian Missions and Colonial Empires Reconsidered: A Black Evangelist in West Africa, 1766–1816." *Journal of Church and State* 51, no. 4 (2009): 663–691.

Apparasu, Srinivasa Rao. "Telangana Dalit Christian Killing." *Hindustan Times*, September 19, 2019. https://www.hindustantimes.com/india-news/for-honour-killing-of-dalit -christian-in-telangana-contract-killer-arrested-from-bihar/story-1KZYMqbG3lQoZX VLIJOFAK.html.

Arendt, Hannah. *The Origins of Totalitarianism.* New York: Harcourt, 1951.

Armitage, Fiona. "The Zionist Movement in Swaziland: Origins and Bid for League Recognition, 1936–1958." Botswana History Workshop, August 1973, unpublished paper.

Arora, Priya. "Mindy Kaling's Netflix Show Tells a New Kind of Story: One Like Hers," *New York Times*, April 27, 2020, updated April 29, 2020, https://www.nytimes.com/2020/04 /27/arts/television/mindy-kaling-never-have-I-ever-netflix.html.

Arrington, Aminta. *Songs of the Lisu Hills: Practicing Christianity in Southwest China.* University Park: Pennsylvania State University Press, 2020.

Asad, Talal. *Formations of the Secular: Christianity, Islam, Modernity.* Stanford: Stanford University Press, 2003.

Asa'l ma'a Mira. Coptic SAT TV, October 23, 2020.

Ashraf, Nava, Colin F. Camerer, and George Loewenstein. "Adam Smith, Behavioral Economist." *Journal of Economic Perspectives* 19 (2005): 131–145.

Astley, Jeff. *Ordinary Theology: Looking, Listening and Learning in Theology.* Burlington: Routledge, 2002.

Aten, Jamie D., Patrick R. Bennett, Peter C. Hill, Don Davis, and Joshua N. Hook. "Predictors of God Concept and God Control after Hurricane Katrina." *Psychology of Religion and Spirituality* 4, no. 3 (2012): 182–192.

Baines, Gary Fred. "New Brighton, Port Elizabeth, c. 1903–1953: A History of an Urban African Community." PhD diss., University of Cape Town, 1994.

Bakker, Janet Kragt. *Sister Churches: American Congregations and Their Partners Abroad.* New York: Oxford University Press, 2014.

Balcomb, Anthony. "From Apartheid to the New Dispensation: Evangelicals and the Democratization of South Africa." *Journal of Religion in Africa* 34, no. 1 (2004): 5–38.

Bara, Joseph. "Colonialism, Christianity and the Tribes of Chhotanagpur in East India, 1845–1890." *South Asia: Journal of South Asian Studies* 30, no. 2 (2007): 195–222.

Barrett, David B. *Schism and Renewal in Africa: An Analysis of Six Thousand Contemporary Religious Movements.* Nairobi: Oxford University Press, 1970.

———. *World Christian Encyclopedia: A Comparative Study of Churches and Religions in the Modern World, 1900–2000.* New York: Oxford University Press, 1982.

Barrett, David B., and Todd M. Johnson. "Annual Statistical Tables on Global Mission: 2002." *International Bulletin of Missionary Research* 26 (2002): 22–44.

Bauman, Zygmunt. *Globalisation: The Human Consequences.* Cambridge: Polity Press, 1998.

Bayoumi, Moustafa. "The Race Is On." *Middle East Report*, Middle East Research and Information Project, March 2010. http://www.merip.org/mero/interventions/race.

Beck, Ulrich. *Risk Society: Towards a New Modernity.* London: Sage, 1992.

Beecher, Lyman. *The Bible a Code of Laws.* Andover: Flagg and Gould, 1818.

Beidelman, T. O. *Colonial Evangelism: A Socio-Historical Study of an East African Mission at the Grassroots.* Bloomington: Indiana University Press, 1982.

Beliso-De Jesús, Aisha, and Jemima Pierre. "Introduction: Special Section: Anthropology of White Supremacy." *American Anthropologist* 122, no. 1 (2020): 65–75.

Benbabaali, Dalel. "Caste Dominance and Territory in South India: Understanding Kammas' Socio-Spatial Mobility." *Modern Asian Studies* 52, no. 6 (2018): 1938–1976.

Bentzen, Jeanet Sinding. "Acts of God? Religiosity and Natural Disasters Across Subnational World Districts." *Economic Journal* 129 (2019): 2295–2321.

Berlant, Lauren. *Cruel Optimism*. Durham, NC: Duke University Press, 2011.

———. "Intimacy: A Special Issue." In *Intimacy*, edited by Lauren Berlant, 7. Chicago: University of Chicago Press, 2000.

———. "Introduction: Compassion (and Withholding)." In *Compassion: The Culture and Politics of an Emotion*, edited by Lauren Berlant, 1–14. New York: Routledge, 2004.

Beti, Mongo. *The Poor Christ of Bomba*. Long Grove, IL: Waveland, 1971.

Bevans, Stephen B., and Robert P. Schroeder. *Constants in Contexts: A Theology of Mission for Today*. Maryknoll, NY: Orbis Books, 2014.

Bhullar, Rajpul, and Bala Rani Bhullar, eds. *Honour Killings & Human Rights in India*. New Delhi: Academic Excellence, 2013.

Bingsheng, Wang. "Resist the Heretics Eastern Lightning." *Tianfeng* 5 (1997): 23.

Biswas, Prasenjit, and Suraj Gogoi. "Racism in India." *Statesman*, February 26, 2017. https://www.thestatesman.com/northeast/racism-in-india-1488142250.html.

Bivins, Jason C. *Religion of Fear: The Politics of Horror in Conservative Evangelicalism*. Oxford: Oxford University Press, 2008.

Blain, Keisha. *Set the World on Fire: Black Nationalist Women and the Global Struggle for Freedom*. Philadelphia: University of Pennsylvania Press, 2018.

Bloom, Paul. *Against Empathy: The Case for Rational Compassion*. New York: Ecco, 2016.

Boellstorff, Tom, Bonnie Nardi, Celia Pearce, and T. L. Taylor. *Ethnography and Virtual Words: A Handbook of Method*. Princeton: Princeton University Press, 2012.

Boltanski, Luc. *Distant Suffering: Morality, Media, and Politics*. New York: Cambridge University Press, 1999.

Boopalan, Sunder John. *Memory, Grief, and Agency: A Political Theological Account of Wrongs and Rites*. New Approaches to Religion and Power. New York: Palgrave Macmillan, 2017.

Booth, Alan. "Lord Selborne and the British Protectorates, 1908–1910." *Journal of African History* 10, no. 1 (1969): 133–148.

Bora, Papori. "The Problem without a Name: Comments on Cultural Difference (Racism) in India." *South Asia: Journal of South Asian Studies* 42, no. 5 (2019): 845–860.

Borthwick, Paul. "Sharpen Your Global Prayers." *WV Magazine*, August–September 1989 10–11.

Bosch, David J. *Transforming Mission: Paradigm Shifts in Theology of Mission*. Maryknoll, NY: Orbis Books, 1991. Reprint, 2011.

Bozeman, Theodore Dwight. *Protestants in an Age of Science: The Baconian Ideal and Antebellum American Religious Thought*. Chapel Hill: University of North Carolina Press, 1977.

Bradley, Mark Philip. *The World Reimagined*. New York: Cambridge University Press, 2016.

Brennan, Christopher. "Rearranging Their Prejudices: The *World Christian Encyclopedia* as a Case Study of Bias in Reference Books." *American Theological Library Association Summary of Proceedings* 57 (2003): 5–58.

Brenneman, Todd M. *Homespun Gospel: The Triumph of Sentimentality in Contemporary American Evangelicalism*. New York: Oxford University Press, 2014.

Brouwer, Steve, Paul Gifford, and Susan D. Rose. *Exporting the American Gospel: Global Christian Fundamentalism*. London: Routledge, 2013.

Bruner, Jason. *Living Salvation in the East African Revival in Uganda*. Rochester: University of Rochester Press, 2017.

Brusco, Elizabeth Ellen. *The Reformation of Machismo: Evangelical Conversion and Gender in Colombia*. Austin: University of Texas Press, 1995.

Burman, Erica. "Innocents Abroad: Western Fantasies of Childhood and the Iconography of Emergencies." *Disasters* 18, no. 3 (1994): 238–253.

Buxton, Meriel. *David Livingstone*. Basingstoke: Palgrave, 2001.

Cabrita, Joel. *The People's Zion: Southern Africa, the USA and a Transatlantic Faith-Healing Movement*. Cambridge, MA: Harvard University Press, 2018.

———. "Writing Apartheid: Ethnographic Collaborators and the Politics of Knowledge Production in Twentieth-Century South Africa." *American Historical Review* 125, no. 5 (2020): 1668–1697.

———. *Written Out: The Erasure of Regina Gelana Twala*. Athens: Ohio University Press, 2023.

Cabrita, Joel, and David Maxwell. "Relocating Christianity." In *Relocating World Christianity: Interdisciplinary Studies in Universal and Local Expressions of the Christian Faith*, edited by Joel Cabrita, David Maxwell, and Emma Wild-Wood, 1–44. Leiden: Brill, 2017.

Campbell, Colin. *The Romantic Ethic and the Spirit of Modern Consumerism*. Oxford: Alcuin Academics, 2005.

Cao, Nanlai. *Constructing China's Jerusalem: Christians, Power, and Place in Contemporary Wenzhou*. Stanford: Stanford University Press, 2011.

Carlsen, Laura. "Mexico's Search Brigades for the Disappeared: Rebuilding Society from the Ground Up." Americas Program, March 2019. https://www.americas.org/mexicos -search-brigades-for-the-disappeared-rebuilding-society-from-the-ground-up/.

Castelli, Elizabeth. *Martyrdom and Memory: Early Christian Culture Making*. New York: Columbia University Press, 2004.

———. "Persecution Complexes: Identity Politics and the 'War on Christians.'" *differences: A Journal of Feminist Cultural Studies* 18, no. 5 (2007): 152–180.

———. "Praying for the Persecuted Church: US Christian Activism in the Global Arena." *Journal of Human Rights* 4 (2005): 1–31.

Chandra, Shefali. "The World's Largest Dynasty: Caste, Sexuality and the Manufacture of Indian 'Democracy.'" *Dialectical Anthropology* 38, no. 2 (June 2014): 225–238.

Chan-Malik, Sylvia. *Being Muslim: A Cultural History of Women of Color in American Islam*. New York: NYU Press, 2018.

Chen, Susanna. "Eastern Lightning Who Worships Female Christ." In *Discerning Truth from Heresies: A Critical Analysis of the Alleged and Real Heresies in Mainland China*, edited by Susanna Chen and Daisy Ho, 94–99. Taipei: Christianity and China Research Center, 2000.

Chesnut, R. Andrew. *Devoted to Death: Santa Muerte, the Skeleton Saint*. New York: Oxford University Press, 2011.

———. "Top Santa Muerte Leader Enriqueta Vargas Is in the Bony Lady's Embrace." *Skeleton Saint*, December 19, 2018. https://skeletonsaint.com/2018/12/19/top-santa-muerte-leader -enriqueta-vargas-is-in-the-bony-ladys-embrace/.

Chiluwa, Innocent, and Presley Ifukor. "'War against Our Children': Stance and Evaluation in #BringBackOurGirls Campaign Discourse on Twitter and Facebook." *Discourse & Society* 26, no. 3 (2015): 267–296.

China Anti-Cult Network. Accessed December 31, 2019. http://www.chinafxj.cn/sp/qns/.

"China Executes Two Cult Members for McDonald's Murder." *BBC News*, February 2, 2015. https://www.bbc.com/news/world-asia-china-31087839.

Chow, Alexander. *Chinese Public Theology: Generational Shifts and Confucian Imagination in Chinese Christianity*. Oxford: Oxford University Press, 2018.

Chow, Christie Chui-Shan. *Schism: Seventh-day Adventism in Post-Denominational China*. Notre Dame, IN: University of Notre Dame Press, 2021.

Christianity in View. "Statistics and Forecasts for World Religions: 1800–2025." Last updated February 22, 2016. http://christianityinview.com/religion-statistics.html.

"The Christian Martyrs in Uganda." *Christian Union*, October 7, 1886.

The Church of Almighty God. Facebook. Accessed May 20, 2022. https://www.facebook.com /godfootstepsen.

———. "Reports on the Chinese Communist Government's Arrest of and Persecution to the Believers of Church of Almighty God." Accessed January 9, 2020. https://www .godfootsteps.org/persecution.html.

———. "2017 Annual Report on the Chinese Communist Government's Persecution of The Church of Almighty God." Accessed December 20, 2019. https://www.cesnur.org/2017 /almighty_china_report.pdf.

———. "2019 Annual Report on the Chinese Communist Government's Persecution of The Church of Almighty God." Accessed March 22, 2020. https://www.holyspiritspeaks.org /news/annual-report-2019/.

"The Church of Almighty God." YouTube. Accessed May 20, 2022. https://www.youtube.com /user/godfootstepsen.

"The Church of Almighty God Releases Report on Persecution in China." ORLIR. November 20, 2017. https://www.orlir.org/church-of-almighty-god-releases-report-on-perse cution-in-china.html.

Cohen, Erik, Yeshayahu Nir, and Uri Aklmagor. "Stranger-Local Interaction in Photography." *Annals of Tourism Research* 19 (1992): 213–233.

Coleman, Simon. *The Globalisation of Charismatic Christianity: Spreading the Gospel of Prosperity.* Cambridge: Cambridge University Press, 2000.

Comaroff, Jean, and John Comaroff. "Millennial Capitalism: First Thoughts on a Second Coming." In *Millennial Capitalism and the Cultural of Neoliberalism*, edited by Jean Comaroff and John Comaroff, 1–56. Durham, NC: Duke University Press, 2001.

Corrigan, John. *Religious Intolerance, America, and the World: A History of Remembering and Forgetting.* Chicago: University of Chicago Press, 2020.

Corrigan, John, and Lynn Neal. *Religious Intolerance in America: A Documentary History*, 2nd ed. Chapel Hill: University of North Carolina Press, 2020.

"The Cover-Up." YouTube video, 50:17. March 3, 2018, https://www.youtube.com/watch?v =ytIIomPECHw.

Cox, George William. *The Life of John William Colenso, D.D., Bishop of Natal.* London: W. Ridgway, 1888.

Curry, David. "A Letter from David Curry, CEO." *World Watch List 2019.* Open Doors. Accessed May 20, 2022. https://revelation-now.org/wp-content/uploads/WWL2019_FullBooklet -1.pdf.

Curtis, Heather. "Depicting Distant Suffering: Evangelicals and the Politics of Pictorial Humanitarianism in the Age of American Empire.'" *Material Religion* 8, no. 2 (2012): 153–182.

———. *Holy Humanitarians: American Evangelicals and Global Aid.* Cambridge, MA: Harvard University Press, 2018.

Dahlfred, Karl. "Why Missionaries Can Never Go Home Again." *Gleanings from the Field: A Missionary Blog.* November 25, 2014. https://www.dahlfred.com/index.php/blogs /gleanings-from-the-field/747-why-missionaries-can-never-go-home-again.

"Dalit Activists, Women's Groups Thrilled; Political Parties Remain Silent [Times Region]." *The Times of India (Online).* December 13, 2017. https://search-proquest-com.ezproxy .princeton.edu/docview/1975805195?accountid=13314.

Darch, John H. *Missionary Imperialists?: Missionaries, Government and the growth of the British Empire in the Tropics, 1860–1885.* Colorado Springs: Paternoster, 2009.

"The Dark Hour Before the Dawn." YouTube video, 55:18. February 23, 2018. https://www
.youtube.com/watch?v=6VwlZsXz3No.

Davis, Edward B., Cynthia N. Kimball, Jamie D. Aten, Benjamin Andrews, Daryl R. Van
Tongeren, Joshua N. Hook, Don E. Davis, Pehr Granqvist, and Crystal L. Park. "Religious Meaning Making and Attachment in a Disaster Context: A Longitudinal
Qualitative Study of Flood Survivors." *Journal of Positive Psychology* 14, no. 5 (2019):
659–671.

Dayam, Joseph Prabhakar, and Peniel Rajkumar. "Mission At and From the Margins: Patterns, Protagonists and Perspectives: A Critical and Constructive Contribution to the
Edinburgh 2010 Conference." In *Mission At and From the Margins: Patterns, Protagonists
and Perspectives*, edited by Peniel Rajkumar, Joseph Prabhakar Dayam, and I. P Asheervadham, 3–9. Oxford: Regnum, 2014.

de Certeau, Michel. *The Practice of Everyday Life.* Translated by Steven Rendall. Berkeley: University of California Press, 2011.

Deibert, Michael. *In the Shadow of Saint Death: The Gulf Cartel and the Price of America's Drug
War in Mexico.* Guilford: Rowman & Littlefield, 2014.

Deliso, Chris. "Ecumenical US Conference Highlights Persecution of Christians." *The Tablet*,
December 5, 2017. https://www.thetablet.co.uk/news/8191/ecumenical-us-conference
-highlights-persecution-of-christians-.

Deol, Satnam Singh. "Honour Killings in Haryana State, India: A Content Analysis." *International Journal of Criminal Justice Sciences* 9, no. 2 (2014): 192–208.

Derrida, Jacques. *Of Grammatology.* Translated by Gayatri Chakravorty Spivak. Baltimore:
Johns Hopkins University Press, 2016.

Desrosières, Alain. *The Politics of Large Numbers: A History of Statistical Reasoning.* Translated
by Camille Naish. Cambridge: Harvard University Press, 1998.

De Waal, Alexander. *Famine Crimes: Politics & the Disaster Relief Industry in Africa.* Bloomington: Indiana University Press, 1997.

Dowell, Oren. "Terrorists Kidnap More Than 200 Nigerian Girls." *USA Today*, April 21, 2014.
https://www.usatoday.com/story/news/world/2014/04/21/parents-234-girls-kidnapped
-from-nigeria-school/7958307.

Du Bois, W.E.B. "The Souls of White Folks." In *Darkwater: Voices from within the Veil.* New
York: Harcourt, Brace, and Howe, 1920.

DuBose, H. C. "Home and Foreign." *Christian Observer*, November 20, 1895.

Dulin, John. "Transvaluing ISIS in Orthodox Christian-Majority Ethiopia: On the Inhibition
of Group Violence." *Current Anthropology* 58, no. 6 (2017): 785–804.

Dunn, Emily. *Lightning from the East: Heterodoxy and Christianity in Contemporary China.*
Leiden: Brill, 2015.

"The Eastern Province Is a Political Time Bomb." *Drum*, October 1956.

Edwards, E. H. *The Reign of Terror in the Western Hills, or Stories of the Persecution of Chinese
Christians in Shansi in 1900, Reprinted from the Shanghai Mercury.* Shanghai" Printed at
the *Shanghai Mercury*, 1901.

Eickelman, D. F. "The Study of Islam in Local Contexts." *Contributions to Asian Studies* 17
(1982): 1–16.

Elisha, Omri. *Moral Ambition: Mobilization and Social Outreach in Evangelical Megachurches.*
Berkeley: University of California Press, 2011.

———. "Saved by a Martyr: Evangelical Mediation, Sanctification, and the 'Persecuted
Church.'" *Journal of the American Academy of Religion* 84, no. 4 (2016): 1056–1080.

Elphick, Richard. *The Equality of Believers: Protestant Missionaries and the Racial Politics of South
Africa.* Charlottesville: University of Virginia Press, 2012.

Eriksen, Thomas Hylland. *Overheating: An Anthropology of Accelerated Change*. London: Pluto Press, 2016.

Etherington, Norman. "Mission Station Melting Pots as a Factor in the Rise of South African Black Nationalism." *International Journal of African Historical Studies* 9, no. 4 (1976): 592–605.

———. *Peasants, Peasants and Politics in Southeast Africa, 1835–1880: African Christian Communities in Natal, Pondoland and Zululand*. London: Royal Historical Society, 1978.

Feuerbach, Ludwig, and Elliot George. *The Essence of Christianity*. Translated by Marian Evans. London: Trubne & Co., Ludgate Hill, 1881. Reprint, 1957.

Fields, Karen, and Barbara Fields. *Racecraft: The Soul of Inequality in American Life*. New York: Verso Books, 2012.

Fieldston, Sara. *Raising the World: Child Welfare in the American Century*. Cambridge, MA: Harvard University Press, 2015.

Fleischacker, Samuel. "Adam Smith's Reception among the American Founders, 1776–1790." *William and Mary Quarterly* 59 (2002): 897–924.

Force, Pierre. "Rousseau and Smith: On Sympathy as a First Principle." In *Thinking with Rousseau: From Machiavelli to Schmitt*, edited by Helena Rosenblatt and Paul Schweigert, 115–131. New York: Cambridge University Press, 2017.

Foxe, John. *Book of Martyrs*. Hartford: E. Hunt, 1851.

France-Williams, Azariah D.A. *Ghost Ship: Institutional Racism and the Church of England*. London: SCM Press, 2020.

Frederick, Marla. *Colored Television: American Religion Gone Global*. Stanford: Stanford University Press, 2016.

Freedom House website. Accessed March 15, 2020. https://freedomhouse.org.

Fulton, Brent. *China's Urban Christians: A Light That Cannot Be Hidden*. Eugene: Pickwick Publications, 2015.

Galtung, Johan, and Mari Holmboe Ruge. "The Structure of Foreign News: The Presentation of Congo, Cuba and Cyprus crises in Four Norwegian Newspapers." *Journal of Peace Research* 2 (1965): 64–91.

Gandhi, Mohandas K. *An Autobiography: The Story of My Experiments with Truth*. Boston: Beacon Press, 1993.

Gardner, Leigh. *Taxing Colonial Africa: The Political Economy of British Imperialism*. Oxford: Oxford University Press, 2012.

Gasset, Ortega y. *The Revolt of the Masses*. New York: W. W. Norton, 1932.

Gaston, Sean. "The Impossibility of Sympathy." *The Eighteenth Century* 51 (2010): 129–152.

Gatti, Mauro, Pasquale Annicchino, Judd Birdsall, Valeria Fabretti, and Marco Ventura. "Quantifying Persecution: Developing an International Law-Based Measurement of Freedom of Religion or Belief." *Review of Faith and International Affairs* 17 (2019): 87–96.

Gershon, Ilana. "Neoliberal Agency." *Current Anthropology* 52, no. 4 (2011): 537–555.

Glendon, Mary Ann. "The Naked Public: A Symposium." *First Things*, November 2004. https://www.firstthings.com/article/2004/11/001-the-naked-public.

God Footsteps. YouTube. Accessed May 20, 2022. https://www.youtube.com/user/godfootsteps. In Chinese.

Gordon, A. J. "Martyr-Seed and Martyr-Fruit in Africa." *Baptist Missionary Magazine*, February 1889, 43–45.

Grace, Pamela. *The Religious Film: Christianity and the Hagiopic*. Malden, MA: Wiley-Blackwell, 2009.

"Grand Banquet, 3rd International Conference on Religious Freedom." Accessed May 26, 2022. https://www.youtube.com/watch?v=JMQqGkbiV4Q&t=1737s.

Graziano, Frank. *Cultures of Devotion: Folk Saints of Spanish America*. New York: Oxford University Press, 2006.

Greiner, Rae. "Sympathy Time: Adam Smith, George Eliot, and the Realist Novel." *Narrative* 17 (2009): 291–311.

Grundemann, R. "Missions: A Story of Persecution in the South." *Independent*, January 11, 1883.

Grupo de estudios sobre la Mujer Rosario Castellanos website. Accessed August 5, 2020. https://www.gesmujer.org/sitio/.

Guillmermoprieto, Alma. "The Vatican and Santa Muerte." *National Geographic*, May 14, 2013. https://www.nationalgeographic.com/news/2013/5/130512-vatican-santa-muerte-mexico-cult-catholic-church-cultures-world/.

Guru, Gopal, ed. *Humiliation: Claims and Context*. New Delhi: Oxford University Press, 2009.

Hage, Ghassan. *White Nation: Fantasy of White Supremacy in a Multicultural Society*. London: Routledge, 2000.

Hanoosh, Yasmeen. *The Chaldeans: Politics and Identity in Iraq and the American Diaspora*. London: Bloomsbury Publishing, 2019.

Harding, Susan F. *The Book of Jerry Falwell: Fundamentalist Language and Politics*. Princeton: Princeton University Press, 2001.

Hassim, Shireen. *The ANC Women's League: Sex, Gender and Politics*. Auckland Park, South Africa: Jacana, 2014.

Hattaway, Paul. "When China's Christians Wish They Were in Prison: An Examination of the Eastern Lightning Cult in China." Asia Harvest website, June 25, 2002. https://asiaharvest.org/when-chinas-christians-wish-they-were-in-prison/.

Haynes, Naomi. "'Zambia Shall Be Saved!': Prosperity Gospel Politics in a Self-Proclaimed Christian Nation." *Nova Religio* 19, no. 1 (2014): 5–24.

Haynes, William C., Daryl R. Van Tongeren, Jamie Alten, Edward B. Davis, Don E. Davis, Joshua N. Hook, David Boan, and Thomas Johnson. "The Meaning as a Buffer Hypothesis: Spiritual Meaning Attenuates the Effect of Disaster-Related Resource Loss on Posttraumatic Stress." *Psychology of Religion and Spirituality* 9, no. 4 (2017): 446–453.

Hefferan, Tara Linn. "Deprofessionalizing Economic Development: Faith-based Development Alternatives through U.S.-Haiti Catholic Parish Twinning." PhD diss., Michigan State University, 2006.

Hertzke, Allen D. *Freeing God's Children: The Unlikely Alliance for Global Human Rights*. Lanham, MD: Rowman and Littlefield, 2004.

Herzog, Jonathan P. *The Spiritual-Industrial Complex: America's Religious Battle against Communism in the Early Cold War*. New York: Oxford University Press, 2011.

Hetta v. Museum of the Bible, Inc. Complaint. Superior Court for the District of Columbia, Civil Division. January 17, 2019. https://d3n8a8pro7vhmx.cloudfront.net/justiceonline/mailings/234/attachments/original/Museum_of_the_Bible_Complaint_public_%280081747xB3827%29.pdf?1547753191.

Hirschkind, Charles. *The Ethical Soundscape: Cassette Sermons and Islamic Counterpublics*. New York: Columbia University Press, 2006.

Hoehler-Fatton, Cynthia. *Women of Fire and Spirit: History, Faith, and Gender in Roho Religion in Western Kenya*. Oxford: Oxford University Press, 1996.

Holden, Dominic. "A Middle Eastern Man Is Suing the Bible Museum for Racial Profiling and Reporting Him to the FBI." *Buzzfeed News*, January 18, 2019. https://www.buzzfeednews.com/article/dominicholden/bible-museum-lawsuit-racial-profiling-fbi.

Holifield, E. Brooks. *The Gentlemen Theologians: American Theology in Southern Culture 1795–1860*. Durham, NC: Duke University Press, 1978.

Hollinger, David. *Protestants Abroad: How Missionaries Tried to Change the World but Changed America.* Princeton: Princeton University Press, 2017.

Hollingshead, Keith. "Surveillance of the Worlds of Tourism: Foucault and the Eye of Power." *Tourism Management* 20 (1999): 7–23.

Honigsbaum, Mark. "Barack Obama and the Empathy Deficit." *Guardian*, January 4, 2013. https://www.theguardian.com/science/2013/jan/04/barack-obama-empathy-deficit.

Horkheimer, Max, and Theodor W. Adorno. "The Culture Industry: Enlightenment as Mass Deception." In *Dialectic of Enlightenment.* Translated by John Cumming, 94–137. New York: Herder and Herder, 1972.

Howell, Sally and Andrew Shryock. "Cracking Down on Diaspora: Arab Detroit and America's 'War on Terror.'" *Anthropological Quarterly* 76, no. 3 (2003): 443–462.

Hsu, Becky, Amy Reynolds, Conrad Hackett, and James Gibbon. "Estimating the Religious Composition of All Nations: An Empirical Assessment of the World Christian Database." *Journal for the Scientific Study of Religion* 47 (2008): 678–693.

Huanxin, Jing. "Tricks Played by the False Christ, Beware of Eastern Lightning the Evil Cult." *Tianfeng* 7 (1999): 20–21.

Human Rights Without Frontiers. *Tortured to Death: The Persecution of The Church of Almighty God in China.* Brussels: HRWF, 2018.

Hutchinson, Mark, and John Wolfe. *A Short History of Global Evangelicalism.* New York: Cambridge, 2012.

INEGI. "Estadísticas a propósito del día internacional de la eliminación de la violencia contra la mujer (25 de noviembre)." Datos nacionales, 2019. https://www.inegi.org.mx /contenidos/saladeprensa/aproposito/2020/Violencia2020_Nal.pdf.

Inouye, Melissa Wei-Tsing. *China and the True Jesus: Charisma and Organization in a Chinese Christian Church.* New York: Oxford University Press, 2018.

"In Response to Persecution: Findings of the *Under Caesar's Sword* Project on Global Christian Communities." University of Notre Dame, Under Caesar's Sword research project, 2020. https://ucs.nd.edu/report/.

Introvigne, Massimo. "Captivity Narratives: Did The Church of Almighty God Kidnap 34 Evangelical Pastors in 2002?" *Journal of CESNUR* 2, no. 1 (January–February 2018): 100–110.

———. "Church of Almighty God and the Visual Arts." *World Religion and Spirituality Project*, December 3, 2017. https://wrldrels.org/2017/12/04/church-of-almighty-god-eastern -lightning-and-the-visual-arts/.

———. *Inside The Church of Almighty God: The Most Persecuted Religious Movement in China.* New York: Oxford University Press, 2020.

———. "Xie Jiao as 'Criminal Religious Movements:' A New Look at Cult Controversies in China and Around the World." *Journal of CESNUR* 2, no. 1 (January–February 2018): 13–32.

Irudayam, Aloysius, Jayshree P. Mangubhai, and Joel G. Lee. *Dalit Women Speak Out: Caste, Class and Gender Violence in India.* New Delhi: Zubaan, 2012.

Irvin, Dale T. "World Christianity: An Introduction." *Journal of World Christianity* 1, no. 1 (2008): 1–26.

Jabine, Thomas B., and Richard B. Claude. *Human Rights and Statistics: Getting the Record Straight.* Philadelphia: University of Pennsylvania Press, 1992.

Jadhav, Sushrut, David Mosse, and Ned Dostaler. "Minds of Caste—Discrimination and Its Affects." *Anthropology Today* 32, no. 1 (2016): 1–2.

Jamir, Sashila. "Christianity in Nagaland." *Word & World* 37, no. 4 (2017): 387–394.

Jaoul, Nicolas. "The 'Righteous Anger' of the Powerless: Investigating Dalit Outrage over Caste Violence." *South Asia Multidisciplinary Academic Journal* 2 (2008): 1–31.

Jars of Clay. Press release, April 20, 2001. http://www.jarchives.com/jartifacts18.htm.

Jenkins, Philip. "How Many Christians?" *Anxious Bench*, September 22, 2017. https://www .patheos.com/blogs/anxiousbench/2017/09/how-many-christians/.

———. *The Next Christendom: The Coming of Global Christianity.* New York: Oxford University Press, 2002.

Jeremiah, Anderson H.M. "Race, Caste, and Christianity." *International Review of Mission* 109, no. 1 (2020): 84–98.

Johnson, Amanda Walker. "Objectifying Measures: Mapping the Terrain of Statistical Discourse in the Hegemony and Racial Politics of High Stakes Testing." PhD diss., University of Texas at Austin, 2004.

Johnson, Kate Bowman. "So Much to Sing About." *Sojourners*, November 2005.

Johnson, Todd M., and Gina Zurlo. "Christian Martyrdom as a Pervasive Phenomenon." *Society* 51 (2014): 679–685.

Jones, Sara. "Memory on Film: Testimony and Constructions of Authenticity in Documentaries about the German Democratic Republic." *European Journal of Cultural Studies* 16, no. 2 (2012): 194–210.

Jongeneel, Jan. "David Barrett's *World Christian Encyclopedia*." *Exchange* 30, no. 4 (2001): 372–376.

Junod, Violaine. "Entokozweni: Managing a Community Service in an Urban African Area." *Human Organization* 23, no. 1 (1964): 28–35.

Kaur, Manpreet. *Honour Killings in India: A Crime against Humanity.* New Delhi: Anamika Publishers, 2015.

Ke-hsien, Huang. "Taming the Spirit by Appropriating Indigenous Culture: An Ethnographic Study of the True Jesus Church as Confucian-Style Pentecostalism." In *Global Chinese Pentecostal and Charismatic Christianity*, edited by Fenggang Yang, Joy K. C. Tong, and Allan H. Anderson, 118–136. Leiden: Brill, 2017.

Kellogg, Sarah Bakker. "Syriac Christianity, Ethnicity, and Secular Legibility." *Current Anthropology* 60, no. 4 (2019): 475–498.

Kemmerer, Lisa. *Animals and World Religions.* Oxford: Oxford University Press, 2012.

Kennedy, Dennis. "Selling the Distant Other: Humanitarianism and Imagery—Ethical Dilemmas of Humanitarian Action." *Journal of Humanitarian Assistance* 28 (2009): 1–25.

Kidd, Thomas. *American Christians and Islam: Evangelical Culture and Muslims from the Colonial Period to the Age of Terrorism.* Princeton: Princeton University Press, 2013.

Kikon, Dolly. "Eating Akhuni in India." In *Farm to Fingers: The Culture and Politics of Food in Contemporary India*, edited by Kiranmayi Bhushi, 80–102. New Delhi: Cambridge University Press, 2018.

King, David P. *God's Internationalists: World Vision and the Age of Evangelical Humanitarianism.* Philadelphia: University of Pennsylvania Press, 2019.

———. "The New Internationalists: World Vision and the Revival of American Evangelical Humanitarianism, 1950–2010." *Religions* 3, no. 4 (2012): 922–949.

Kingsbury, Kate. "At Death's Door in Cancun: Sun, Sea, and Santa Muerte." *Anthropology and Humanism* (2021): 1–22.

———. "Death Is Women's Work: Santa Muerte, a Folk Saint and Her Female Followers." *International Journal of Latin American Religion* 5 (2021): 43–63.

———. "Doctor Death and Coronavirus: Supplicating Santa Muerte for Holy Healing." *Anthropologica* 63, no. 1 (2021): 1–23.

Kingsbury, Kate, and R. Andrew Chesnut. "Syncretic Santa Muerte: Holy Death and Religious Bricolage." *Religions* 12, no. 3 (2021): 220.

Klein, Christina. *Cold War Orientalism: Asia in the Middlebrow Imagination.* Berkeley: University of California Press, 2003.

Kleinman, Arthur, Veena Das, and Margaret Lock, eds. *Social Suffering.* Berkeley: University of California Press, 1997.

Kleist, Nauja, and Stef Jansen. "Introduction: Hope over Time—Crisis, Immobility and Future-Making." *History and Anthropology* 27, no. 4 (2016): 373–392.

Kraidy, Marwan M. "The Projectilic Image: Islamic State's Digital Visual Warfare and Global Networked Affect." *Media, Culture & Society* 39, no. 8 (2017): 1194–1209.

Kruse, Peter. "Miscellaneous Communications. Proposed Wesleyan Mission to China." *Wesleyan Methodist Magazine*, Vol. 2: *1833–1854*. London: John Mason, 1854.

Kumar, Deepa. *Islamophobia and the Politics of Empire.* Chicago: Haymarket Books, 2012.

Kumar, R. Vimal. "'Honour' Killing of Dalit Youth Shankar in Tamil Nadu: Death for Six, including Father-in-Law." *Hindu*, December 12, 2017. https://www.thehindu.com/news/national/tamil-nadu/shankar-murder-case-father-in-law-gets-death-sentence/article21478790.ece.

Kuper, Hilda. *Sobhuza II, Ngwenyama and King of Swaziland: The Story of an Hereditary Ruler and His Country.* London: Duckworth, 1978.

———. *The Uniform of Color: A Study of White-Black Relationships in Swaziland.* Johannesburg: University of Witwatersrand Press, 1947.

Kupper, Kristin. "Images of Jesus Christ in Christian Inspired Spiritual and religious Movements in China since 1978." In *The Chinese Face of Jesus Christ*, vol. 3b, edited by Roman Malek, 1365–1375. Sankt Augustin, Germany: Institut Monumenta Serica and China-Zentrum, 2007.

Kznaric, Roman. *Empathy: Why It Matters and How to Get It.* New York: TarcherPerigee, 2014.

LaCapra, Dominick. *Writing History, Writing Trauma.* Baltimore: Johns Hopkins University Press, 2001.

LaFranchi, Howard. "What Role for US in Efforts to Rescue Nigeria's Kidnapped Girls?" *Christian Science Monitor*, May 5, 2014. https://www.csmonitor.com/USA/Foreign-Policy/2014/0505/What-role-for-US-in-efforts-to-rescue-Nigeria-s-kidnapped-girls.

Langworthy, Harry W. "Joseph Booth, Prophet of Radical Change in Central and South Africa, 1891–1915." *Journal of Religion in Africa* 16, no. 1 (1986): 22–43.

La Santa Muerte. Directed by Eva Aridjis. Dark Night Pictures, 2007.

Latourette, Kenneth Scott. *A History of the Expansion of Christianity*, 7 vols. New York: Harper and Brothers, 1937–1945.

Lausanne Committee Issue Group. "LOP 32: The Persecuted Church." 2004 Forum Occasional Papers. Pattaya, Thailand: Lausanne Committee for World Evangelization, 2004. http://www.lausanne.org/documents/2004forum/LOP32_IG3.pdf.

Lee, Joel. "Odor and Order: How Caste Is Inscribed in Space and Sensoria." *Comparative Studies of South Asia, Africa and the Middle East* 37, no. 3 (2017): 470–490.

Lee, Joseph Tse-Hei, and Christie Chui-Shan Chow. "Methodological Reflections on the Study of Chinese Christianities." In *World Christianity: Methodological Considerations*, edited by Martha Frederiks and Dorottya Nagy, 113–134. Leiden: Brill, 2020.

Leonard, Dickens. "Spectacle Spaces: Production of Caste in Recent Tamil Films." *South Asian Popular Culture* 13, no. 2 (2015): 155–173.

Lichtenberg, Judith. "Absence and the Unfond Heart: Why People Are Less Giving Than They Might Be." In *The Ethics of Assistance: Morality and the Distant Needy*, edited by Deen K. Chatterjee, 82–87. New York: Cambridge University Press, 2004.

Livingstone, David. *Missionary Travels and Researches in South Africa.* New York: Harper & Bros, 1858.

Lodge, Tom. *Black Politics in South Africa since 1945.* New York: Longman, 1983.

Longkumer, Arkotong. "'Nagas Can't Sit Lotus Style': Baba Ramdev, Patanjali, and Neo-Hindutva." *Contemporary South Asia* 26, no. 4 (2018): 400–420.

"The Long Road of Exile." YouTube video, 39:42, June 6, 2018. https://www.youtube.com/watch?v=Ok1Rk_GWVT8.

Lubiano, Wahneema. "Affect and Rearticulating the Racial 'Un-Sayables.'" *Cultural Anthropology* 28, no. 3 (2013): 540–543.

Ludwig, Frieder and J. Kwabena Asamoah-Gyadu. *African Christian Presence in the West: New Immigrant Congregations and Transnational Networks in North America and Europe.* Trenton: Africa World Press, 2011.

Ma, Li, and Jin Li. *Surviving the State, Remaking the Church: A Sociological Portrait of Christians in Mainland China.* Eugene: Pickwick Publications, 2018.

Mabee, Charles. *Reading Sacred Texts through American Eyes.* Macon, GA: Mercer University Press, 1991.

Maclean, Ruth, and Andrew Esiebo. "Eat, Pray, Live: The Lagos Megachurches Building Their Very Own Cities." *Guardian*, September 11, 2017. https://www.theguardian.com/cities/2017/sep/11/eat-pray-live-lagos-nigeria-megachurches-redemption-camp.

Macmillan, Hugh. "A Nation Divided: The Swazi in Swaziland and the Transvaal, 1865–1986." In *The Creation of Tribalism in Southern Africa,* edited by L. Vail, 289–323. Berkeley: University of California Press, 1989.

———. "Swaziland, Decolonization and the Triumph of Tradition." *Journal of Modern African Studies* 23, no. 4 (1985): 643–666.

Magaziner, Dan. *The Art of Life in South Africa.* Athens: Ohio University Press, 2016.

Mahmood, Saba. *Politics of Piety: The Islamic Revival and the Feminist Subject.* Princeton: Princeton University Press, 2004.

Marsden, George. *The Evangelical Mind and the New School Presbyterian Experience.* New Haven: Yale University Press, 1970.

———. *Fundamentalism and American Culture.* New York: Oxford University Press, 1982.

Marshall, Paul, with Lela Gilbert. *Their Blood Cries Out: The Untold Story of Persecution Against Christians in the Modern World.* Dallas: Word Publishing, 1997.

Marshall, Paul, Lela Gilbert, and Nina Shea. *Persecuted: The Global Assault on Christians.* Nashville: Thomas Nelson, 2013.

Marshall, Ruth. *Political Spiritualities: The Pentecostal Revolution in Nigeria.* Chicago: University of Chicago Press, 2009.

Martos, J.A.F. "Iconografías Emergentes y Muertes Patrimonializadas en América Latina: Santa Muerte, Muertos Milagrosos y Muertos Adoptados." *Revista de Antropología Iberoamericana* 9, no. 2 (2014): 115–140.

"The Martyr Church of Madagascar." *Scribner's Monthly,* April 1871, 639–646.

Maxwell, David. "Historical Perspectives on Christianity Worldwide: Connections, Comparisons and Consciousness." In *Relocating World Christianity: Interdisciplinary Studies in Universal and Local Expressions of the Christian Faith,* edited by Joel Cabrita, David Maxwell, and Emma Wild-Wood, 47–69. Leiden: Brill, 2017.

McAlister, Melani. *Epic Encounters: Culture, Media, and U.S. Interests in the Middle East since 1945.* 2nd ed. Berkeley: University of California Press, 2005.

———. *The Kingdom of God Has No Borders: A Global History of American Evangelicals.* New York: Oxford University Press, 2018.

———. "The Persecuted Body: Evangelical Internationalism, Islam, and the Politics of Fear." In *Facing Fear: The History of an Emotion in Global Perspective,* edited by M. Laffan and M. Weiss, 133–161. Princeton: University of Princeton Press, 2012.

———. "What Is Your Heart For?: Affect and Internationalism in the Evangelical Public Sphere." *American Literary History* 20, no. 4 (2008): 870–895.

McClymond, Michael J. "Making Sense of the Census: What 1,999,563,838 Christians Might Mean for the Study of Religion." *Journal of the American Academy of Religion* 70, no. 4 (2002): 875–890.

McCracken, John. *A History of Malawi, 1859–1966.* Suffolk: James Currey, 2012.

———. *Politics and Christianity in Malawi: The Impact of the Livingstonia Mission in the Northern Province.* Kachere Monographs. Zomba: Kachere Series, 2008.

McDonic, Susan. "Witnessing, Work and Worship: World Vision and the Negotiation of Faith, Development, and Culture." PhD diss., Duke University, 2004.

McDuie-Ra, Duncan. *Debating Race in Contemporary India.* New York: Palgrave Macmillan, 2015.

McDuie-Ra, Duncan, Elaine Lynn-Ee Ho, Tanya Jakimow, and Bittiandra Chand Somaiah. "Collaborative Ethnographies: Reading Space to Build an Affective Inventory." *Emotion, Space and Society* 35 (2020): 1–10.

McIver, Moira. *Memory, Memorial.* Belfast: Artefact, 1997.

McKay, Holly. "Nigeria's Christian Community Slowly Being Erased as Militants Step up Vicious Killings, Kidnappings." *Fox News*, June 18, 2018. https://www.foxnews.com/faith-values/nigeria-christian-militants-isis-erased-killings-kidnappings.

Merry, Sally Engle. *The Seductions of Quantification: Measuring Human Rights, Gender, Violence, and Sex Trafficking.* Chicago: University of Chicago Press, 2016.

Meyer, Birgit. "Mediation and Immediacy: Sensational Forms, Semiotic Ideologies, and the Question of the Medium." *Social Anthropology* 19, no. 1 (2011): 23–39.

Meyer, Birgit, and Annelies Moors, eds. *Religion, Media, and the Public Sphere.* Bloomington: Indiana University Press, 2005.

Miner, Luella. *China's Book of Martyrs: A Record of Heroic Martyrdoms and Marvelous Deliverances during the Summer of 1900.* Cincinnati: Jennings and Pye, 1903.

"Miscellaneous: Monthly Concert." *Religious Intelligencer*, September 5, 1835, 210.

Moeller, Susan D. *Compassion Fatigue: How the Media Sell Disease, Famine, War and Death.* New York: Routledge, 1999.

Moore, Johnnie. *The Martyr's Oath: Living for the Jesus They're Willing to Die For.* Carol Stream, IL: Tyndale House, 2018.

Morgan, David. *Key Words in Religion, Media and Culture.* New York: Routledge, 2008.

———. "The Look of Sympathy: Religion, Visual Culture, and the Social Life of Feeling." *Material Religion* 5 (2009): 132–154.

Morrison, Toni. "On the Backs of Blacks." *Time Magazine*, December 2, 1993.

Mozingo, Joe. "Slain Egyptian Was a Fixture in San Gabriel." *LA Times*, September 19, 2001. http://articles.latimes.com/2001/sep/19/local/me-47275.

Mwase, George Simeon, and Robert I. Rotberg. *Strike a Blow and Die: The Classic Story of the Chilembwe Rising.* Cambridge: Harvard University Press, 1975.

Naber, Nadine. "Imperial Whiteness and the Diasporas of Empire." *American Quarterly* 66, no. 4 (2014): 1107–1115.

Nanay, Bence. "Adam Smith's Concept of Sympathy and Its Contemporary Interpretations." *Essays on the Philosophy of Adam Smith: The Adam Smith Review* 5 (2010): 85–105.

National Association of Evangelicals. "Statement of Conscience of the National Association of Evangelicals Concerning Worldwide Religious Persecution, January 23, 1996." PCA Historical Center. Accessed February 17, 2020. http://pcahistory.org/pca/studies/3-476.html.

Neill, Stephen. *Colonialism and Christian Missions.* New York: McGraw Hill, 1966.

Newton, A. Taylor, and Daniel N. McIntosh. "Associations of General Religiousness and Specific Religious Beliefs with Coping Appraisals in Response to Hurricanes Katrina and Rita." *Mental Health, Religion & Culture* 12 (2009): 129–146.

Noll, Mark A. "Common Sense Traditions and American Evangelical Thought." *American Quarterly* 37 (1985): 216–213.

———. "Review: *World Christian Encyclopedia*." *Church History* 71 (2002): 448–454.

Norget, Kristin. *Days of Death, Days of Life: Ritual in the Popular Culture of Oaxaca*. New York: Columbia University Press, 2006.

Obadare, Ebenezer. *Pentecostal Republic: Religion and the Struggle for State Power in Nigeria*. London: Zed Books, 2018.

Obiezu, Timothy. "More Than 100 Chibok Girls Still Missing Seven Years Later." *Voice of America*, April 15, 2021. https://www.voanews.com/africa/more-100-chibok-girls-still-missing-seven-years-later.

Observatorio Ciudadano Nacional del Feminicidio. Accessed June 5, 2022. http://observatorio feminicidio.blogspot.com/p/publicaciones.html.

Office of the High Commissioner of Human Rights. "Official Statistics and Human Rights: 'Statistics Matter for Human Rights and Human Rights Matter for Statistics.'" United Nations, 2014. https://www.ohchr.org/Documents/Issues/HRIndicators/StatisticsAnd HumanRights.pdf.

Oguntola, Sunday. "Leah Sharibu Inspires Nigeria's Christians, Faces Execution by Boko Haram." *Christianity Today*, October 15, 2018. https://www.christianitytoday.com/news /2018/october/free-leah-sharibu-boko-haram-execution-dapchi-nigeria.html.

Olutokunbo, Adekalu Samuel, Turiman Suandi, Oluwaseyitan Rotimi Cephas, and Irza Hanie Abu-Samah. "Bring Back Our Girls, Social Mobilization: Implications for Cross-Cultural Research." *Journal of Education and Practice* 6, no. 6 (2015): 64–75.

Omer-Cooper, John D., A. E. Afigbo, E. A. Ayandele, R. J. Gavin, and Robin Palmer. *The Making of Modern Africa: The Growth of African Civilisation*, vol. 2. New York: Longman, 1968.

O'Neill, Kevin. *Secure the Soul: Christian Piety and Gang Prevention in Guatemala*. Berkeley: University of California Press, 2015.

Oosterbaan, Martijn. "Virtually Global: Online Evangelical Cartography." *Social Anthropology* 19, no. 1 (2011): 56–73.

Open Doors. "How the Scoring Works." Accessed February 15, 2020. https://www.open doorsusa.org/christian-persecution/world-watch-list/about-the-ranking/.

———. "Open Doors World Watch List 2022: The Fifty Countries Where It Is Most Dangerous to Follow Jesus." Accessed May 20, 2022. https://www.opendoorsusa.org/christian -persecution/world-watch-list/.

Ove, Peter. "Change a Life, Change Your Own: Child Sponsorship, the Discourse of Development, and the Production of Ethical Subjects." PhD diss., University of British Columbia, 2013.

Ownby, David. *Falun Gong and the Future of China*. New York: Oxford University Press, 2008.

Palmer, Catherine, and J.-A. Lester. "Stalking the Cannibals: Photographic Behavior on the Sepik River." *Tourist Studies* 7 (2007): 83–106.

Palmer, David. *Qigong Fever—Body, Science, and Utopia in China*. New York: Columbia University Press, 2007.

Panorama sociodemográfico de Oaxaca 2020. INEGI. https://www.inegi.org.mx/contenidos /productos/prod_serv/contenidos/espanol/bvinegi/productos/nueva_estruc /702825197933.pdf.

Pansters, Wil G., ed. *La Santa Muerte in Mexico: History, Devotion, and Society*. Albuquerque: University of New Mexico Press, 2019.

Parkinson, Joe, and Drew Hinshaw. "Whispered Prayers, Hidden Bibles, Secretly Scribbled Verses: Inside the Resilient Faith of the #BringBackOurGirls Hostages." *Christianity Today*, June 21, 2020. https://www.christianitytoday.com/ct/2021/july-august/bring -back-our-girls-parkinson-hinshaw-nigeria-boko-haram.html.

Pease, Joshua. "The One Thing the Persecuted Church Doesn't Need from You." *Open Doors*, May 30, 2017. https://www.opendoorsusa.org/christian-persecution/stories/one-thing -persecuted-church-doesnt-need/.

Penner, Glenn M. *In the Shadow of the Cross: A Biblical Theology of Persecution & Discipleship.* Bartlesville, OK: Living Sacrifice Books, 2004.

"Persecution of Christians and Possible Solutions." Session 2. Accessed May 26, 2022. https:// www.youtube.com/watch?v=10iToAH4Z-k.

Peters, John Durham. "Information: Notes toward a Critical History." *Journal of Communication Inquiry* 12, no. 2 (1988): 9–23.

Peterson, Jeanette Favrot. "The Virgin of Guadalupe: Symbol of Conquest or Liberation?" *Art Journal* 51, no. 4 (1992): 39–47.

Pew Research Center. "Global Christianity—A Report on the Size and Distribution of the World's Christian Population." Dec. 19, 2011. https://www.pewforum.org/2011/12/19 /global-christianity-exec/.

———. "Rising Restrictions on Religion—One-Third of the World's Population Experiences an Increase." August 9, 2011. https://www.pewforum.org/2011/08/09/rising-restrictions -on-religion2/.

Philpott, Daniel, and Timothy Samuel Shah, eds. *Under Caesar's Sword: How Christians Respond to Persecution.* Cambridge: Cambridge University Press, 2018.

Pillay, Kavita. "Love And Marriage: Rebels against an Indian Tradition That Endures in the U.S." Accessed May 1, 2020. https://www.wgbh.org/news/national-news/2019/02/27/love -and-marriage-rebels-against-an-indian-tradition-that-endures-in-the-us?00000161 -8b7f-d670-ad6f-abff33b10000-page=2.

Plaatje, Sol. *Native Life in South Africa.* Northlands, South Africa: Picador Africa, 2007.

Preston, Andrew. *Sword of the Spirit, Shield of Faith: Religion in American War and Diplomacy.* New York: Knopf, 2012.

Preston-Whyte, E. M. "Land and Development at Indaleni: A Historical Perspective." *Development Southern Africa* 4, no. 3 (1987): 401–427.

Price, P. E. "The Persecution in China." *Christian Observer*, January 23, 1901, 7–8.

Puar, Jaspir. *Terrorist Assemblages: Homonationalism in Queer Times.* Durham, NC: Duke University Press, 2007.

Rabbitts, Frances. "Give and Take? Child Sponsors and the Ethics of Giving." In *Child Sponsorship: Exploring Pathways to a Brighter Future.* edited by Brad Watson and Matthew Clarke, 280–296. New York: Palgrave Macmillan, 2014.

Ram, Kalpana. *Fertile Disorder: Spirit Possession and Its Provocation of the Modern.* Honolulu: University of Hawai'i Press, 2013.

Rana, Junaid. "Anthropology and the Riddle of White Supremacy." *American Anthropologist* 122, no. 1 (2019): 99–111.

———. "The Racial Infrastructure of the Terror-Industrial Complex." *Social Text* 129 34, no. 4 (2016): 111–138.

Ransford, Oliver. *David Livingstone: The Dark Interior.* London: J. Murray, 1978.

Rao, Smitha. "Saffronisation of the Holy Cow: Unearthing Silent Communalism," *Economic and Political Weekly* 46, no. 15 (2011): 80–87.

"Report on Statistics." *Evangelical Repository* 12 (June 1873).

Respinti, Marco. "The Bloody Tribute Paid by The Church of Almighty God." *Bitter Winter*, March 13, 2019. https://bitterwinter.org/the-bloody-tribute-paid-by-the-church-of -almighty-god/.

Robert, Dana L. *American Women in Mission: A Social History of Their Thought and Practice.* Macon, GA: Mercer University Press, 1996.

———. "Shifting Southward: Global Christianity since 1945." *International Bulletin of Missionary Research* 24, no. 2 (2000): 50–58.

Roohi, Sanam. "Caste, Kinship and the Realisation of 'American Dream': High-Skilled Telugu Migrants in the U.S.A." *Journal of Ethnic and Migration Studies* 43, no. 16 (2017): 2756–2770.

Roush, Laura. "Santa Muerte, Protection, and 'Desamparo': A View from a Mexico City Altar." In "Lived Religion and Lived Citizenship in Latin America's Zones of Crisis," special issue, *Latin American Research Review* 49 (2014): 129–148.

Runciman, Walter Garrison. *The Social Animal.* Ann Arbor: University of Michigan Press, 2000.

Rycroft, David. "*Zulu Zion and Some Swazi Zionists* by Bengt Sundkler." *Bulletin of the School of Oriental and African Studies* 41, no. 1 (1978): 205–206.

Sahoo, Sarbeswar. *Pentecostalism and Religious Conflict in Contemporary India.* New Delhi: Cambridge University Press, 2018.

Salinas, Jennifer J., Soham Al Snih, Kyriakos Markides, Laura A. Ray, and Ronald J. Angel. "The Rural-Urban Divide: Health Services Utilization among Older Mexicans in Mexico." *Journal of Rural Health* 26, no. 4 (2010): 333–341.

Sam, Jillet Sarah. "Caste Diasporas beyond National Boundaries: Digital Caste Networks." *Perspectives on Global Development and Technology* 16, nos. 1–3 (2017): 145–159.

Sanneh, Lamin O. *Translating the Message: The Missionary Impact on Culture.* American Society of Missiology Series. Maryknoll, NY: Orbis Books, 1989.

———. *West African Christianity: The Religious Impact.* Maryknoll, NY: Orbis Books, 1983.

Sarbeswar, Sahoo. *Pentecostalism and the Politics of Conversion in India.* Cambridge: Cambridge University Press, 2018.

Sathyamala, C. "Meat-Eating in India: Whose Food, Whose Politics, and Whose Rights?" *Policy Futures in Education* 17, no. 7 (2019): 329–351.

Sauer, Christof. "Researching Persecution and Martyrdom." *International Journal of Religious Freedom* 1 (2008).

Sayre-McCord, Geoffrey. "Hume and Smith on Sympathy, Approbation, and Moral Judgment." In *Sympathy: A History,* edited by Eric Schlesser, 208–246. New York: Oxford University Press, 2015.

Scarles, Caroline. "The Photographed Other: Interplays of Agency in Tourist Photography in Cisco, Peru." *Annals of Tourism Research* 39 (2012): 928–950.

Scarry, Elaine. *The Body in Pain: The Making and Unmaking of the World.* New York: Oxford University Press, 1985.

Schramm, Wilbur, ed. *The Process and Effects of Mass Communication.* Urbana: University of Illinois Press, 1954.

Seamands, John T. "Christianity's Answer to the Muslim Challenge." *WV Magazine,* May 1964.

Sedra, Paul. "Class Cleavages and Ethnic Conflict: Coptic Christian Communities in Modern Egyptian Politics." *Islam and Christian-Muslim Relations* 10, no. 2 (1999): 219–235.

———. "Writing the History of the Modern Copts: From Victims and Symbols to Actors." *History Compass* 7, no. 3 (2009): 1049–1063.

Selod, Saher. *Forever Suspect: Racialized Surveillance of Muslim Americans in the War on Terror.* New Brunswick: Rutgers University Press, 2018.

Senior, Jennifer. "Have a Heart, but Be Careful Not to Lose Your Head." *New York Times*, December 7, 2016.

Shah, Alpa. "The Dark Side of Indigeneity?: Indigenous People, Rights and Development in India." *History Compass* 5, no. 6 (2007): 1806–1832.

Shea, Nina. *In the Lion's Den*. Nashville: B and H Publishing, 1997.

Shenoda, Anthony. "Cultivating Mystery: Miracles and the Coptic Moral Imaginary." PhD diss., Harvard University, 2010.

Shepperson, George. "Review: Ethiopianism and Zionism in Southern Africa." *The Journal of African History* 20, no. 1 (1979): 142–145.

Shepperson, George, and Thomas Price. *Independent African: John Chilembwe and the Origins, Setting and Significance of the Nyasaland Native Rising of 1915*. Kachere Monographs. Blantyre: Christian Literature Association in Malawi, 2000.

Simpson, Thula. "The Bay and the Ocean: A History of the ANC in Swaziland, 1960–1979." *African Historical Review* 41, no. 1 (2009): 90–117.

Singh, Nikhil Pal. *Black Is a Country: Race and the Unfinished Struggle for Democracy*. Cambridge, MA: Harvard University Press, 2004.

Sluka, Jeffrey A., and Antonius C. G. Robben. "Fieldwork in Cultural Anthropology: An Introduction." In *Ethnographic Fieldwork*, edited by Antonius C. G. Robben and Jeffrey A. Sluka, 1–48. Malden, MA: Blackwell, 2007.

Smith, Adam. *The Theory of Moral Sentiments*. London: T. Cadell, 1767.

Smith, Andrea. *Unreconciled: From Racial Reconciliation to Racial Justice in Christian Evangelicalism*. Durham, NC: Duke University Press, 2019.

Smith, Bruce W., Kenneth I. Pargament, Curtis Brant, and Joan M. Oliver. "Noah Revisited: Religious Coping by Church Members and the Impact of the 1993 Midwest Flood." *Journal of Community Psychology* 28, no. 2 (2000): 169–186.

Smith, Christian. "Evangelicals Behaving Badly with Statistics." *Books and Culture* 13 (2007).

Smith, David, and Harriet Sherwood. "Military Operation Launched to Locate Missing Nigerian Girls." *Guardian*, May 14, 2014. https://www.theguardian.com/world/2014/may/14/nigeria-launches-military-operation-to-find-kidnapped-girls.

Smith, James. "Industrial Training in India." *Missionary Herald* 4 (April 1900): 168–172.

Smith, Lacey Baldwin. *Fools, Martyrs, Traitors: The Story of Martyrdom in the Western World*. New York: Alfred A. Knopf, 1997.

Smith, Saphora. "China Forcefully Harvests Organs from Detainees, Tribunal Concludes." *NBC News*, June 18, 2019. https://www.nbcnews.com/news/world/china-forcefully-harvests-organs-detainees-tribunal-concludes-n1018646.

Sontag, Susan. *AIDS and Its Metaphors*. New York: Farrar, Straus and Giroux, 1989.

———. *Regarding the Pain of Others*. New York: Picador, 2004.

Sookhdeo, Patrick. *A People Betrayed: The Impact of Islamisation on the Christian Community in Pakistan*. Pewsey, U.K.: Isaac Publishing, 2002.

"The Spread of the Gospel and the Conversion of the World." *Andover Review* 4 (1885).

Staples, James. "Beef and Beyond: Exploring the Meat Consumption Practices of Christians in India." *Ethnos* 82, no. 2 (2017): 232–251.

Starr, Chloë. *Chinese Theology: Text and Context*. New Haven: Yale University Press, 2017.

Steffen, Tom, and Lois McKinney Douglas. *Encountering Missionary Life and Work: Preparing for Intercultural Ministry*. Grand Rapids, MI: Baker Academic, 2008.

Stetzer, Ed. "Defining Evangelicals in Research." National Association of Evangelicals, Winter 2017–18. https://www.nae.net/defining-evangelicals-research/.

———. "Why You Should Use Stats in Ministry." *Exchange*, July 27, 2016. https://www.christianitytoday.com/edstetzer/2016/july/how-to-use-stats.html.

Stewart, Kathleen. *Ordinary Affects*. Durham, NC: Duke University Press, 2007.

Stoddard, Theodore Lothrop. *The Rising Tide of Color against White World-Supremacy*. New York: Charles Scribner's Sons, 1921.

Sundkler, Bengt. *Bantu Prophets in South Africa*. London: Lutterworth Press, 1948.

———. *Zulu Zion and Some Swazi Zionists*. Oxford: Oxford University Press, 1976.

"Sympathy for the Heathen." *Baptist Missionary Magazine*, May 1842, 131.

Taiwan Roman Catholic Bishops Committee. *Biographies of China's Catholic Martyr Saints*. In Chinese. Taipei: Tianzhujiao Taiwan diqu zhujiaotuan, 2000.

Tedlock, Dennis, and Bruce Mannheim, eds. *The Dialogic Emergence of Culture*. Urbana: University of Illinois Press, 1995.

Teltumbde, Anand. *Khairlanji*. New Delhi: Navayana Publishers, 2008.

———. *The Persistence of Caste: The Khairlanji Murders and India's Hidden Apartheid*. New York: Zed Books, 2010.

Telugu Association of North America website. Accessed May 1, 2020. https://www.tana.org/services/matrimonials-listing.

Thangaraj, Stanley. "Playing through Differences: Black-White Racial Logic and Interrogating South Asian American Identity." *Ethnic and Racial Studies* 35, no. 6 (2012): 988–1006.

Thomas, Sonja. "Cowboys and Indians: Indian Priests in Rural Montana." *Women's Studies Quarterly* 47, nos. 1–2 (2019): 110–131.

Thornton, Patricia M. "The New Cybersects: Resistance and Repression in the Reform Era." In *Chinese Society, Chang, Conflict, and Resistance*, edited by Elizabeth J. Perry and Mark Selden, 215–238. New York: RoutledgeCurzon, 2003.

"Thoughts on Various Methods of Advancing the Cause of Christ by Missionaries at Bombay." *Panoplist* 12, no.1 (January 1816): 34–39.

"To the Brink and Back." YouTube video, 47:35. March 5, 2018. https://www.youtube.com/watch?v=TG2qmA6kaso.

"Trial in Gokulraj Murder Begins." *Times of India*, August 31, 2018. http://timesofindia.indiatimes.com/articleshow/65615115.cms?utm_source=contentofinterest&utm_medium=text&utm_campaign=cppst.

Tsing, Anna L. *Friction: An Ethnography of Global Connection*. Princeton: Princeton University Press, 2005.

Turek, Lauren Frances. *To Bring the Good News to All Nations: Evangelical Influence on Human Rights and U.S. Foreign Relations*. Ithaca: Cornell University Press, 2020.

———. "To Support a 'Brother in Christ': Evangelical Groups and U.S.-Guatemalan Relations during the Ríos Montt Regime." *Diplomatic History* 39, no. 4 (2015): 689–719.

U.S. Commission on International Religious Freedom. "Nigeria." *USCIRF Annual Report 2021*. Accessed July 2, 2021. https://www.uscirf.gov/sites/default/files/2021-05/Nigeria%20Chapter%20AR2021.pdf.

U.S. Department of State—Bureau of Consular Affairs, "DV 2018—Selected Entrants." Accessed May 26, 2022. https://travel.state.gov/content/travel/en/us-visas/immigrate/diversity-visa-program-entry/dv-2018-selected-entrants.html.

Vala, Carsten T. *The Politics of Protestant Churches and the Party-State in China: God above Party?* New York: Routledge, 2018.

Van Rheenen, Gailyn. *Missions: Biblical Foundations and Contemporary Strategies*. Grand Rapids. MI: Zondervan, 2014.

Verdery, Katherine. *Secret and Truths: Ethnography in the Archive of Romania's Secret Police*. Budapest: Central European University Press, 2014.

Verstraelen, Frans J. "Calculation and Surprise in the *World Christian Encyclopedia*." *Missiology: An International Review* 12, no. 1 (1984): 55–62.

"Violence against Inter-Caste Couples: The Need for A New Law." October 18, 2018. https://www.youtube.com/watch?v=2RRRiIyJIsA&feature=emb_logo.

Von Eschen, Penny. *Race against Empire: Black Americans and Anticolonialism, 1937–1957.* Ithaca: Cornell University Press, 1997.

Walls, Andrew. *The Missionary Movement in Christian History: Studies in the Transmission of the Faith.* Maryknoll, NY: Orbis Books, 1996.

Walton, Jonathan L. *Watch This! The Ethics and Aesthetics of Black Televangelism.* New York: NYU Press, 2009.

Wang, Yiman. "The Amateur's Lightning Rod: DV Documentary in Postsocialist China." *Film Quarterly* 58, no. 4 (2005): 16–26.

Wariboko, Nimi. *Nigerian Pentecostalism.* Rochester: University of Rochester Press, 2014.

Watney, Simon. "Making Strange: The Shattered Mirror." In *Thinking about Photography,* edited by Victor Burgin, 154–176. London: Macmillan, 1982.

"The Way of the Cross." YouTube video, 55:18. February 23, 2018. https://www.youtube.com/watch?v=6VwlZsXz3No.

Weinstein, Jack Russell. "Sympathy, Difference, and Education: Social Unity in the Work of Adam Smith." *Economics and Philosophy* 22 (2006): 79–111.

WGBH and Public Radio International. "Caste in America." *The World.* June 28, 2021. https://www.pri.org/categories/caste-america.

White, Landeg. *Magomero: Portrait of an African Village.* New York: Cambridge University Press, 1987.

Whitehead, Andrew, and Samuel Perry. *Taking America Back for God: Christian Nationalism in the United States.* Oxford: Oxford University Press, 2020.

"Who Forced Her to the End of the Road?" YouTube video, 34:12. March 3, 2018. https://www.youtube.com/watch?v=covKrONHyuE.

Wickeri, Philip L. *Reconstructing Christianity in China: K. H. Ting and the Chinese Church.* Maryknoll, NY: Orbis Books, 2007.

Winerip, Michael. "Our Towns; a Terrorist at the Shell Station? No, but That Goatee Looks Suspicious." *New York Times,* September 30, 2001. https://www.nytimes.com/2001/09/30/nyregion/our-towns-a-terrorist-at-the-shell-station-no-but-that-goatee-looks-suspicious.html.

Winter, Deborah Du Nann, and Dana C. Leighton. "Structural Violence: Introduction." In *Peace, Conflict, and Violence: Peace Psychology for the 21st Century,* edited by Daniel J. Christie, Richard V. Wagner, and Deborah Du Nann Winter. Upper Saddle River, NJ: Prentice Hall, 2001.

Woods, Paul, ed. *Shaping Christianity in Greater China: Indigenous Christians in Focus.* Oxford: Regnum Books International, 2017.

World Religion Database. Accessed February 15, 2020. https://worldreligiondatabase.org/wrd/#/homepage/wrd-main-page.

World Vision. "Our Work." Accessed May 20, 2022. https://www.worldvision.org/our-work.

"World Vision U.S. 2019 Annual Review." Accessed May 20, 2022. https://s3.us-east-2.amazonaws.com/wvusstatic.com/2020/landing-pages/financial-accountability/pdfs/2019+Annual+Report+Brochure-F_updated-final.pdf.

"World Watch List: Nigeria." Open Doors International website. Accessed July 2, 2021. https://www.opendoorsusa.org/christian-persecution/world-watch-list/nigeria/.

Wuthnow, Robert. *Boundless Faith: The Global Outreach of American Churches.* Berkeley: University of California Press, 2010.

———. *The Restructuring of American Religion: Society and Faith since World War II.* Princeton: Princeton University Press, 1990.

Xi, Lian. *Redeemed by Fire: The Rise of Popular Christianity in Modern China.* New Haven: Yale University Press, 2010.

Yang, Fenggang. "The Red, Black, and Gray Markets of Religion in China." *Sociological Quarterly* 47, no. 1 (2006): 93–122.

Yangwen, Zheng. *Sinicizing Christianity.* Leiden: Brill, 2017.

Young, Liam Cole. "'What's in a List?' Cultural Techniques, Logistics, Poesis." PhD diss., University of Western Ontario, 2014.

Young, Neil J. *We Gather Together: The Religious Right and the Problem of Interfaith Politics.* Oxford: Oxford University Press, 2015.

Young, Richard Fox, and Jonathan Seitz, eds. *Asia in the Making of Christianity: Conversion, Agency, and Indigeneity, 1600s to the Present.* Leiden: Brill, 2013.

Zito, Angela. "Religion Is Media." *Revealer.* April 16, 2018. https://therevealer.org/religion-is -media/.

Zurlo, Gina A. "The Legacy of David B. Barrett." *International Bulletin of Mission Research* 42 (2017): 29.

NOTES ON
CONTRIBUTORS

SUNDER JOHN BOOPALAN is an assistant professor of biblical and theological studies at Canadian Mennonite University.

JASON BRUNER is an associate professor of religious studies in the School of Historical, Philosophical and Religious Studies at Arizona State University.

JOEL CABRITA is an associate professor of history in the Department of History and the director of the Center for African Studies, both at Stanford University.

CHRISTIE CHUI-SHAN CHOW received her doctorate in religion and society from Princeton Theological Seminary and is an independent scholar of global Christianity and Chinese religions.

JOHN CORRIGAN is the Lucius Moody Bristol Distinguished Professor of Religion and a professor of history at Florida State University.

OMRI ELISHA is an associate professor in the Department of Anthropology at Queens College–CUNY.

HILLARY KAELL is an associate professor of anthropology in the Department of Anthropology at McGill University.

KATE KINGSBURY is an adjunct professor of anthropology at the University of British Columbia.

DAVID C. KIRKPATRICK is an associate professor of religion in the Department of Philosophy and Religion at James Madison University.

HARVEY KWIYANI is chief executive officer of Global Connections.

CANDACE LUKASIK is an assistant professor of religion in the Department of Philosophy and Religion at Mississippi State University.

MELANI McALISTER is professor of American studies and international affairs in the Department of American Studies at George Washington University.

INDEX

Acquired Immunodeficiency Syndrome (AIDS), 59, 184
affect: and caste-based violence, 9, 12, 126, 142–155; and intimacy, 57; and persecution narratives, 2, 44, 108, 166, 181–182; production of, 17, 44, 108, 126, 142–155, 166, 178, 181–182; and quantification, 17–18, 29, 31. *See also* caste system; Coptic Christianity; media
African National Congress (ANC), 80–82
Alexander Low Bruce Estates. *See* Bruce, Alexander Low
Allison, James, 76–77
American Board of Commissioners of Foreign Missions, 24, 54
Amnesty International, 43, 178
Anglicanism, 1, 5, 139
apartheid, 76, 79–82, 183. *See also* race
Assemblies of God. *See* Pentecostalism

Baptists, 127, 131, 181
Barrett, David B., 28, 31
Beshara, Madgy, 114–115
Beti, Mongo, 137–138
Bharatiya Janata Party (BJP), 153–154
Bhengu, Nicholas, 80–81, 84–85. *See also* Pentecostalism
bin Laden, Osama, 113, 180. *See also* Islam
Blantyre Mission, 128–129, 131–132
body, the: and antipersecution activism, 42, 48, 108, 110; and Dalits, 147, 153; and persecution narratives, 11, 48, 108, 110–112; and race, 112–113; and violence, 11, 73–74, 144, 147. *See also* martyrdom; media; Protestant internationalism
Boko Haram, 1–4, 44, 48. *See also* Islam
Boltanski, Luc, 27, 33
Book of Martyrs (1563). *See* Foxe, John
Booth, Joseph, 133–134, 137–138
Boxer Uprising (1899–1901), 22, 167
Bruce, Alexander Low, 127, 129–130, 132–133, 138
Buddhism, 62, 160, 165

Cable News Network (CNN), 53, 62, 181
capitalism, 33, 134, 178
caste system: and affect, 126, 142–144, 147, 150–151, 182; Christian resistance of, 143,

148; and Dalit Christian ethics, 9, 12, 148; and food, 153–154; function of, 144, 146, 152; global reach of, 144–146, 149; and violence, 9–10, 12, 142–144, 147, 149–151, 154–155. *See also* affect; Hinduism
Catholicism: and American politics, 119; antipersecution activism in, 22, 30–31, 34, 179; census taking in, 28; and child sponsorship organizations, 55–59, 61, 63–65; enchanted internationalism in, 110; martyrdom in, 167; and missions, 137; and modern media, 181–182; and race, 113–114; and Santa Muerte, 92–97, 100, 104
ChildFund. *See* Christian Children's Fund (CCF)
Chilembwe, John, 11, 127–131, 133, 137–138
Christian Children's Fund (CCF), 54–55
Christian Herald (1878–1992), 23, 54
Christian Right, 73, 108, 116–120
Church Missionary Society (CMS), 135–136
Church of Almighty God (CAG): development of, 126, 159; global scale of, 160, 162–163, 171; media coverage of, 159; media productions of, 161–163, 166–167, 170–171; membership of, 162; and persecution narratives, 160, 164–167, 170–171; relationship with Chinese state, 159–160, 164, 168–169; social networking of, 159, 163, 165–166; teachings of, 160, 179. *See also* media
Church of England. *See* Anglicanism
Cold War, 43, 109, 178–179
colonialism. *See* empire
communism, 43, 159–161, 164, 167, 177
Compassion International, 55, 57, 62–63
Coptic Christianity: and antipersecution activism, 47, 108; and persecution narratives, 31, 47, 108–109, 111; and post-9/11 America, 11, 109, 112–114, 181, 183; and Protestant internationalism, 73, 108, 110; transnational networks of, 4, 11, 107–109, 116–120, 179. *See also* Islam; martyrdom; 9/11; race
culture wars, 118–119
Curtis, Heather, 23, 54

Defiance Campaign, 81, 83
democracy, 49, 109, 145, 160, 164, 171